Presented to Purchase College
by
Gary Waller, PhD Cambridge

State University of New York
Distinguished Professor

Provost 1995-2004
Professor of Literature & Cultural Studies
Professor of Theatre & Performance
1995-2019

New Poems by Shakespeare

Order and meaning restored to the Sonnets

New Poems by Shakespeare

*Order and meaning restored
to the Sonnets*

JOHN PADEL

THE HERBERT PRESS

ISBN 0 906969 10 7

Contents

Preface   6

Part I: The Argument   9

1   Reasons for this new edition   9

2   The discovery of the order   12

3   The identity of 'Mr. W. H.'   14

4   The Herbert family
    and William's two engagements   17

5   A provisional dating of the sonnets;
    the significance of the tetrad   21

6   The method of reconstructing the story   25

7   The story
         (i)   The first commission   28
         (ii) The second commission   44
         (iii) Herbert's engagement and its outcome   53
         (iv) The Drama of 1598   57
         (v)   Tetrads for eight birthdays (1599–1606)   100

8   The publication of Q in 1609   119

9   Reconstructing the real relationships   125

Bibliography   133

Notes   135

Part II: The Sonnets in their poems   143

Indexes from and to the traditional order   284

Preface

This edition of the sonnets is intended for the general reader; but being radically new it is addressed also to the student and the scholar. It is based upon my claim to have discovered the original order of the sonnets – Shakespeare's order of design – and upon the further claim that the order is validated first and foremost on poetic grounds, that is to say on the grounds of pattern and unfolding sense.

Although I came to the discovery from an old hypothesis – namely that the young man to whom most of the sonnets are addressed was William Herbert, later the third Earl of Pembroke – and from working out some of the striking implications of that hypothesis, yet the order itself does not rest upon it; it stands independently. In fact, the order is a set of sequences of simple structures, which contribute so much to the meaning of their component sonnets that none of the traditional problems of interpretation is unaffected by that order. The sequences of poetic structures do tend to confirm the original hypothesis, to establish the dating of the groups of sonnets, and ultimately to reveal the human relationships behind their composition; but it is the poetry which matters and the structures require to be judged as poems and not for the identities, the dates, or even the relationships which may be deduced from them.

This book was first intended to be two books, and the second part – the text of the sonnets arranged in tetrads and triads with notes upon each – may indeed be published separately later on; but the first part, which gives the detailed background and undertakes to prove by literary methods the order of the sonnets in every structure and sequence, demands a text set out in the order it is proving.

Although the order is radically different from any proposed before, yet it is based upon that of the first edition, which was, I argue, a *careful* disarrangement of it. The text is that of the first edition with modern spelling and punctuation. The few textual changes (mostly proposed by Tucker) are noted as they occur, along with the reasons for them.

In scholarship this edition does not pretend to be self-sufficient and students will need to refer to other editions for a history of the text, for an account of the many theories and interpretations which the sonnets have stimulated, and for the wealth of linguistic analysis which has been mined from them, around them, and for their sake. My aim here is to make the sense of the sonnets clearer, and to make them more directly intelligible than ever before, and to do so by restoring poems that had been dismembered.

The two cross-reference tables at the end of the book (Indexes I and II) make it easy to refer to and from any other edition using the traditional order.

Somebody who has come newly, as I have, to a field which was not his own but had been intensively cultivated by others, owes many debts. First, there is the support I have had from people who, knowing the field well themselves, have generously recognized the value of the new ideas brought to it. The late Professor C. L. Barber was the first to give immediate and enthusiastic reception to my findings and work; I only wish I could still repay him. Professor Gāmini Salgādo put some of my discoveries to the searching test of use with senior students; and I am more than grateful for his encouragement and for his readiness to support my ideas not only among his Shakespearean colleagues but also publicly. Mr Michael Kustow and Mr Simon Callow have put the order to quite a different test – public recitations at the National Theatre, London, from March to September 1980. I am most obliged to them for the enthusiasm and expertise they devoted to the four cycles and the one marathon performance which they put on.

For myself, and I believe for others, the recitations have proved two things – first, that the sonnets are far more readily understandable heard than read silently (especially when recited by somebody so gifted as Callow) and therefore that they were indeed composed to be heard rather than seen on the page; second, that audiences are excellent judges of what flows properly and coheres. My friends and relatives had made most helpful provisional audiences and I am truly grateful to them.

Then there are debts, direct and indirect, of scholarship. J. Dover Wilson's edition and Martin Seymour-Smith's, which actually preceded his, were my first sources of information and references; the next was Thomas Tyler's of 1890. My order for the sonnets to the man was found early in 1976, just after my article in *The Times Literary Supplement* of December 1975, and the theories were nearly all developed with that order in mind. All the editions I have been able to discover and all the books about the sonnets have been of enormous value in testing both the order and the theories. Stephen Booth's *An Essay on the Sonnets* gave me an immediate conviction that I had been right to look to the limit for pattern – variation in sameness. Peter Jones's fine choice of essays for his *Shakespeare, The Sonnets* in the Casebook Series provided some excellent material for rethinking the personal relationships in the last section of my Argument. Every modern editor is indebted to the thoroughness of H. E. Rollins's edition of 1942. My own preferred older edition is T. G. Tucker's of 1924; of the modern ones Seymour-Smith's (*Poetry Bookshelf*) is very valuable for its informative, balanced introduction and for its text so close in spelling and puctuation to that of the first edition. Professor M. M. Mahood's book, *Shakespeare's Wordplay*, suggested to me the sign 'w-p', which I use freely in the notes.

Professor S. Schoenbaum has put everybody in his debt with his *William Shakespeare: A Documentary Life* (1975) and his *William Shakespeare: A Compact Documentary Life* (1977); it is a debt for usable and reliable facts and also for sheer enjoyment.

Finally, I am delighted that this work appears in England under the imprint of The Herbert Press. There is a poetic rightness if the true order is at last revealed by a member of the *other* branch of the Herbert Family.

Part I: The Argument

1 Reasons for this new edition

Shakespeare's sonnets are wonderful poetry and yet are little known. A few of them are very familiar and greatly loved but most are usually put aside as obscure and difficult, or as frustrating, because they seem to be telling a story which they never quite convey. Indeed from the time of their first publication in 1609, seven years before Shakespeare's death, the sonnets have been one of the mysteries of English literature. So much about them is still disputed by editors and scholars – not merely the meaning of certain passages and the restoration of the text, but the interpretation of the human relationships portrayed or implied, the assignment of dates and identities, and the significance of the dedication. Not even the basic circumstances of publication have been settled.

The sonnets are beset with problems, not the least of which is the insistence of some recent editors that the text is as healthy as need be, that careful scholarship and linguistic expertise have solved most of the problems, and that any that remain are probably insoluble and anyway unimportant for the literary appreciation of the poetry. Some prominent scholars of today even contend that dates, persons, and situations are irrelevant to the literary experience of reading the poems.

But how if *nobody has ever yet seen the poems in print*? One aim of this book is to show that the sonnets individually are component units of disorganized poems, not complete poems in themselves. The original poems are here set out for the first time.

The first edition of the sonnets, a small quarto book usually known as 'Q', is our only source of the text – except for the text of two which had been printed ten years earlier, in a pirated anthology of 1599. Besides the 154 sonnets Q contains a poem entitled 'A Lover's Complaint, by William Shakespeare'. It follows the sonnets and consists of forty-seven seven-line stanzas; so it is as long as twenty-three and a half sonnets.

In Q the sonnets are numbered consecutively but are arranged in two unequal groups. The last twenty-eight (i.e. two elevenths of the whole collection) follow a kind of 'envoi', Q's 126, not itself a strict sonnet but a twelve-line valedictory poem that seems to round off the preceding 125 sonnets addressed to a fair young man who is handsome, high-born, and wealthy. Seventeen of the last twenty-eight are to a woman (or to women) and seven are about her (or about them). Two are versions of a Byzantine Greek epigram and two are meditative poems, one on the power of sexual lust, the other renouncing earthly lusts for things divine.

For various reasons, many people have been convinced that the order of the sonnets in Q is not the order in which they were originally written; and during the last 150 years more than thirty editions have been published printing them in different orders and offering different versions of the events and personalities to which they seem to refer or relate. The trouble with almost all these editions was that, although the story in each case supported the order and the order the story, there was no independent way of validating either. Sir Denis Bray's edition of 1925 and later was different. He tried to reconstitute the order on linguistic grounds, making each new sonnet pick up the rhyme or last key-word of the one before. Although his attempt appealed to many people, it did not last, because he ignored strong links of other kinds between adjacent sonnets and broke up too many pairs or longer sequences which were tied to each other by sense. Nevertheless he gave much-needed attention to the possibility of using poetics to discover the original order.

The reasons why Q's order has so often been thought wrong are three, each strong but together very strong indeed. First, the sequence is uneven in texture. Some pairs or longer runs are very closely linked to each other by sense, rhyme, key words, and themes, but some isolated sonnets or pairs interrupt the themes, and there are a few abrupt and inexplicable changes of tone. Some runs of sonnets have no connecting thread at all. Second, the sense of many of the sonnets appears to depend for proper understanding on a knowledge of the situations and events to which they seemingly refer, but the reader is left in a tantalizing uncertainty of the story. Third, some widely separated sonnets seem to relate to the same situation and must belong closely together in time.

The most serious thing about the order is that it affects the tone and the sense of the poetry. In a review the late C. L. Barber wrote of the sonnets, 'that there is an uncertainty about the tone of many of them is evident from the different ways that competent readers have taken them. And the tone we hear in a sonnet can change as we read those around it.' Therefore if the order is wrong, we are probably being misled about the tone and sense. With the order restored, irrelevant uncertainties are, I believe, eliminated simply by the context of each sonnet, and those that remain are part of the poetry 'working to transform or cope with situations' by making 'gestures towards others'.[1]

This edition presents an order which is for the first time independently validated. It can be seen at a glance in Index II. It makes the poetry immediately accessible and shows the sonnets as having a single coherence and direct intelligibility unrealized from their first publication until now. Its certainty is based on the newly printed poems, literary structures which use repeated patterns. Not only that, but the sequence of the groups arranged in their patterns implies a certain series of events, which is confirmed by the evidence of letters, and suggests the likelihood of certain situations. Even more, it makes an overwhelmingly strong case for dating the sonnets between April 1597 and April 1606, when Shakespeare was almost thirty-three and almost forty-two, and for identifying the young man addressed in most of them as William, elder son and heir to Henry Herbert, the second Earl of Pembroke, the third Earl himself from 1601. But the most important thing about the discovered order is the justice it does to the poetry; besides removing many of the ambiguities, it enhances the poetic value of almost all the sonnets and often supplies meaning that was missing until now.

Here two obvious questions need to be asked and answered: How was the original, coherent sequence disturbed – by chance or deliberately?[2] And why has it not been reconstituted before? The provisional answers are that it was deliberately disordered (indeed there is in Q too much coherence of short groups for chance to have been at work) but that it was also carefully reordered to suggest a false account of the situations underlying the poems and some false links between consecutive sonnets. The young man and his family had something to hide and they hid it well by arranging to have published an artful text with almost nothing changed except the order.

The third obvious question is: Why did they publish it at all and not simply keep quiet or otherwise suppress the whole series or part of it? The short answer is that publication blocked any other publication and thus neither Shakespeare himself, even if he had wished, nor his heirs would be able legally to publish the true version of the sonnets, which might reveal the family's scheming. Besides, a clever falsification of the sequence would set people speculating upon wrong lines and would mask the true story with a blurred confusion far more effective than silence or suppression.

The story will be told in section 7. In the meantime something will be said of the discovery of the original order and of the identity of 'Mr W. H.', to whom the first edition was dedicated.

2   The discovery of the order

A brief personal account is required of how it is that a non-Shakespearean, a psychiatrist and psychoanalyst who in a previous career taught Latin and Greek, has ventured upon a field which a Shakespearean friend warned him was 'a minefield on which six machine-guns are also trained'.

It so happened that I had just re-read the introduction to J. Dover Wilson's *New Cambridge Shakespeare* edition of the sonnets when there appeared[3] Geoffrey Bullough's review of S. Schoenbaum's *William Shakespeare: a Documentary Life*. The review mentioned the date of Hamnet Shakespeare's death. Why, I wondered, had no editor of the sonnets, especially none who held the Pembroke-theory, connected the death of Shakespeare's only son with their composition? Searching in the Herbert–Sidney families (Lady Pembroke was a Sidney) for a solution to the *hue-Hugh* mystery of Q's 20, which might confirm the Pembroke-theory, I turned to W. A. Ringler's *The Poems of Sir Philip Sidney*,[4] to which a *Times Literary Supplement* review had persuaded me some years before, and there, in his introduction, commentary, and bibliography, found information about Hugh Sanford and about Nicholas Hilliard's links with the Sidney family. I wrote an essay on the object-relations psychology of the sonnets.[5]

Already in that essay I pointed out the series of sets of four which make up roughly the last quarter of the sonnets to the young man. I had taken the hypothesis of sets of four from Sir Edmund Chambers and J. Dover Wilson and (being a psychotherapist!) hit upon the idea of working backwards from the later sonnets to the earlier. The middle and later groups have been least disturbed and Q's 18–39 the most, so that, once the later sonnets are removed from that early series, it is less hard to remake the fours.

Wilson's suggestion that the first seventeen sonnets had been commissioned for William Herbert's seventeenth birthday also seemed worth testing, and it worked so well with 95–125 to take each group of four as offered for a different birthday, that I could at once assign to Herbert's eighteenth birthday the early group of four which I had pointed out in the essay and which was accompanied by a gift (Q's 77, 122, 30, 31).

By this time the early sources for William Herbert's life and for his mother's were necessary. It was a surprise to discover that no holder of the Pembroke-theory had yet tried to bring together all the bits of information to be got from contemporary letters and to correlate them with the possible dates of the sonnets.

Q's last twenty-eight sonnets were a harder problem than the first 126, until I took together the seven sonnets which were not obviously about or to the Dark Woman. One of these seven has short lines of eight syllables, and the other six form three pairs. The remaining twenty-one could then be arranged in convincing groups of three (triads) and the groups in sequence. These groups had been more thoroughly and more carefully disarranged than any of the others.

It was advisable to recypher the groups of sonnets and not simply to renumber the sonnet sequence in a way that might cause confusion with the traditional numbering. All the sonnets to the young man are here arranged – as they were composed – in sets of four, in 'tetrads'. There are thirty-one tetrads, which are cyphered te 1–te 31. The sonnets in each tetrad are denoted *a–d*. There is one epilogue, which belongs after te 4, and one 'envoi', a farewell-poem of six rhyming couplets; it rounds off the eighteen tetrads te 6–te 23. The three pairs are now pr 1–pr 3, *a* and *b*. There are strong reasons to think that the single sonnet of short lines was composed by Shakespeare for recitation at his own wedding breakfast of 30 November or early December 1582. It is a version, for the benefit of the guests, of how Shakespeare had won the consent of his bride, Anne Hathaway. The three pairs, I hope to show, were the earliest sonnets brought to birth by 'Mr. W. H.'

The recyphering calls for two indexes. The first is from Q's numbers to tetrads, triads, and pairs, and to pages. The second is from the groups, arranged chronologically, to Q's numbers. The indexes make it easy to refer from any edition using Q's order to this one and from this to any other such edition.

3   The identity of 'Mr. W. H.'

'Mr. W. H.', 'the onlie begetter of these insuing sonnets' (so the dedication of the original edition calls him), has remained elusive, as he was
probably intended to remain. The most obvious person, suggested
about 150 years ago,[6] is William Herbert, third Earl of Pembroke from
a few weeks before his twenty-first birthday. He and his brother
received the dedication of the First Folio of Shakespeare's plays in
1623, seven years after the poet's death. The only objection to the
suggestion that Herbert was 'Mr. W. H.' has been that, before his
father died, on 19 January 1601, he was always known as 'Lord
Herbert', and Thomas Thorpe, the publisher, would not have dared to
change his title. Clearly this objection has no force if it was the young
Earl himself who supplied Thorpe with the copy and with directions
about the publication, the wording of the dedication, and its signature.
His mother was a most likely rearranger of sonnets; it was almost a
family trait! Both her brothers had rearranged their own sonnets and
she kept changing the details and the arrangement in her elder
brother's works which she was publishing. Of her, more later. The
dedication itself, if not actually worded in advance for Thorpe, would
certainly have required the approval of the Herbert family.

The suggestion that 'W. H.' stood for 'William Himself' may be
absurd if taken to mean William Shakespeare, as D. Barnstorff, who
proposed it in 1860, intended, but the initials might convey just what
some contemporaries understood, when taken to refer to William
Herbert. In 1613 George Wither published his first book, of satirical
poems, with the dedication, 'G. W. to himself wisheth all happiness'. It
seems intended to refer to the dedication of the sonnets and to suggest
that 'W. H.' had in effect caused them to be dedicated to himself,
though 'T. T.' had signed the dedication. Then in 1616 Ben Jonson
published his book of epigrams and opened its longish dedication to
'the most noble William, Earl of Pembroke', with words implying that
a previous dedicator had changed Pembroke's title, used a cipher, and
taken shelter under his patronage because there was danger in the
contents of his book. So Jonson, by hinting that 'T. T.' *had* been the
real dedicator of the sonnets, is absolving Pembroke from the slur of
self-dedication – or trying to. He received £20 each New Year's Day
from Pembroke to buy books and, as a writer, would have been a
useful person to scotch a rumour by hinting at a different version of the
facts.

Only two other candidates for the identity of 'Mr. W. H.' need detain us. Over the past thirty years or so, Leslie Hotson has urged the case for a certain William Hatcliffe, a Yorkshire squire's son and law student who, for the Christmas festivities of one of the Inns of Court, had been made 'Prince of Purpoole'. This involves dating the sonnets to the years 1588–1591/2. The theory and the supporting scholarship are most ingenious but the dating is far out, as we shall see.[7]

The earliest name proposed was that of Henry Wriothesley, third Earl of Southampton from a few days before his eighth birthday. As a boy he had soon become the ward of William Cecil, Lord Burghley, the Lord High Treasurer, who was guardian to several wealthy young aristocrats and organized their education. Along with the guardianship, which included the profitable management of his ward's estates, went his 'marriage', i.e. the right of his guardian to negotiate a bride for him and to be paid handsomely for doing so.[8] On Southampton's sixteenth birthday, 6 October 1589, Burghley proposed for his bride his own eldest granddaughter, Elizabeth Vere. She, though daughter of the Earl of Oxford, lived with her two younger sisters in Burghley's household. Southampton declined the proposal but was given a year to think about it. An apologetic letter to Burghley survives, dated 15 July 1590, from Sir Robert Stanhope, acknowledging that he has proposed his own daughter's marriage to Southampton but had not realized Burghley's claim and intention, which he thinks right and proper. It is an honest admission and withdrawal. Another letter to Burghley, dated 19 September 1590 (less than three weeks before Southampton turns seventeen and has to give his answer, his year of grace being expired), is from Viscount Montague, Southampton's maternal grandfather. He answers Burghley at some length, that he has been pressing his grandson to marry Elizabeth Vere. Both men apparently believe Burghley to be suspicious and potentially angry if his claim is ignored or not pressed at this eleventh hour.[9]

On becoming seventeen Southampton persisted in his refusal and faced four painful years, until he came of age, in which he could not marry without his guardian's consent or manage his own estates; even for the urgent repair of a manor for a friend who was his tenant he had to advise his friend to write to Burghley. He knew that at the end of the four years Burghley would exact from him a huge sum in compensation for the loss of his 'marriage'; the threat of it was part of Burghley's pressure upon him. In fact as soon as he became twenty-one, Burghley demanded the immediate payment of £5,000 on account of his refusal of 'the Lady Vere'.[10] The payment impoverished him for some years. Before he was twenty-two he had fallen in love with Elizabeth Vernon, one of the Queen's ladies-in-waiting.[11] He was faithful to her and dashed back from Paris to marry her, when she was pregnant, late in August 1598. He went back to France at once to continue his service under Essex, but Queen Elizabeth was angry when she heard the news, as we learn from two letters of 3 September. She commanded his return to England and, after he had taken his time over coming, had him imprisoned in the Fleet on 11 November. Eleven days later he was about to be released.[12]

Those who have held the theory that the sonnets were written to Southampton have argued that his reluctance to marry was the reason for Shakespeare's seventeen marriage sonnets. But they have never faced the fact that there is no time after 1590 appropriate for their composition. If they belonged to the four-year period in which Southampton and Burghley were estranged, the young man, still a minor, could marry nobody without his guardian's consent and was awaiting Burghley's savage bill of 1594. Shakespeare could have written them only advocating marriage with Elizabeth Vere and there would have been no surer way to alienate Southampton. It would have seemed to him either impudence or a professional job done by Burghley's hireling. If they belonged to 1594–5, it would have been a mockery of the young Earl, who could not now afford to marry and before his twenty-second birthday was in love with Elizabeth Vernon.

Nor was Southampton's patronage worth much after 1594. In 1593 Shakespeare had dedicated to him his long poem *Venus and Adonis*. Christopher Butler and Alastair Fowler showed, in a fascinating paper of 1964, that the number 20 was used repeatedly in that poem; they proposed that this was in honour of Southampton's coming twentieth birthday.[13] The dedication of *The Rape of Lucrece* to Southampton in 1594 suggests that Shakespeare had been well enough paid for the earlier poem. It is doubtful if he received any money for the later one. Southampton had none to spare.

The argument from the marriage problem is indeed a strong argument *against* Southampton's being the man addressed in the sonnets. But the story was a warning to other aristocratic families. Patronage, birthdays, and the threat of wardship are clues which will help us with the Pembroke theory.

16

4 The Herbert family and William's two engagements

William Herbert, the elder son and heir of Henry Herbert, second Earl of Pembroke, and of Mary *née* Sidney, his Countess and third wife, was educated at New College, Oxford, from 1593 to 1595. As he was born on 8 April 1580, he would then have been thirteen to fifteen years old. In the next two years his parents made two documented attempts to get him married. Whatever personal motives, conscious and unconscious, they may have had, their overriding reason must have been that, in the event of the Earl's death, William's wardship would be bestowed by the Queen upon some magnate who made a bid for it and would certainly intend to profit from it both by management of the estates and by arranging the young man's marriage. It was still unlikely that a widow would be awarded such an important wardship.

A wardship of several years' duration would be sure to diminish considerably the fortunes of a family, and the only reliable way to avoid that was to marry the minor in good time into a family whose head would thereby acquire strong title to the wardship and would have an interest in preserving the family estates intact for the young couple. The likelihood of a father's death was talked about and provided against, much as it is now between a man and his insurance agent or solicitor, and the most secure provision for the whole family (for his house therefore) was the timely marriage of his heir, if he acquiesced in their choice of a suitable bride.

The first Earl of Pembroke had acquired big estates in the south-west. He had been given the Abbey of Wilton, near Salisbury, the Abbey of Ramsbury (also in Wiltshire) and Cardiff Castle with the ancient Crown lands belonging to it. Under Queen Mary he had had to give back Wilton to the nuns and cried 'peccavi' ('I have sinned') on his knees to the Lady Abbess. But, says Aubrey, 'Upon Queen Mary's death the Earl came to Wilton (like a tiger) and turned them out, crying out, "Ye whores, to work; to work, ye whores; go spin"'.

He rebuilt Wilton but, as an upstart and a soldier of fortune, was not easily accepted by the gentry round about, although he had been Henry VIII's brother-in-law and had become Lord President of Wales. By Aubrey's account he was always in fear of losing Wilton and even died saying, 'They would have Wilton, they would have Wilton'. He died in 1570.[14] Although there was a great fire in the 1640s which destroyed the front of the house, it is still one of the show-pieces of

England, no worse perhaps for the new façade and for Inigo Jones's double-cube room, in which hang many of the beautiful pictures collected chiefly by the fourth Earl, Willlam Herbert's younger brother, Philip.

Henry Herbert, the second Earl, was chronically ill with recurrent bouts of an illness which it was more than once believed was about to end his life. Among the remedies he tried were visits to the waters near Bristol, surgery at the hands of an eminent London man, Dr Goodrich, and treatment by the Queen's own physician, Dr Gotherous, whom she sent down to Wilton in September 1599.[15]

The first young woman whom William's parents chose for him was Elizabeth Carey, daughter of Sir George Carey and granddaughter of Lord Hunsdon, the Lord Chamberlain. Negotiations for this came to decision in the autumn of 1595 when, from early October to the end of November, the Earl of Pembroke was in London with his son William and with Hugh Sanford, his secretary and agent. (Lady Mary had not come with them; she was ill at Wilton with a swelling in the throat. Dr Goodrich went down from London and cured her by lancing what was perhaps a quinsy.)[16] Besides arranging for William's marriage, Pembroke was concerned to urge the importance of fortifying Milford Haven against a possible Spanish invasion and to negotiate the purchase of some of Northwood Park from the Earl of Essex. Sanford acted for him in this and offended Essex's agents, who complained that his tone was peremptory, but Sanford justified himself by saying that he had said only what his lord had told him to say.

The contract of marriage was frustrated at the last minute by William, who did not like the girl when they met (he was fifteen and a half and she was nineteen). The reason of course had to be concealed (Rowland Whyte reports it in a letter of 5 December to William's uncle, Sir Robert Sidney, in Flushing; Whyte was in close touch with the Herberts and was acting as agent to Sidney). Pembroke provided a face-saving reason by suddenly demanding a big increase in the dowry required. The Careys were angry and, as Rowland Whyte wrote to Sidney, 'Truly I heard that if my Lord of Pembroke should die, who is very pursive and maladise [sc. 'breathless and sickly'], the tribe of Hunsdon do lay wait for the wardship of the brave young lord'. That is to say, they would more than get their own back, when William's father died, by applying for the wardship and basing their claim on the wrong done them in the earlier negotiations. So, although the Queen good-humouredly supported Pembroke before he left London and sent a jewel to the Countess, it had become far more urgent than before to get William married and to find ways to overcome his reluctance.[17]

Perhaps just over a year later his parents found another suitable candidate in Bridget Vere, the second daughter of the Earl of Oxford and Lord Burghley's granddaughter, younger sister of that Elizabeth whose hand Southampton had refused more than six years earlier. Bridget was only thirteen, so William could not object to her on the ground of her greater age, as he probably had to the Carey girl. Nevertheless, there would have to be considerable gentle persuasion exerted to get him to change his mind to the extent of agreeing even to entertain once more the idea of marriage. It is contended by those who hold the Pembroke-theory of the sonnets that the seventeen sonnets urging marriage were part of that preliminary persuasion urged upon him and that his parents commissioned them of Shakespeare in time for his seventeenth birthday (Dover Wilson suggested that this was the reason for the number). His birthday was held at Wilton, not at Baynard's Castle, the Herberts' huge residence in London, as we can tell from the letters which Whyte wrote to Sidney in April 1597.[18]

From one sonnet[19] we can deduce that Shakespeare's own presence added to the persuasive message of his poems. We may also guess that permission for William to live in London from the following spring (i.e. 1598), a permission which later in the April of 1597 Whyte mentions twice in letters to Sidney, was a concession which his parents made in getting him to agree to their arranging for him to meet Bridget in London later that year. There is no saying whether his parents' promise or Shakespeare's recitation weighed more with young Herbert.

The visit to London was made this time in July 1597, but not by the Earl of Pembroke, who was again ill. The Countess and William, now seventeen years and three months, accompanied by Sanford, who usually prepared the suites of rooms in Baynard's Castle, seem to have travelled up and negotiated their business well, probably helped by the Queen's secretary, Sir Robert Cecil, who introduced them to the Court. In mid August, back at Wilton, they both wrote to thank Cecil for his kindness. From the convolutedly inarticulate gratitude of the Countess's letter we may perhaps infer that she had then persuaded Cecil to agree to take over the wardship of William, if the Earl died. William and Bridget liked each other well enough, as another letter from the Countess, this time to Lord Burghley, indicates. So negotiations proceeded between Pembroke and Burghley, specifying the financial settlements and the household in which Bridget was to reside after the wedding, until she was old enough to consummate the marriage. While William was travelling abroad, she would live with his parents at Wilton. Bridget's father, the Earl of Oxford, gave his approval on 8 September.[20]

The four-yearly Parliament was to be held in 1597, from October to December, and William's father wrote on 3 September to Burghley, answering point by point a letter he had received from him about the marriage, asking to be excused from the Parliament, and saying, 'Lastly, my sonne himself at the beginning of the parliament shall come up both to attend her Ma^tes pleasure for his intended travell (whereunto he shall accordingly prepare himself) and also to performe what by yo^re Lp. and me shall be agreed upon for his purposed marriage".[21] But it is certain that William did *not* come up to London in early October. In the first place his mother wrote on 29 September to Sir Robert Cecil, Bridget's uncle, defending herself against the charge, which she had heard he had made, that she had disclosed the confidential information that he hoped to take the title of Lord Cranborne (in fact he did take this title a few years later, before he became Lord Salisbury).[22] William would have been chary of going alone to London to attend the Queen for his passport, when the very man who had introduced him to the Court two months before had just become annoyed with his mother. Secondly, although over this engagement the only *documented* evidence we have about its miscarrying is the news twice reported to Sidney by Whyte that Burghley was blaming Pembroke for suddenly demanding a much bigger marriage-portion, it is obvious that William had again refused to marry; and, meditating refusal, he would have been far too reluctant to go to London to meet the Cecils and Veres alone and to approach the Queen for her permission to travel overseas, if he was not committed to the scheme. Thirdly, Whyte's Letter of 5 November says that whoever had told Sidney that Herbert would be coming to London had been wrong.

So his father had again to raise the dowry required and made Burghley break off negotiation in anger.[23] Even if it did not cost him compensation, the Earl, and presumably the Countess, must have been furious with their son that he had again frustrated the plans they had been carefully implementing to get him suitably married and so to insure the family's fortunes. We have therefore every reason to suppose that the Earl at this juncture would have treated William with no greater indulgence than in the preceding April and would certainly not have advanced the date from which he had agreed to let him live in London – the spring of 1598.

So we can say with some confidence that the first three opportunities that William Herbert and Shakespeare had of meeting each other were:

(1) on, and perhaps just after, Herbert's seventeenth birthday in

April 1597 at Wilton (the marriage sonnets and perhaps a few others would belong to this time);

(2) during a week or so near the end of July 1597, when Herbert was in London with his mother to meet Bridget Vere and the Cecils (we shall find a few sonnets belonging to this visit);

(3) onwards from 23 March 1598, when Robert Sidney arrived in England to join his wife and family and to stay at Baynard's Castle in a suite of rooms prepared for him in advance by his sister's orders, a suite overlooking the Thames at Blackfriars.[24] It seems likely that his sister Mary and William his nephew came up to London to welcome him there and that William stayed on attending the Court. Whyte's letters naturally cease, now that Sidney was in London, but there is in the Salisbury Papers an informative letter written on 18 June 1598 by the Earl of Pembroke at Wilton to Sir Robert Cecil as secretary to the Queen.[25] He apologizes for his own sudden return to Wilton from duty in Wales owing to 'want of health' and also for his son's being at home and absent from the Court because he was 'distempered in his body'. He goes on, 'As it is, I must for some few days stay him till he perfectly recover'. This implies that William had previously been attending the Court over some time; so we have no reason to suppose that the Earl's original plan for William's residence in London had not been followed.

In effect the earliest continuous time over which Shakespeare could have written sonnets to William Herbert independently of his parents began in the spring of 1598.

5   A provisional dating of the sonnets; the significance of the tetrad

So far we have a hypothetical date for the beginning of the sonnets – 8 April 1597 – and so an equally hypothetical date for the third anniversary of the meeting of Herbert and Shakespeare – 8 April 1600. The anniversary is recorded in te 25 d (Q's 104), the first of three sonnets which all have the same rhyme for their couplet – (un-)bred/dead. The other two are Q's 108 and 112 (te 28 d and te 27 d). These three, occurring in the series of four in Q's numbering, give one of the hints of the existence of groups of four.

A late dating has been suggested by several scholars for two other sonnets, 1603 for Q's 107 (te 28 c) and 1606 for Q's 124 (te 31 c). They have taken line 5 of the former to mean 'Queen Elizabeth has died' but several other meanings have been proposed for it and other references and dates suggested. Lines 5 and 6 need to be considered together:

> The mortal moon hath her eclipse endured
> And the sad augurs mock their own presage.

Line 6 means simply 'And the sad prophets mock their own prediction'. Those who say that line 5 does *not* mean 'Queen Elizabeth has died' but refers to an earlier crisis, cannot have the prophets being sad *because* they had been wrong in their prediction, because that would mean that they were sad that the Queen had survived or that the Armada had not defeated the British navy! So they say that 'the sad augurs' means 'the prophets of death or disaster'. Clearly the prophets' prediction has been wrong and they would have to admit it if challenged, but this is not the right meaning for 'mock'. There is a simple, natural meaning for line 6, which as far as I can discover has not been suggested before. It is that the prophets' prediction had been that the Queen would *recover* and now by their very mourning (sadness) they were giving the lie to their own forecast; they were mutely proclaiming it wrong. This gives a proper sense to 'mock' ('contradict') and confirms that the Queen's death is what is announced in the line before.

The execution of the Guy Fawkes conspirators on 31 January 1606 has been taken as the reference in the couplet of Q's 124:

> To this I witness call the fools of time,
> Which die for goodness, who have lived for crime.

Again, several other allusions have been suggested but none as well known.

It is revealing to see what happens when we take the late dates proposed for these two references and assign each set of four to one of William Herbert's birthdays, beginning from 1606 and working backwards but observing these two suggested dates. 1606 has the last tetrad (Q's 121, 125, 124, 123). Tetrad 30 (Q's 119, 117, 118, 120) falls to 1605 and tetrad 29 (Q's 113, 114, 116, 115) to 1604. 1603 has the tetrad 28 (Q's 106, 105, 107, 108) because of its reference to the Queen's death. So tetrad 27 (Q's 110, 109, 111, 112) falls to the next free year, 1602, and 1601 gets tetrad 26 (Q's 95, 96, 69, 70), its first pair referring to William Herbert's disgrace for his seduction of one of the Ladies-in-Waiting (which was lampooned on the streets):

> That tongue that tells the story of thy days,
> Making lascivious comment on thy sport,
> Cannot dispraise but in a kind of praise:
> Naming thy name blesses an ill report.

'Sport' was slang for a sexual affair. A lampoon is extant in two versions; both name Pembroke's name and would belong to the first quarter of 1601, when the pregnancy and Pembroke's part in it had become known.

That leaves for 1600 tetrad 25 (Q's 98, 99, 97, 104), including the third anniversary sonnet, and for 1599 tetrad 24 (Q's 100–103). Before that come the 'farewell' groups (te 21–te 23), so it is appropriate that te 24 is the first group that apologizes for an unusually long interval since the last 'singing'.

Three more points can be made about this series of eight tetrads, each being taken as made for one of the birthdays from 1599 to 1606.

The first is that five of them mention a time interval since the last communication and the other three at least imply new situations. The second is that the tetrads for the years 1602 and 1603 have been inverted. Whether that was done to bring the sonnet announcing the Queen's death, a sonnet in which some have seen reference to the wording of the 107th Psalm, into the position of Q's 107, nobody can say.[26] Lady Pembroke certainly knew her Psalms (she was continuing her late brother's translation of them), but inversion was a frequently used dodge of the rearranger of the sonnets; it obscured sequence and was therefore more likely when references to known events might be recognized.

The third point is that the group which has fallen to 1604 includes the sonnet which begins

> Let me not to the marriage of true minds
> Admit impediments.

Young Pembroke was to be married on 4 November 1604. Negotiations for this had gone on throughout the previous autumn and winter,[27] so the engagement could have been announced in March and could have been the piece of news which disoriented Shakespeare in the way that the first sonnet of te 29 (a = Q's 113) describes. 'The marriage of true minds' will then have both a literal and a metaphorical meaning. Similarly the metaphor of *crowning*, used in *b* and *d* of that tetrad, may have been prompted by the coronation of James I on 15 March.

By all these 'coincidences' our original hypothesis for the dating is strengthened. Moreover, we discover how much the theory of tetrads helps us in the restoration of order and assignment of dates; it reduces by a factor of four the number of intervals between poems. Each poem makes it possible to say something more definite about the change of situation since the last poem and to infer some events that may have occurred in the interval. This principle will be of even greater help when we come to the year 1598, to which we must assign the bulk of the terads.

These eight groups show very plainly what a tetrad is, not just a 'linked quartet' of sonnets, as Dover Wilson called Q's 97, 98, 99, and 104 (in that order) and Q's 36–9 – loose groups sharing rhymes and themes. A tetrad has an organic unity. It opens suitably, either dramatically with an exclamation:

How sweet and lovely dost thou make the shame . . . ! (te 26 *a*)

Alas, 'tis true! I *have* gone here and there . . . ! (te 27 *a*),

What potions have I drunk of Siren tears . . . ! (te 30 *a*),

or in a measured way, perhaps conveying the situation (maybe dramatically also):

Where art thou, Muse, that thou neglect'st so long . . . ? (te 24 *a*),

From you I have been absent in the Spring . . . (te 25 *a*),

When in the chronicles of wasted time . . . (te 28 *a*),

Since I left you, mine eye is in my mind . . . (te 29 *a*),

and occasionally with a generalization:

'Tis better to be vile than vile esteemed . . . (te 31 *a*).

The couplets of the last sonnet of each tetrad close convincingly and positively. Those of other sonnets may make a half-close, or state a negative or a warning sentiment, but the couplets of all *d* sonnets are strong and satisfying. This feature of the structure therefore rescues the Shakespearean sonnet from the common accusation of weakness in its ending; only one in four of the couplets is to be accounted a true ending.[28]

A tetrad is nearly always made of two pairs, *ab cd*. A pair is often so closely bound together in sense that it cannot be separated or inverted. Eight pairs have accordingly survived intact in this series of te 24 – te 31. Pairs slightly less closely bound have been inverted by the dis-arranger (three in this series). The pairs of a tetrad are linked to each other in various ways, by sense, theme, rhyme, key words, and tone.

The laws of probability guarantee that the tetrads are an aspect of Shakespeare's original design. We shall soon see from where he may have got the idea. The tetradic form was never used again because Shakespeare had kept his sonnet poems private and because the editors of the first edition took pains to break up or to camouflage the sets of four.

6   *The method of reconstructing the story*

There are three kinds of material from which I have pieced together the story which follows in section 7. The first and most extensive is Shakespeare's poetical response to the situations in which he found himself. It was a response elaborated in a series of sonnets and is therefore equivalent to one side of a telephone conversation. Hitherto the difficulty has been that his response was scrambled: there has been no way of telling (a) the sequence, (b) the length of the pauses between the bouts of talk, (c) who was on the other end of the line. But Shakespeare's response, *when put in the order of tetrads*, gives a manageable number of units to arrange chronologically, some indication of intervals between them, and strong evidence of their being arranged in groups.

Second, the family situations of the Herberts and Sidneys provided part of the chronological framework in which to order the tetrads. Third, other facts afford a series of datable events to which allusions may be made in the tetrads; some of these may overlap with the family situation. The reconstruction and provisional dating of te 24– te 31 show the method to be pursued. The datable events in the third class were the first rising of Saturn in opposition in April,[29] the Mary Fitton scandal, the death of Queen Elizabeth, Pembroke's marriage, and the execution of the Guy Fawkes conspirators.

It must be emphasized that all this is in the nature of an extended hypothesis. But methodologically there is all the difference in the world between *multiplying hypotheses* (i.e. making a second depend on a first and a third on the second), when the probabilities become smaller and smaller, receding from unity, and *adding the deductions from a hypothesis*, when the probabilities become greater, as with placing the pieces of a jigsaw puzzle; they then approach unity.

The sequence was found *from working backwards* and I think that any systematic test of the results would have to pursue the same path through the 126 which address the young man.

The groups which in Q immediately precede the annual groups are two sets of four which show deteriorating relations between poet and patron and contain a farewell sonnet. When these are logically rearranged with the farewell at the end and the calm generalizations at the beginning, they reveal a gap which is best filled with the tetrad of jealousy. Three tetrads therefore lead up to the break.

Before them come nine sonnets traditionally known as the 'rival-poet' series; 77 and 81 do not belong to it but three earlier in Q should be brought to join it, viz. 23, 32, and 38. These twelve again make three highly wrought tetrads.

Before these should come two tetrads, the first of return from a journey and discovery of sexual supplanting, the second of forgiveness; it leads naturally on to a third tetrad with the theme 'When I am dead and laid in grave', a group which has not been displaced or broken up like the other two.

The ten sonnets now standing before the group just mentioned are a group conveying melancholy over loss, over the destructive power of time, and over the degenerate days that make one long for death. Another sonnet on Time (19) and one on Death (81), when added appropriately, bring the total to twelve sonnets – three convincing tetrads which, it will be argued, belong to Shakespeare's visit to Stratford in 1598.

Nine of the ten sonnets now standing just before the melancholy groups are about a journey. When given three more – 18, 27, and 28 – they can be arranged in three tetrads, the first describing the setting out, the second thoughts on receiving a portrait by messenger, and the third the night before arrival.

The eight sonnets now remaining before the journey need to be joined by four left unused in our backward course through the series – 122, 77, 75, and 52. These twelve sonnets again make three good tetrads, the third of which appropriately is a leave-taking and an insistence upon the need to live separately; the first offers a gift and was therefore well suited for Herbert's birthday of 1598 (8 April). The middle one will be shown to record experiences at the Easter service; in 1598 this was on 16 April.[30] The gap between the birthday and Easter, plus two days allowed for composition of the Easter poem, would be one of ten days and this can be used as an indication of the interval between successive tetrads. There would on this reckoning be three tetrads a month from April to September inclusive, and grouping of tetrads by theme into sets of three would correspond with the successive months. The 'envoi' (126) would round off the eighteen tetrads, which form a drama of six acts.

What is left consists of the seventeen marriage sonnets, now assigned to the seventeenth birthday (8 April 1597), and a group of four sonnets, three of which start with allusions to painting and the remaining one to a mirror. When put in the order 21, 20, 24, 22, this group makes a significant tetrad, which, it will be argued, belongs to the fourth week of July 1597, when Herbert came to London with his mother to meet Bridget Vere.

To complete the sonnets to the young man, 1–17 in Q can be arranged as four tetrads and an epilogue. No. 8 is the epilogue; it is the only one that will pair with no other of the seventeen, the only one that mentions the complete family – 'sire and child and happy mother', and the only one which indicates that Shakespeare has met William Herbert, heard him talk and watched the play of emotion on his features as he listened to music. The four tetrads that preceded it were written to a painted miniature of Herbert before Shakespeare actually met him; there are several indications of this, which will be pointed out later.

Q's order has with one main exception preserved the approximate chronological sequence of the first 125 sonnets. The chief exception is the poet's discovery of sexual transgression and his forgiveness for it. But Q's last twenty-eight are in an order very far from chronological. When convincingly rearranged, there are eighteen sonnets in six triads ostensibly addressing a Dark Woman. The triads form a double poem, tr 2–tr 4 and tr 5–tr 7. The editors of Q must have first inverted the halves and arranged them as (tr 5, 6, and 7) + (tr 2, 3, and 4), before they lightly mixed the groups leaving as much poetic coherence as possible. Then, together with the wedding sonnet (145), the individual sonnets of tr 1 (148, 130, 138) and of the pairs were sprinkled in. The last twenty-eight sonnets in Q are almost like a well-mixed plum pudding but the basic structure of the double poem is still discernible.

The first triad, **tr** 1, will be shown to go with **te** 5 and therefore to belong like it to the fourth week of July 1597.

For pure interest in the recovery of time past the three pairs and the wedding sonnet are unequalled. They are, I believe, a relic of the first meeting of Shakespeare with William Herbert's parents in the absence of their son and they give us a glimpse of Shakespeare's powers and speed of composition. The story begins there.

7   *The story*[31]

(i)   The first commission

During the first week of April 1597 Shakespeare arrived at Wilton House to do the job for which the Earl and Countess of Pembroke had summoned him. Since his purchase of New Place at Stratford was completed just one month later, on 4 May, clearly he had been negotiating it beforehand knowing that he could count upon enough ready money for the purpose. He would have had advance notice of the sum he would receive and presumably of the reason for the invitation – to compose birthday poetry which would prevail upon William Herbert, the Pembrokes' heir, to fall in with his parents' second attempt to arrange a marriage for him. It was not Shakespeare's first poetry for a birthday, if *Venus and Adonis* was written for the Earl of Southampton's twentieth, as Christopher Butler and Alastair McIntyre argued in 1964. But we know nothing of the circumstances of that composition. To perform the Pembrokes' commission Shakespeare may have re-read the passages in T. Wilson's *The Art of Rhetorique* which reproduce Erasmus's arguments in favour of marriage. Sir Philip Sidney, the Countess's late brother, had used them in Book III of his *Arcadia* so they would be most appropriate. From a comparison of Shakespeare's known sources and the texts of his plays it can be seen that he had tremendous powers of verbal and thematic recall, but such recall is nearly always something that fades with lapse of the time since a text has been read. At any rate the seventeen marriage sonnets do recall Wilson's arguments in words and thought – more vividly than Venus's arguments urging Adonis to forgo his sexual self-sufficiency.

It was probably Shakespeare's first visit to Wilton, because, as he makes clear in the third anniversary sonnet, he had not met William Herbert before. Herbert had been at New College, Oxford, from 1593 to 1595 and he would have reported the vogue at the Universities for Shakespeare's two long poems, published in those years. So Shakespeare was a clever choice of his mother's – she being the literary figure in the family – to put the most persuasive pressure on her son. Various people in London could have done the preliminary negotiations; Rowland Whyte, her younger brother's agent there, was quite probably one of them, since he was in constant touch with Arthur Massinger, the dramatist's father, house-steward at Wilton, and regularly passed on to Sir Robert Sidney the family news from there. Arthur Massinger is reported by his son Philip to have been the person who was negotiating for the marriage of William with Burghley's granddaughter.[32]

It is fruitful to wonder whether Shakespeare went alone to Wilton or on tour with some of his company. Lent was over – Easter had been on 27 March – so it is likely that the Lord Chamberlain's company was on the road. The arrival of the Players in *Hamlet* II.ii must have been distilled from many such visits to country mansions but it can rarely have been associated with a special commission, as it is in Hamlet (first version probably 1597) and perhaps was at Wilton. If one fits that scene to the occasion and puts the old Earl in the position of Hamlet calling for a speech and alluding to the old courtiers who call for 'a jig or a tale of bawdry' from a visiting player, it makes excellent material from which to imagine the way in which Shakespeare was greeted at his first interview (and later taken off to lodging by Hugh Sanford, the pedantic secretary, a likely source of some ingredients for Polonius):

> We'll e'en to it like French falconers,
> fly at anything we see; we'll have a (sonnet) straight:
> come give us a taste of your quality; come a passionate (sonnet).

The Earl was about twenty-seven years older than his Countess, whose great love had been her brother, Philip, seven years her elder. She was still mourning him more than ten years after his death, re-editing his works with Sanford's assistance, and continuing his translation of the Psalms, which in the following year she would arrange to have written by a calligraphist on vellum for presentation to Queen Elizabeth on the visit she planned to pay at Wilton.[33] Nobody who saw *Twelfth Night*, probably first played in January 1601, and who knew Mary Lady Herbert, could have failed to associate her with Olivia's seven years' mourning for a brother. Perhaps Shakespeare played a part com-

parable to the Fool's in that play in weaning her from her too prolonged grief.

Like Olivia, Lady Pembroke seems to have been an hysterical
character. Aubrey reports that 'old Sir Walter Long of Draycot and old
Mr Tyndale' asserted that she had lain with her brother Philip and that
young Philip, her second son and fourth child, was his son and named
after him.[34] The naming is right but if there had been brother–sister
incest, it was more likely that William was their son than Philip. Before
Philip was conceived, Sir Philip had taken up with Penelope Rich
('Stella') and then married Sir Francis Walsingham's daughter,
Frances, whereas before and just after William was born he and his
sister had been very close. Indeed a house at Ivy Church, four miles
from Wilton, had been specially furnished for brother and sister to live
in during Sidney's prolonged visit to Wilton at the time of William's
birth and during the months that followed it. He began and wrote
much of the *Arcadia* for her then.

Aubrey records that she had a salacious nature and had a room
specially built along one side of Wilton House so that she could view
the mares and stallions copulating and be excited by them to copulate
herself with her 'stallions' (viz. her gallants). Although such rumours
that Aubrey quotes are not all to be believed, such a mild perversion in
a beautiful, gifted, and intellectual woman is not so unusual. Like
many an hysteric she tended to remain unusually identified with her
children. In 1609, on hearing that her son Philip had been insulted and
whipped across the face by a Scottish courtier and had not retaliated,
she tore her hair – at the age of 46! The story is told by Francis
Osborne, reminiscing of what he had heard as a youth of fourteen
residing in Wilton.

Her husband Henry, the second Earl, held the command of much of
the south-west of England and of south Wales. Like his father, he was a
general of the Queen, even if his more important service had been legal
rather than military. He had acted in the trials of the Duke of Norfolk
and of Mary, Queen of Scots. He had also accepted the patronage of a
company of actors, then called the Earl of Pembroke's Men; to have
such companies enrol under the names of a few leading men was
Queen Elizabeth's way of avoiding the imposition of censorship and
the suppression of plays, for which the Puritans agitated and the
powerful Corporation of the City of London often called. Pembroke
had been devoted to Sir Philip Sidney, twenty years younger than
himself and the son of a far more cultured father (once the boyhood
companion to the future Edward VI, whose tutor and household
steward had been *his* father, Philip and Mary Sidney's grandfather). In

1601 Samuel Daniel wrote a 'dump' (an elegy) on Earl Henry's death, in which he enumerated the services he had done to the late Sir Philip Sidney; it was presumably another of the Countess's commissions.

It is worth asking how Lady Pembroke had managed to convince herself and her husband that Shakespeare was the right choice for their purpose in 1597. She had to make sure that he could do what they wanted. It must have been her scheme, for she was the highly literate one and she it was who had built up at Wilton, partly with her brother's advice and help initially but with her husband's money, a magnificent library of English and foreign books and manuscripts, many of which are still treasures of the Bodleian Library at Oxford. A commission for sonnets would be a tribute to her brother, who by his posthumous sonnet sequence had prompted the sonnet craze, which was lessening by the later 1590s and which Shakespeare had gently satirised in the first production of *Love's Labours Lost*.

Lady Pembroke herself knew Latin and Greek, French and Italian, and Hebrew too. She had translated and published a verse translation of a French tragedy, *Antonie*, and with her husband's wealth became patroness and benefactor to a number of poets and writers, including Spenser, Donne, Daniel, and Jonson. The epitaph upon her death in 1621 runs:

> Underneath this sable hearse
> Lies the subject of all verse,
> Sidney's sister, Pembroke's mother;
> Death, ere thou hast slain another
> Fair and learn'd and good as she,
> Time shall throw a dart at thee.

Her own verse was not of this quality and it is worth adding that Aubrey thought her as good a chemist as poetess and that she seems to have had the same kind of restless curiosity for scientific knowledge as her brother Philip.

The first interview with Shakespeare will have required the Pembrokes to state their family reasons for the urgency of their heir's marriage. The Earl was sick with a recurrent urinary complaint and if he died soon the long wardship of William might ruin the fortunes of his house. He had tried repeated cures by taking the waters at Bath but they had not really worked.

Questions to Shakespeare about himself were also a natural opening and the information that his only son, Hamnet, had died just eight months before would have struck a note of kinship in grief with Lady

31

Pembroke. Besides the deaths of her father, mother, and elder brother (all in 1586) she too had lost a child – her second, the elder daughter, who died aged three on the very day on which she had borne Philip. Thinking of her brother she perhaps asked what was the first sonnet that Shakespeare had ever written – one for his own wedding speech in 1582! She would have recalled her brother's sonnet sequence dating from the same period and told Shakespeare that she had, still unpublished, another sequence of his poems, mostly sonnets. She must then have shown him the manuscript, which included a special group of four sonnets that perhaps suggested an idea for Shakespeare's own composition for their son's birthday two or three days later. It could have been Shakespeare who urged the publication of *Certain Sonnets* in Sidney's collected works, which Lady Pembroke and Hugh Sanford were re-editing for publication the next year. A set of four in that sequence, nos. 8–11, is introduced by the epigraph:

> These four following sonnets were made when his Lady
> had pain in her face.[35]

Four sets of four and an epilogue would be most appropriate for William's seventeenth birthday, if Shakespeare agreed. He did agree and they also settled that music should be played while he recited – or at least before the epilogue.

Shakespeare will have needed some information about young Herbert's nature and attitude to marriage and to women. He was lent a portrait of him for the composition of the seventeen sonnets; it will have been a miniature painted by Nicholas Hilliard in the autumn of 1595, a picture of William at fifteen and a half standing in a garden, and inscribed on the bottom of the frame with the words *Happy Hours* – in English or in Latin. It would have been intended as a wedding gift for Elizabeth Carey. (These statements are all inferences from the re-ordered sonnets but they are well founded, as will be argued later.)

The final topic at that interview would have been the Pembrokes' admiration that Shakespeare really could manage to write such a series in the specified form in so short a time. Taking this as his cue for assurance that the feat was really possible, he offered – or perhaps they asked for – a display of *ex tempore* composition, which was in vogue at the time.

The chief clue to this event is the existence in Q of 153–4 (**pr** 1 *b* and *a*). They stand last in the traditional order and present a puzzle in the series. They are the only pair of obviously literary sonnets, the sort of thing Shakespeare would never have written unless he had to. They are both adaptations of the same Greek epigram, an obscure little poem composed by the fifth-century Byzantine lawyer, Marianus. It had not been translated before into English, but an Italian translation of it had been published by Fausto Sabeo in a collection of epigrams at Rome in 1556 (and twenty years later Sir Philip Sidney had brought over many Greek and Italian books, which accrued to the Wilton House library). There had also been an early Latin imitation of it in praise of Baiae, and Italian and French translations of that had already been published, but Shakespeare's poems are closer to the Fausto Sabeo and in one detail even closer to the Greek. There are two problems: where had Shakespeare met the Greek epigram, a text still very rare in England, and why did he choose to write two versions of it? It is not enough to say, 'He was practising the sonnet form'. For Shakespeare that was certainly unnecessary and we also need to know why he chose to adapt only one epigram from the Greek anthology.

The whole point of an *ex tempore* display is that the audience is sure that the performer does not know in advance the themes they are going to set him. Asked to produce a poem that Shakespeare could not have met, Lady Pembroke will have taken down from the library shelves the Planudean anthology published in Florence in 1484, turned to a poem she had been studying with the help of Fausto Sabeo's translation (this explains why Shakespeare reproduces Fausto's misunderstanding of a verbal prefix in the second line), and translated it aloud to her husband and Shakespeare, who then and there wrote two sonnet versions of the poem. Music was played while he wrote (the model for this is in *The Merchant of Venice; Portia:* 'Let music sound while he doth make his choice').

Shakespeare's two versions have often been dismissed as academic but may seem different if we imagine the occasion and the situation in which he could have written them. He was, I believe, incapable of not responding to a situation and of not using it in whatever he thought, re-thought, and wrote. Marianus's Greek epigram has only six lines, three elegiac couplets, and Shakespeare has added to it, almost certainly using what he recalled of one of Giles Fletcher's sonnets, no. 27 from *Licia*, published in 1593, a sequence he could have been reading in preparation for his *ex tempore*.

Here is an English version of the Greek:

Here underneath the plane-trees, held in gentle sleep, Eros
    slumbered,
His torch deposited with the nymphs. The nymphs to each other
Said, 'Come on! Let's quench his fire and along with it

The fire of human hearts.' But the torch set alight
The waters too, and from that source now the water
Which the love-nymphs draw for baths is hot.

In his sonnets Shakespeare made some changes before adding ideas. In 153 only one nymph (of Diana's) is mentioned. The description takes only six and a half lines. In 154 the act is of a single nymph, the fairest of a band; the chastity of the nymphs is specified, so is the virgin hand of the nymph who acts; the disarming of Cupid is dwelt on. This all takes ten lines.

New ideas in both are that the bath was a remedy for men's diseases and that the poet needed it but found it didn't help. 154 ends with a general statement of his discovery

> Love's fire heats water, water cools not love

but 153 with the personal conclusion

> the bath for my help lies
> Where Cupid got new fire, my mistress' eyes.

Lines 9–12 of Fletcher's sonnet are:

> I searched the cause and found it to be this:
> *She* touched the water and it burned with love;
> Now by her means it purchased hath that bliss
> Which all diseases quickly can remove.

It is likely that 154 was written before 153, because, given a poem that had to be expanded, it would have been natural – safer, on the spur of the moment – to pad out initially in the first version and then afterwards, in the second, to contract the early part and to amplify the new ideas. A scholar called James Hutton came to the same conclusion for a different reason.[36] Having discussed the possible sources for Shakespeare's two sonnets in great detail, he said that the first two lines of 154 are absurd – to lay aside a torch *while sleeping* – and 153 corrects the absurdity; so it was the later.

154 seems specially intended for the Countess, lingering as it does upon the fairest votary's maiden hand, and 153 rather for the Earl, because it dwells more on men's strange maladies; not only might he appreciate the *double entendre* of love sickness and venereal disease, but, suffering himself from a chronic urinary complaint, he would ap-

34

preciate also the notion of the poet's own failed treatment – at Bath! The sexual meaning of both sonnets would have been quite as plain to Elizabethans as nowadays; *brand, heart-inflaming, hot desire*, and *disarming by hand* do not need a psychoanalyst to interpret them.

Lady Mary was two and a half years, her husband thirty years, older than Shakespeare, and we might read 154 as a flirtatious sally and both, especially 153, as men's tavern jokes. The editor who put them at the end along with 151 (**pr 2** *b*) was relegating the sexual to the back of the book – and indeed hiding it there, since 150 and 152 (**tr 4** *a* and *b*) effectively embed 151 and make it appear a moment in Shakespeare's personal love-life, while 154 and 153 in isolation and in reversed order have been almost unanimously considered products of his immaturity rather than the set improvisation which they probably were.

It is hard to imagine 151 (**pr 2** *b*) as a moment in Shakespeare's love-life. There is something ridiculous in making him say it to a woman with whom he is already intimate. It is equally absurd to think of him describing his erections as a preliminary to seducing her. Like 154 and 153, 151 must have been a *risqué* sonnet written to amuse. Its tone is wrong for 150 and 152 (**tr 4** *a* and *b*), which run on perfectly from one to other without it, and the phrase 'betraying me' in line 5 cannot have the same sense as it would in those two sonnets, where it would mean betrayal *with a third person*. In 151 the betrayal is not with a third person but is a betrayal of the self, of the personal resolve. The sense is that of 'betray' at the end of the line; it means *tempt, encourage to transgress* – encourage by look, touch, word, or gesture – or by grace of movement, perhaps in playing the virginals!

For indeed 151 goes perfectly as the second of a pair with 128 (**pr 2** *a*) before it. For its first rhyme – *is/amiss* – it picks up the last rhyme of 128 – *this/kiss* – , an unusual rhyme in Shakespeare's sonnets, used in only five other places, but one which had been the fifth in Fletcher's sonnet – *this/bliss*. The pair (**pr 2** *a* and *b* = 128 and 151) repeats as many as six rhymes of the first pair (and the four sonnets together repeat four of the rhymes of Fletcher's sonnet). The unusually big number of shared rhymes suggests that Shakespeare took up a challenge – or challenged himself – to turn his first pair into a technical tetrad. He continued to amuse his hosts by sexual imagery, which is obvious without being blatant in 128, though some scholars have thought it the more indecent. In 151 the menial-bodyguard metaphor for erection and its loss would have been as suitable to aim at an old general of the Queen as to style Cupid 'the general of hot desire'. We may infer from the epilogue to the seventeen marriage sonnets (Q's 8) that there was a virginalist at Wilton House, perhaps Lady Pembroke herself (her younger brother

35

adored Dowland's music). So we may imagine the Earl, asked for a subject for the next pair to be improvised, exclaiming, 'The virginalist! and make them as irresistible as the lady! give me a pair to woo her with!'

There is another nice link with the Giles Fletcher. His couplet had been

> Then if by you these streams thus blessèd be,
> Sweet grant me love, and be not worse to me.

Shakespeare's couplet to 128 is

> Since wooden jacks so happy are in this,
> Give them thy fingers, me thy lips to kiss.

Each poet begs that the *things* blessed by the touch of the woman be not treated better than himself.

For his finale Shakespeare did a very daring thing. He composed aloud, without writing them down, new versions of the last two of Sidney's *Certain Sonnets*, a pair never published before. His hosts would know that he had only just been shown them and that they themselves held the only manuscript of *C.S.* 32 (31 exists in another manuscript in Sidney's own hand but had never been published, as some earlier of the series had been by Henry Constable).[37]

Q's 129 upon Lust (**pr** 3 *a*) matches Sidney's 31 upon Desire and shares with it certain technical features like the repetition of words:

> . . . lust in action, and till action lust . . .
> (*C.S.* 31.5: Desire, Desire I have too dearly bought);

> Past reason hunted . . .
> Past reason hated. . . .
> (*C.S.* 31.9–11: But yet in vain . . .
> In vain thou madest me . . .
> In vain thou kindlest . . .).

(Also Shakespeare's sonnet shares two rhymes with Fletcher's quoted above and the prominent words 'bliss' and 'woe'.)

The other sonnet of Shakespeare's pair (**pr** 3 *b* = Q's 146) has just as close affinities with the second of Sidney's pair. The theme is the same, as J. W. Lever and others have pointed out, though nobody has ever asked where Shakespeare could have met *C.S.* 32 or seen that the two *pairs* match in themes and words. Sidney's 32 begins

> Leave me, O love which reachest but to dust,
> And thou, my mind, aspire to higher things;
> Grow rich in that which never taketh rust;
> Which ever fades but fading pleasure brings.

These lines are surely echoed by Shakespeare's third quatrain:

> Then soul, live thou upon thy servant's loss,
> And let that pine to aggravate thy store;
> Buy terms divine in selling hours of dross;
> Within be fed, without be rich no more.

There is a famous corruption in the text of the second line of Shakespeare's sonnet. Its first three words repeat the last three words of the first line and the second line is two syllables too long:

> Poor soul, the centre of my sinful earth,
> My sinful earth these rebel powers that thee array.

Clearly these three words have displaced two syllables (one word or two) that began the second line. The usual way to emend the text recently has been to put a participle + 'by' – e.g. 'Foiled by'. But this makes a vocative of two lines, which is clumsy compared with all other vocatives in the sonnets. A one-line vocative is better and matches Sidney's first-line vocative. Besides, when Shakespeare in the sonnets has a series of short staccato questions, he almost always establishes a two-line sentence pattern early and has a four-line sentence in the second or third quatrain. Therefore an imperative, which several scholars have suggested, makes a much more characteristic pattern for the sonnet as a whole.[38]

We require a verb that fits the three meanings of 'array' in Shakespeare's day – *attire with display, afflict, defile* – and also the military metaphor for the sexual meaning of 'these rebel powers'. We should also like a word that, as C. K. Pooler hoped, would pick up the economic image of '*Poor* soul', an image that is continued in lines 3–12, especially in the words, *pine, costly, cost, spend, loss, pine, store, selling, rich.* I believe that the lost word is 'Disperse'. It fits the image of scattering rebels; its pun on 'dis-purse' (*disburse*) satisfies Pooler's wish; it suits the subsidiary meanings of 'array'; and in terms of consonantal types it is identical with 'these . . . powers' – dental, sibilant, labial, liquid, sibilant – a linguistic device which Stephen Booth noted Shakespeare was inclined to.[39]

We shall have to account for the mistake, which is extremely unlikely to have been a copyist's or typesetter's error, but may be one of the most suggestive clues to the circumstances of the composition.

I am maintaining that Shakespeare composed his pair of sonnets aloud and that some scribe, perhaps Lady Pembroke herself, took them down as he did so and made certain mistakes natural in the circumstances, once putting a comma where there was a hesitation for thought, failing to put commas lest pauses were only for thought, and being in doubt over what seemed, or was, a repetition.

The text of **pr** 3 *a* (Q's 129) 7–12 runs

> Past reason hated as a swallowd bayt
> On purpose layd to make the taker mad.
> Made In pursuit and possession so,
> Had, having, and in quest, to have extreme,
> A bliss in proofe and proud and very woe,
> Before a ioy proposd behind a dreame.

Here there are three certain mistakes – the capital 'I' of 'In pursuit' (a unique typographical error in the sonnets' text, which is very consistent on initial capitals and nowhere else gives one to a preposition which does not begin a line or a sentence), the comma after 'in quest', and the 'and' before 'very woe'. They all indicate certain pauses *in oral composition*, wrongly taken by the scribe to be punctuational pauses in the sense. The first also indicates the scribe's momentary uncertainty whether 'Made' was simply the poet's pensive repetition of 'mad' at the end of the line before (they were then pronounced alike and punned on). After writing 'Made' he would suddenly have thought that after all the line began at 'In pursuit', so put a capital, but realized it did not before he crossed out 'Made'.

Editors who change 'Made' to 'Mad' have decided there is a fourth mistake, but I think they are wrong, because 'extreme' would be weak by comparison, whereas it should be the climax of the two lines. Besides, to take 'so' as meaning 'the same' (i.e. 'mad'), 'as well', or 'also' is prose, not poetry. Shakespeare was fond of the anticipatory *so* – 'like this: at every time extreme: a bliss . . . a woe, a joy . . . a dream').

The second mistake arose from the poet's pause, in doubt whether he could afford to have the extra two syllables of 'in quest *to have*', before he found the dissyllabic 'extreme'. Similarly the third came from his slight pause after 'prov'd', making the scribe think that the sense was 'A bliss in proof and proved'; so that he tacked on 'very woe' with 'and', not realizing the mirror symmetry between the two halves of the line.

In composing the second sonnet the poet paused after the first line and this time really did pensively repeat its last three words while he searched for the verb *Disperse*. In writing them out again the scribe probably never even heard 'Disperse' owing to its assonance with 'sin . . . earth'.

With 'Disperse' to begin line 2 the sense of Shakespeare's first two lines and that of Sidney's opening

> Leave me, O love which reachest but to dust,

is one and the same – the renunciation of physical sexuality.

In this sonnet we find the strong metaphors of *eating up* and of inheritance, which are just as prominent (worms and all) in the first of the tetrads which Shakespeare was about to compose for the birthday ceremony of 8 April. But the strongest metaphor of all

> Why so much cost, having so short a lease,
> Dost thou upon thy fading mansion spend?

was surely derived from Shakespeare's currently negotiated purchase of New Place, his first house – an event to make one think on death. Moreover,

> Buy terms divine in selling hours of dross

was a way of describing what the poet was doing at that very moment – prostituting his talents to provide his family with a better home!

Love's Labours Lost, which we know only in its amplified version written for performance at Christmas 1597, has examples of extemporal composition both written and oral. They may or may not be Shakespeare's own allusion to his performance earlier that year, but I believe that we have Ben Jonson's humorous allusion to it in *Every Man in his own Humour*. In that play put on by Shakespeare's company in 1598 a character claims to have written *ex tempore* ten or a dozen sonnets at a sitting but is shown up later as an impostor by being challenged at oral *ex tempore*. Moreover some of the fragments which the pseudo-poet stole were from *Delia* by Samuel Daniel, another poet whom the Pembrokes had patronized.[40]

The *ex tempore* given, Shakespeare turned to composing the birthday tetrads. From them, once put in order, the strong likelihood emerges that he composed them having before him a miniature portrait of William Herbert and that he did not meet him in person until the ceremony, at which he may have recited the tetrads but certainly did recite the epilogue, which he purported to extemporize.

The epilogue is Q's sonnet 8. It differs in three important ways from the other sixteen. It will not pair with any other; it is the only sonnet to mention human sound and facial expression; it is the only one to speak of the complete family – 'sire and child and happy mother'. But the editors who placed it before Q's sonnet 9 forged a powerful false link which has kept the first seventeen from being restored to their original order. It has always been thought that the last five words of 8 – 'thou single wilt prove none' – led on to the first two lines of 9, which seem to pick up the word *single*. But once 8 is removed, it is easy to spot a much more appropriate couplet – that of Q's 3 – which leads on to the opening of 9:

> But if thou live remembred not to be,
> Die single and thine image dies with thee.

> Is it from fear to wet a widow's eye
> That thou consum'st thyself in single life?

Besides the word *single* the later lines share the concepts of living and dying. Now 2 runs on to 3 and 9 to 10; so to bring these two pairs together reconstitutes a tetrad – the second.

With 2 and 3 put back to join 9 and 10, 1 and 4 are left next to each other and run on well; 5 and 6 are a pair and run on, but clearly the couplet of 6

> Be not self-willed, for thou art much too fair
> To be death's conquest and make worms thine heir

is picked up by the opening of Q's 1

> From fairest creatures we desire increase,
> That thereby beauty's rose might never die,

> But as the riper should by time decease,
> His tender heir might bear his memory.

The link is made particularly by the words *fair* and *heir* as well as later by expansion of the idea of 'self-willed'. With the order of the pairs reversed, the two halves of this tetrad are bound together by the same device as the two halves of the second tetrad. We can now see what an appropriate opening to the whole series Q's 5 provides. It is the only sonnet of the seventeen which has neither first nor second person pronoun. The second person enters at **te** 1 *b* and the first person pronoun not till **te** 2 *d* (except in the anticipated speech of William Herbert as an old man – **te** 2 *a*). **Te** 1 shows William Herbert as extremely narcissistic – 'contracted to (his) own bright eye'. **Te** 2 features the woman as mother, wife, and perhaps widow.

Te 3 is concerned with the father. We now have sonnets 7, 11, 12 together. The missing pair to 7, which has for its chief image the course of the sun across the sky, is 14, the astronomical sonnet. Then the opening of 11 – 'As fast as thou shalt wane' – picks up the astronomical image of the first pair. This sonnet also makes the transition from the astronomical images for human continuity to the agricultural, which had been prefigured in line 12 of 14 (*b*):

> If from thyself to store thou would'st convert.

So in **te** 3 *c* we get 'when thou from youth convertest' and 'whom nature hath not made for store'. Seed-corn yields to harvest and in *d* we find

> summer's green all girded up in sheaves
> Born on the bier with white and bristly beard.

The final tetrad, after a glance at astronomy, changes the image of growth to horticulture and then, via the flowers of the 'painted counterfeit', to painting and poetry as ways of handing on a likeness of the self, but ways which are inadequate if the likeness is not also transmitted to offspring. *Thou* and *thee* of the first three tetrads in the fourth become *you*, perhaps then a more emotionally heightened form of address; the epilogue returns to *thou*.

The tetrads have had no living model, only a miniature portrait to teach the pen its business. True to the situation, they reproduce no human sound or movement, only the sound of a clock that tells the time. But the epilogue breaks the spell. Its first four words address

Herbert as 'Music to hear' (we imagine his voice) and the rest of the line asks about the sadness on his face as he listens to music. Shakespeare's portrait can outdo paint in these two ways and its chief image for the complete family is one of musical notes.

Clues to the painted portrait are strewn about. The most obvious is in **te** 4 *b*, where the children Herbert will beget shall be

> Much liker than your painted counterfeit.

Then in line 10 the words

> this (time's pencil or my pupil pen)

refer to what Shakespeare was looking at and to what he was writing *taught by* the miniature portrait; for he had nothing else to go upon in describing Herbert's 'outward fair'.

Once Shakespeare's use of the miniature portrait is entertained as a serious hypothesis, it illumines several passages. A miniature was a small framed water-colour behind glass and sometimes called 'a jewel'. It was painted with delicate touches of a 'pencil' (a fine hair brush) – the 'heav'nly touches' of **te** 4 *d*. In fact the whole of that sonnet, in which the writing is spoken of in the language of painting, is an expanded fusion of the words bracketed in *b*:

> (time's pencil or my pupil pen).[41]

Lines 5–8 of *b*

> Now stand you on the top of happy hours,
> And many maiden gardens yet unset
> With virtuous wish would bear your living flowers
> Much liker than your painted counterfeit.

make a marvellous sense if the miniature showed the youth standing in a garden with painted flowers and had on the frame below the picture the words *Happy Hours* (or *Horae felices*). The phrase 'stand you on the top' then literally describes the miniature as well as being a metaphor for the youth on the border of adolescence and adult life. Now the opening lines of **te** 1 *a* are enriched and seen as the perfect opening for the whole series:

> Those hours that with gentle work did frame
> The lovely gaze where every eye doth dwell . . . .

The word *hours* on the frame have supplied the metaphor. The hours that the painter had spent limning the youth are equated with the time that had gone to the boy's rearing (if not begetting).

A liquid prisoner pent in walls of glass

are marvellous words to describe the distilled essence of flowers but still richer if the word-play lets us think of a framed water-colour. In the next sonnet the distillation will become the foetus in a womb.

An anniversary sonnet is an appeal to the person addressed to recall the first occasion of the meeting of himself and the poet. The appeal is stronger if it includes something that both would remember, and stronger still if that something was a joke or phrase then used by the one appealed to. Shakespeare's phrase recalling the occasion of the third anniversary is

when first your eye I eyed.

Many have thought this one of Shakespeare's worst lapses from taste and euphony but such a judgment is utterly irrelevant if the words were intended to remind Herbert of his own joke on his seventeenth birthday after hearing Shakespeare recite: 'What was that line, Mr Shakespeare? I have it – "The lovely gaze where every eye doth dwell". So you wrote all those sonnets eying my eye!'

Tetrad 5, which belongs to the next meeting, in July, opens

So is it not with me as with that Muse
Stirred by a painted beauty to his verse.

The Muse referred to has been sought here and there among the poems and poets of the 1590s, but vainly, for the lines are Shakespeare's claim that he is no longer his professional past self of the marriage sonnets, when he was inspired by the painted beauty of the miniature: 'I am not now as I was then.' Indeed the openings of the first three sonnets of te 5 add up to Shakespeare's gently teasing response to Herbert, a teasing that would be unthinkable if the young aristocrat had not first teased him: 'How can I believe a compliment from the man who wrote so many sonnets to my painted portrait before he'd even met me?'

But that second meeting lay three and a half months ahead. After 8 April they separated, Shakespeare perhaps on tour, but if so, a tour time-tabled for him to take possession of his fading mansion, his new house in Stratford, on 4 May. The Pembrokes had time to think of what was to come: William had his parents' promise to let him live in London and attend the Court from the spring of 1598 but with the prospect of an early marriage for the sake of the family; his parents had gained William's agreement to meet Bridget Vere and consider marriage but with inevitable doubts whether he would go through with their scheme. Lady Mary knew she had made a valuable ally in Shakespeare, while the Earl was probably exasperated at William's self-willed attitude. It is reasonable to suppose that Shakespeare had left with instructions to call upon them at Baynard's Castle in the fourth week of July, when they would come to London.

(ii) The second commission

However and exactly when the second meeting began, it is easy to say how and when it ended. On Thursday 28 July the Privy Council made an order for the 'final suppressing of all stage plays' and the closing and dismantling of all theatres in and around London.[42] The dismantling was not enforced but the theatres were all closed and, in effect, had a suspended sentence; it lasted three months, for the order was rescinded on 31 October. No historical reason has yet been given why the Privy Council should suddenly have done what the Puritan Corporation of the City of London had been agitating for and demanding for years. The reason alleged was the seditious character of a play, *The Isle of Dogs*, written jointly by Thomas Nashe and Ben Jonson and put on at the Swan Theatre by the Earl of Pembroke's Men; but if that had been all, the closing down of the play and the imprisonment of the authors (which was in fact carried out, though Nashe evaded imprisonment for a time by taking refuge in Yarmouth) would have been quite enough. Failing hard evidence it sometimes helps to ask, not *cui bono?*, but *cui malo?* The order would have hit Pembroke's Men specially hard, for some of the actors were imprisoned besides the authors, and it would have been a warning to Pembroke, their patron, to keep a better control of his Men.

And of his son? For if William Herbert had been seen around in Shakespeare's company, especially at the 'seditious' play, which it would have been natural for him to attend, put on as it was by his father's company, Lord Burghley could have decided to crack a whip

44

to remind the youth who had come up to pay court to his grand-daughter that he should choose his companions more carefully. So for three months we find

> art made tongue-tied by authority.

Shakespeare must have received a message from Baynard's Castle on 28 July to say that in view of the Order in Council he should stay away from the Herbert family for the present. In April of the next year he was to write of

> those blots that do with me remain

and say

> I may not evermore acknowledge thee
> Lest my bewailèd guilt should do thee shame.

He could find in the recall of that incident of July a perfect excuse for living apart, for not accepting an invitation to take up his residence in the Herbert mansion.

Since William had come up with his mother, escorted almost certainly by Hugh Sanford, it is unlikely that he made arrangements without reference to them. Even three years later, so Rowland Whyte writes to his uncle, there is a risk that Mr Sanford will suggest 'some pedantic invention' for William's shield device on entering the tilting lists, unless his uncle can suggest one first. Like many narcissistic youths he seems to have been dependent on others for suggestions about the right way to do things. It may have been at his mother's suggestion that he gave Shakespeare a notebook ('tables') at this time.

Shakespeare's first poem of 1598 contains an explanation of his having given the notebook away. By then it contained something besides its 'vacant leaves'; tetrad 5 (Q's 21, 20, 24, 22) is the natural supposition and also, or perhaps only, triad 1 (148, 130, 138). It has often been suggested that 21 and 130 were written at the same time. The third rhyme of 21 *compare/rare* is used for the couplet of 130:

> And yet, by heav'n, I think my love as rare
> As any she belied by false compare.

And there is a similarity of tone in 21's couplet:

Let them say more that like of hearsay well;
I will not praise that purpose not to sell.

But there is a stronger reason for dating them together. Both are to be used later for self-quotation. To quote an opening verse of one's own poems is as valid a way to remind the recipient of the occasion of that poem as to quote a remark of his. The first line of te 5 *d* (22) is

My glass shall not persuade me I am old.

The first line of te 6 *a*, fixed for the quite other reasons as the beginning of Shakespeare's next poem to Herbert, is

Thy glass shall show thee how thy beauties wear.

Besides that the opening rhymes of te 5 *a* are *Muse/verse/use/rehearse*. The opening rhymes of a later poem of 1598 – te 18 *a* (78) – are *Muse/verse/use/disperse*. And there are reasons to think that George Chapman and his poetry were in the minds of Shakespeare and Herbert on both occasions. Again, the opening two lines of tr 1 *a* (148) are

O me, what eyes have love put in my head,
Which have no correspondence with true sight?

Which are surely recalled by the opening two lines of tr 2 *a* (137):

Thou blind fool Love, what dost thou to mine eyes,
That they behold and see not what they see?

Moreover such recall is silly unless there is a point to it and unless a fair time interval has elapsed. In each of the three cases of self-quotation we shall find the point of the recall in the new situation itself.

The sonnets of te 5 are linked to each other quite differently from those of any other tetrad or triad. Each sonnet appears to refer to a different man who was of some importance to William Herbert, *a* to Chapman, *b* to Sanford, *c* to Hilliard, and *d* to Shakespeare himself (this needs to be argued for *a, b,* and *c*). Secondly, the first three sonnets open by alluding to painting:

a 2   stirred by a painted beauty

b 1   A woman's face with Nature's own hand painted;

c 1   Mine eye hath played the painter;

and *d* 1   has Shakespeare's image in his mirror.

We saw above that a good reason for this would be that Herbert had teased Shakespeare about writing sonnets to his portrait. This idea gives a valuable hint about the tone of this tetrad. It is light-hearted and at least starts teasingly. William Herbert had come up with his mother to court a young lady, a situation in which teasing is traditional. The image which binds the elements of the tetrad together is entirely consistent with this; it is the image of mother and baby:

a   my love is as fair
       As any mother's child;

b   (gestation) Nature while she wrought thee fell a-doting
       And by addition me of thee defeated
       By adding one thing to my purpose no-thing

       (i.e. she went crazy over you and added a penis, though
       she'd intended making a girl);

c   Which in my bosom's shop is hanging still, . . .
       Mine eyes have drawn thy shape, and thine for me
       Are windows to my breast, where-through the sun
       Delights to peep to gaze therein on thee.

(allowing for the *sun-son* pun, we may take this as Shakespeare's recall of his mother's subsequent pregnancies, visualizing the baby in her body, imagining it in his own, and later peeping at it in its crib)

d   Bearing thy heart, which I will keep so chary
       As tender nurse her babe from faring ill.

Robert Gittings pointed out that George Chapman was probably referred to in *a*. He used exaggerated and over-ornate language; he was fond of inventing words in *-ure* like *rondure*; and he was perhaps referred to as a pedlar, which Chapman means, in the last five words – 'who purpose not to sell'.[43] To this we may add that there was a family connection; Chapman's patron had been Sir Thomas Walsingham,

47

cousin to the father of Sir Philip Sidney's widow. A narcissistic young intellectual recently down from Oxford may well have had a penchant for Chapman's learned style.

In *b* there is a pun on *Hew* (i.e. hue and Hugh). Line 7, omitting the disputed syllables runs

> A . . . hew all *Hews* in his controlling

i.e. a hue surpassing (*or* dominating) all Hughs in its hue. *Hue* here certainly includes the meaning 'complexion' but would be enriched by word-play on the Spenserian meaning of 'shape'.

The missing syllables in Q are 'man in' but various editors have suggested that Shakespeare wrote 'maiden' (cf. 'maiden hand' of **pr** 1 *a* − 154). The reasons are firstly that each two lines of the first eight refers to a female feature:

1–2	a woman's face
3–4	a woman's gentle heart
5–6	an eye more bright than theirs
7–8	a maiden hue . . .

and line 9 is a climax – 'And for a woman wert thou first created'. If line 7 had begun 'A man in hue', line 9 would have had to begin 'But for a woman . . .' Finally, it is a *maiden* hue which steals men's eyes (and 'which' would be very awkward stylistically if it referred to a noun in an earlier prepositional phrase rather than to the principal noun of the whole line before). We may suppose that the change was made deliberately and possibly by Hugh Sanford himself, who could have been the Pembrokes' first editor – he died in 1607.

For some purposes a miniaturist corresponded to a modern Court photographer. A young man about to marry would present his bride with his portrait, especially if early separation was anticipated, as it was for Herbert, who was going to travel abroad after his wedding and before his conjugal life began. We have seen the probability of a miniature of Herbert painted in November 1595 when marriage with Elizabeth Carey was in view. Now we may suppose that he sat for another such portrait to give to Bridget Vere. If Shakespeare escorted him to Nicholas Hilliard's studio (or 'shop'), it would probably have been at Lady Pembroke's suggestion. There are strong indications in **te** 5 *c* (24) that that did happen and that in this sonnet Shakespeare has used what he heard and saw there.

Hilliard composed his *Treatise on the Art of Limning* between about 1597 and 1601. (It was first printed in 1911.) Under its title he added the words 'Written at the request of R. Haydocke who publisht in English a translation of Paolo Lomazzo on painting in 1598'. Hilliard quotes Dürer very often and Dürer had published in 1525 his *Textbook of Proportion and Perspective*, setting out for German readers the principles formulated first by Alberti. Lomazzo had written his textbook on painting about fifty years after Dürer. Hilliard may well have been the one who first brought the artistic application of proportion and perspective to England on his return from the continent in 1576. Sidney had visited him probably in the autumn of 1579 or the winter following; he was taking an interest in scientific subjects then, being out of favour at Court. Earlier he had attended John Dee's lectures and Dee had taught the mathematics of proportion and perspective as early as 1570. Hilliard recalls a question that Sir Philip Sidney had put to him. He says he cannot forbear to record it though his 'book is great already'. It was whether you could tell from seeing two figures of men, each in a six-inch miniature, which was the tall man and which the short. Hilliard had said you could; as children use grammar correctly without having learned the rules, so 'our eye is cunning and learned by long use' to tell by proportion. It would have been very likely for Hilliard to recall the incident at the visit of Sidney's nephew and Shakespeare and so to have it fresh in his mind while writing his treatise.[44]

Dürer has prints of artists using a lattice frame for looking through at their models, a nude in one case and a lute end-on in another, and even measuring with string, to get perspective and proportion right. This is probably the meaning of 'frame' in line 3:

My body is the frame wherein 'tis held.

The next line

And perspective it is – best painter's art

is probably a joke on 'perspective', a term which Hilliard would have used in telling them of Sidney's question or of the use of the frame. As an art term it was probably brand new, though it had long been used to mean an instrument for looking through. This would account for the joke in the next two lines:

For through the painter must you see his skill,
To find where your true image pictured lies.

Dover Wilson suggested that if these words were a kind of maxim –
'you' and 'your' for 'one' and 'one's' – it would be a reason for finding
'thy', 'thine', and 'thee' in the rest of the sonnet. So I suggest that here
Shakespeare is deliberately garbling an explanation that Hilliard had
given them of the frame's use, e.g. 'To delineate well a man by drawing
you must know and use the rules of proportion and perspective. Your
skill as an artist is to hold his form in your frame and stell his image in
table – fix it on paper. And to find where any feature truly lies, you
transfer it from the square through which you see it onto the corresponding square of your paper.'

Haydock uses the word *stell* to translate the Italian *delineare*. The
O.E.D. quotes him (I.16): 'Before you begin to Stell, delineate and
trick out the proportions of a man, you ought to know his true quantity
and stature.' Nouns and verbs *stell* were in use at the time (the German
stellen means *put, place*, or *fix*). Later *a stell* was used for *an outline*.

The spelling in Q is 'steel'd' and may have a most interesting source.
It is twice used in the draft of the Herald's description of the coat of
arms granted to Shakespeare's father in October 1596 – 'a spear
steeled *argent*' on the shield and 'a spear *gold* steeled as aforesaid' supported by the falcon of the crest.[5] It probably meant '(represented as)
having a steel tip' but suggested 'represented' and could have afforded
word-play to Shakesepare, who had used 'stelled' in 1594 to mean
'shown', 'set down', or 'represented':

To this well-painted piece is Lucrece come
To find a face where all distress is stelled.
(*R. of L.* 1443–4)

There is probably similar word-play in te 27 *d* (112), written in 1602, as
we have argued. There 'my steeled sense' can mean both 'my hardened
attitude' and 'the sense I have set down (i.e. inscribed in earlier
poems)'. It may not be a coincidence that in 1602 the wording of the
Herald's grant was fresh in Shakespeare's mind; 1602 was the year in
which the York Herald tried to invalidate several grants of arms
(including Shakespeare's) which his London colleague had made.[46]
The matter is described by S. Schoenbaum (1975, pp. 167–73).

To realize the wit and humour of te 5 *d* as well as the shared
experience that probably lay behind it, let us catch its tone, consistent

with the gentle teasing of *a* and *b* and not the love tribute it might otherwise be thought.

It is worth remarking how *c* leads on to *d*. In *c* we have the loan of eyes:

> Now look what good turns eyes for eyes have done . . .

Its couplet is

> Yet eyes this cunning want to grace their art:
> They draw but what they see, know not the heart.

So in *d* we get the exchange of hearts, the chief image of the sonnet, which ends with the playful joke:

> Presume not on thy heart when mine is slain;
> Thou gav'st me thine not to give back again.

From this tetrad we can suppose three things that Shakespeare did in the fourth week of July – attended the Herberts at Baynard's Castle, there meeting Hugh Sanford as a matter of course and quite possibly George Chapman, accompanied Herbert to Hilliard's studio for a sitting, and escorted him to the theatre. Lady Pembroke would not only have approved all this but have encouraged or prompted it. She and her husband had further need of Shakespeare's influence upon William.

They must have realized by this time how likely it was that William would back out of the marriage they were planning. The Earl was probably exasperated at the thought that William might ruin everything and refuse again because of not liking the girl and not wanting to be married. Such a magnate is still ready in some countries to arrange for his son's sexual initiation, tactfully or impatiently according to the youth's attitude. At the very least the Pembrokes would insure against a repetition of their scheme's failure. There must be ways of overcoming William's reluctance to know a woman and Shakespeare would know of them; weren't actors classed with whores?

Shakespeare would certainly know the problem for different reasons. On the stage women's parts were played by boys and there must often have been boy leads who preened themselves and preferred to steal the eyes of older men than to face their own inexperience with the other sex, acknowledging their own untutored youth. Such an attitude and behaviour quickly provokes in others a wish to bring the beauty low. When a youth admires a man it is tempting for others to make him jealous and to bring him up against the man's mistress. In an acting company there was probably a great deal of teasing, also regular ways of making sure that a proud boy-lead lost his virginity to a woman. But a fairly kind way to begin was to help him lose his dread of the female by emphasizing her ordinariness and the ordinariness of heterosexual life, to tell him about so-and-so's woman – or even your own – without making out she's anything wonderful – or particularly unapproachable.

Shakespeare's first triad seems as if it could have had just that function. It plays down the wonder of the woman, while still saying she's special to the man who loves her, and so makes life with a woman seem ordinary and nothing so dreadful if she did have other men. But it also must have served to arouse Herbert's curiosity to know more of Shakespeare's love-life and to see his woman.[47] Its three sonnets are the only ones that tell the hearer, half whimsically and half jauntily, about the mistress without any complaining of her. And they run on perfectly from one to another, *a* to *b* with the image of the sun's eye, *b* to *c* with word-play on falsehood and truth:

> And yet, by heav'n, I think my love as rare
> As any she belied with false compare.
> When my love swears that she is made of truth,
> (maid)
> I do believe her, though I know she lies.

In short this triad gave the right sort of encouragement to Herbert in his courtship of Bridget Vere but it also prepared the ground for his sexual temptation if he evaded marriage.

The last sonnet of the triad (**tr** 1 *c* = 138) is one of the two printed in *The Passionate Pilgrim*, Jaggard's pirated anthology of 1599. It is worth wondering how Jaggard got hold of it. The other sonnet (**te** 7 *c* = 144) in that anthology differs from the text in Q only in unimportant ways, which could be explained by supposing that a hearer had remembered it and written it down soon after; but Jaggard's text of this sonnet has been thought by several editors to be Shakespeare's own earlier version of Q's 138. If triad 1 was written in the notebook given by Herbert to Shakespeare in July and given away by him, as he tells in **te** 6 *b* (122), long before Herbert asked after it (or rather after the poem he had seen written in it), we should have a way of accounting both for the escape of the earlier text and for Shakespeare's offering a new text, perhaps written in the new notebook which he presented to Herbert on his eighteenth birthday, when he recited te 6. It was unlike Shakespeare not to keep a better guard over the poetry written for his patrons, so my personal guess is that he had given the first notebook, containing the triad, to Lady Pembroke to take and show to her husband and that *he* enjoyed and quoted it; it matches **pr** 2 in tone and bawdy wit, and **pr** 2, it has been argued, was written specially for the Earl.

(iii)   Herbert's engagement and its outcome

Shakespeare very possibly left London upon the closing of the theatres on 28 July. He would have been told that he would receive a message saying whether the composition of further triads was required, as it would be if William Herbert did not go through with this engagement.

We know an unusual amount about the engagement, for letters are extant to Sir Robert Cecil from William and Lady Mary Herbert, thanking him for his sponsorship of them at Court, and to Lord Burghley from Lady Mary, saying the young people had liked each other well enough, and from the Earl of Pembroke replying point by point to a letter from Burghley to him, concerning details of the dowry and settlement and concerning Bridget's residence after the wedding while William was travelling abroad. Other points from that letter were given earlier. There is also a letter from Bridget's father, Edward Vere, Earl of Oxford, indicating his warm approval of the match. The first hint we have that things were not still going smoothly is the letter from Lady Pembroke to Sir Robert Cecil answering him that she was not the person responsible for divulging Cecil's hope of becoming Lord Cranborne. Finally the engagement is broken off in the third week of October, presumably for the same reason as the courtship of Elizabeth Carey – William's not liking, although this time all we have is the news of Burghley's anger with Pembroke for suddenly insisting on more dowry.[48]

Shakespeare would receive the news and begin the triads by early November. He would have been revising *Love's Labours Lost* for performance before the Queen at Christmas. (Although the Quarto's date of *L.L.L.* is 1598 and this *could* mean up to 24 March 1599, making the Christmas before that the Christmas of 1598, it is unlikely.) Many people have remarked not only on the verbal similarities of the teasing of Rosaline to the denigration of the sonnets' Dark Woman but also on their similar sentiments about fairness and darkness. The passages about Rosaline's darkness may be among the additions to the original play or may have suggested the theme of darkness and foulness for the sonnets. The character of the two women is certainly similar, fascinating but a wanton,

> one that will do the deed
> Though Argus were her eunuch and her guard.

In Q the triads have been expertly hidden. Even with the wedding sonnet (145), the pairs (154, 153; 128, 151; 129, 146), and triad 1 (148, 130, 138) removed, the triadic structure is not obvious. The first step in making it clear is to put two sonnets which mention the friend back among the four which are concerned with him – 143, which is about escape, pursuit, and catching, to round off the theme of imprisonment in 133–4 (**tr** 6), and 144, which ends with the bitter joke about 'one angel in another's hell' (i.e. their sexual intercourse), to round off the pair fraught with word-play on *will* in the sense of *genitals* (135–6). Then all that this half of the poem requires is the inversion of 131 and 132. The black eyes that seem mourners in 127 (**te** 2 9–14) are at once continued as the theme of 132 (*b* 1–8). So that sonnet's closing desire for pity comes up against the woman's tyrannous and cruel nature in 131 (*c* 1–2) and the poet's *groans* of *c* 6 and 10 are picked up at once in the first line of the next triad (**tr** 6 *a*1 = 133), besides the rhyme *groan/alone* being used to link the new triad to the old. Triads 5, 6 and 7 are then quite distinct in themes – blackness, imprisonment, and sexual insatiability.

Triads 2, 3, and 4 become obvious once 141–2 are brought to join 137 (**tr** 2), leaving 139–40 next to 147 (**tr** 3). The links between 2 *a* and *b* are in their openings:

> Thou blind fool Love, what dost thou to mine eyes . . . ? (127)

> In truth I do not love thee with mine eyes . . .   (141)

and in their couplets:

> In things right true my heart and eyes have erred
> And to this false plague are they now transferred.   (127)

> Only my plague thus far I count my gain,
> That she that makes me sin awards me pain.   (141)

Then *c*'s opening is at once linked to *b*'s couplet:

Love is my sin and thy dear virtue hate,
Hate of my sin, grounded on sinful loving,   (142)

Tr 2 *c* ends with the poet urging pity against the woman's denial of it.
Tr 3 *a* opens with

                              the wrong
That thy unkindness lays upon my heart.   (139)

The advice of *a*'s couplet

                  since I am near slain,
Kill me outright with looks and rid my pain.

is continued in *b*'s opening

Be wise as thou art cruel; do not press
My tongue-tied patience with too much disdain;
Lest sorrow lend me words and words express
The manner of my pity-wanting pain.   (140)

   The sonnet continues the threat, which, after the image of a sick man
and his doctor, becomes the threat of telling the truth in madness. This
supplies the chief image of *c* (147):

My love is as a fever . . .

The prognosis is desperate because the patient has not followed the
prescriptions of reason, his doctor.

     Past cure I am, now reason is past care

(nicely echoed by a line in *L.L.L.*V. ii. 28). The madness returns in the
next three lines.
   Only one more change is needed – to put te 4 *c* (149) back after *a* and
b (150 and 152). The idea that binds together the sonnets of tr 4 is that
of swearing falsely and being for‿sworn. The close of tr 4 *c* has two
features that hark back to the opening of tr 2 *a*: the rhyme *despise/eyes*
(2 *a*'s first rhyme was *eyes/lies*) and its answer to 'thou blind fool Love' –
'and I am blind'.
   The two halves of the whole double poem of eighteen sonnets were
certainly exchanged for publication in Q. It is an absurd come-down

55

to go from an explicit statement of the woman's infidelity with the poet's friend to general statements about the woman's untrustworthiness and promiscuity. With the halves reversed from Q's order, there are two enormous gains. First, the woman's infidelity with the friend is a climax, heralded by the accusation (after compliments)

In nothing art thou black – save in thy deeds.

Secondly, we see the structure of the whole poem to be carefully contrived; its first and second halves begin each with a third-person sonnet and all the others except the very last address the woman directly; **tr** 7 *c* speaks *of* her again and utters the final insult, the worst of all. This formal symmetry is striking. Another planned feature of the first half is that its second and third triads (**tr** 3 and 4) open with the exclamatory 'O'; its last sonnet also has 'O cruel' but not at the beginning of the line.

All this makes it utterly unlikely that the Dark Woman series is the record of an experience already lived or being lived. But it could very well have been the script for an experience still to be lived, its first half a charm to lure and bind the friend to the woman and its second half a charm to unloose him, the number nine being characteristic of black magic. (There is an emphasis on 'thrice three' in **tr** 6 *a*; there is a teasing passage in *L.L.L.* V. ii. 488–99 between Berowne and Costard over whether thrice three makes nine or not; and in *Macbeth* we shall hear

> Thrice to thine and thrice to mine
> And thrice again to make it nine:
> Peace! the charm's wound up.

A young man's curiosity already aroused by **tr** 1, if he was later sent at intervals triads 2–4, could scarcely have withstood the temptation to go alone and visit the woman who had so bewitched and tortured the poet, especially if the poet himself had taken him to see her. For that, I believe, was Shakespeare's scheme, a contingent scheme which he must have devised in outline to meet the Earl's demand and must have discussed with Lady Pembroke back in July. But it was a scheme that he could not implement until Herbert was living in London, and that would be from the next April onwards. The six triads were to be kept till then and the number of their eighteen sonnets would have the same significance as that of the seventeen marriage sonnets, a compliment to Herbert's age. Moreover, the number of tetrads written for Herbert during 1598 will also be shown to be eighteen. They make a drama of six acts, each of three scenes, a script to be played with Herbert as junior lead, entirely unaware that he was playing a role at all, especially a role in a new piece written and produced by Shakespeare. For Shakespeare's task in 1598 would be to create the opportunity to use the six triads; he might count on Lady Mary's help in stage management.

(iv) The Drama of 1598

Episode 1: Celebrations and leave-taking (tetrads 6–8)

The letters to Sir Robert Sidney, who was military governor of Flushing in the Low Countries, from his agent in London, Rowland Whyte, make up much of the Sidney papers of the time. They reveal how impatient Sidney was in the autumn and winter of 1597–8 for leave in England. Again and again Whyte assures him that Lady Pembroke had urged various important figures, who had the opportunity, to 'move the Queen' to let her brother return on long overdue leave. At last Elizabeth relented and it seemed that Sidney would be back early in March; at all events his sister ordered rooms to be prepared for him in Baynard's Castle by 6 March. On 10 and again on 17 March Whyte reports that they are ready, but it does not look as if Sidney arrived until about the 23rd.[50]

Lady Pembroke had sent Hugh Sanford up to London to prepare a suite overlooking the Thames for her brother and his family, who came up from Penshurst in Kent. This suite served as their London home for the months that Sidney was on leave. His arrival and stay there were especially convenient for the Pembroke family, since he and his wife would be able to keep an eye on their nephew during the first months of his independent residence in London to attend the Court. Lady Pembroke apparently came up to London again with William, naturally to welcome her brother and to hold William's eighteenth birthday in Baynard's Castle. There is no way to tell whether or not the Earl came with her this time.

She must have engaged Shakespeare to recite a new poem at William's birthday celebrations, for he had ready both a poem – tetrad 6 – and a birthday present. The second sonnet of the tetrad (122) suggests that he had received a message which also asked after the notebook ('thy tables') that Herbert had given him in July, presumably for the sonnets that were written in it. If the sonnets had been those of

57

triad 1, it would suit the plan of Lady Pembroke and Shakespeare that William should again be reminded of the poem about the mistress, since he had to be made curious again in preparation for his introduction to her. The request to produce it gave Shakespeare the chance to write an improved version of its third sonnet:

> When my love swears that she is made of truth . . .

To choose a novelty notebook as a birthday present for Herbert was a graceful way of making restitution for having given away his earlier present and also an ingenious means of calling his attention freshly to the triad, which could be the content of the new notebook's 'non-vacant' leaves. The first sonnet of the birthday tetrad describes the present quite carefully and also encourages Herbert to develop the habit of writing – writing verse, presumably, which he did in his youth.

Te 6 consists of two pairs of sonnets (77, 122; 30, 31). The first pair deals with gifts, the second with reflection and mourning. But a double theme unites the whole tetrad – remembrance and the grave. All four sonnets are concerned with both but *b* has five different synonyms for *memory*. The tetrad is tightly bound together also by rhyme links and word repetition.

The structure of *a* is unique and an American poet, Yvor Winters, pronounced it the most successful of all Shakespeare's sonnets.[51] Certainly it is far more than the occasional piece it appears at first sight and it greatly repays memorizing. Its first line is clearly intended to establish continuity by recalling the first line of the last sonnet of the July tetrad. Its first four lines are statements about the recipient's mirror (one line), his dial (one line), and the vacant leaves of the book presented (two lines). The next eight lines repeat the three sentiments in augmentation (a musical term for restatement at greater length): lines 5–6 restate line 1, 7–8 restate 2, and 9–12 restate 3–4. There is a special device in line 4 to make it clear that the mirror and the dial are not separate from the book.

> And of this book this learning may'st thou taste.

The first 'this' simply refers to the book, which offers '*this learning*' – i.e. the lessons that follow; now, since the first and second lessons are taught by the mirror and by the dial, it follows that they must both be parts of the book, presumably its front and back covers. If the back cover was a sundial which could be set with the book face down, it would have had a hinged gnomon to fold away when the book was written in and to serve as a support when it was stood on its edge for the mirror of the front cover to be used.

Lines 9–12 of *c* have their own special device. In each line a syllable is repeated: 'grieve at grievances', 'woe to woe', 'bemoaned moan', 'pay as if not paid'. The effect is as of the tolling of a bell. The couplet releases from mourning, and the sonnet has even been criticised for this by contrast with *d*, sustained in tone to the end. Such criticism of course fails to take account of *c* as part (the third element) of a tetrad; the function of its couplet is precisely to prepare for the resolution of mourning in *d*.

The last line of *d* has a phrase that must have specially appealed to the Countess and helps to confirm that she was present to hear the poem on William's birthday. The line is

And thou – all they – hast all the all of me.

The Countess's echo of it comes in a dedication to her elder brother's *Angel Spirit* (lines 32–6):

As little streams with all their all do flow
    to their great sea, due tribute's grateful fee,
    so press my thoughts my burdened thoughts in me
To pay the debt of infinits I owe
To thy great worth.[52]

She composed the poem of thirteen seven-line stanzas to prefix to a copy of Sir Philip Sidney's version of Psalms 1–43. She had the copy beautifully hand-written by John Davies of Hereford for presentation to Queen Elizabeth, who intended to visit her at Wilton in 1599. Unfortunately, as W. A. Ringler records in his edition of *The Poems of Sir Philip Sidney*, Countess Mary was such 'an inveterate tinkerer who found it difficult to make up her mind' that the manuscript could not be presented 'because the many corrections made in the process of copying marred its appearance'.[53]

Te 6 would have been recited on 8 April, a Saturday. Holy Week followed and we are able to infer that Shakespeare was given a place at the Easter service held in St Paul's Cathedral on the 16th. To hold it there will have been the Queen's way of honouring the memory of Sir Philip Sidney in the presence of his brother and family. The next tetrad (*te* 7 = 75, 52; 29, 25) is again of two pairs linked overtly by rhymes but at a deeper level by a consistent attitude of exaggerated dependence upon the young man addressed. The exaggeration is lessened for us when we see William Herbert as the representative of the Herbert and Sidney families, before whom Shakespeare was reciting the poem. Lady Mary was, I believe, encouraging her son to practise patronage, a relationship she knew to be mutually rewarding; and Shakespeare was playing his part. Once this is understood, the poem is seen to derive the unity of its four sonnets from the experience of the Easter service, attended a day or two before by all who heard them.

In *b* (52) Shakespeare compares his seldom seeing Herbert to a miser's deliberately rare treat of surveying his treasure, to the rare feast-days in the year, and to the spaced-out, principal jewels in a necklace or coronet. The last two comparisons are expressed in the lines:

> Therefore are feasts so solemn and so rare
> Since, seldom coming, in the long year set
> Like stones of worth they thinly placèd are,
> Or captain jewels in the carcanet.

Another comparison follows, a comparison not of the thing contained but of the container:

> So is the time that keeps you as my chest

and a fifth comparison immediately, first of the container (the time in which the poet did not see Herbert) and then of the brilliant thing it contained:

> Or as the wardrobe which the robe doth hide,
> To make some special instant special blest
> By new unfolding his imprisoned pride.

The robe is the priestly robe of gold, put on at one special moment in the Christian year – during the Easter Mass, when the dark purple robe of mourning is exchanged for it to symbolize the Resurrection.

H. C. Beeching, in his 1904 edition of the sonnets, noted the parallel passage in *King Henry IV*, Part 1 (III. ii 56–9), part of the King's speech warning Prince Hal not to be lavish of his appearances in public, as he himself had gained charisma 'by being seldom seen':

> My presence like a robe pontifical,
> Ne'er seen but wondered at, and so my state,

> Seldom but sumptuous, showed like a feast
> And won by rareness such solemnity.

These lines, besides sharing the theme of appearances the more valued for their infrequency, have five key words in common with te 7 *b*: 'robe', 'seldom', 'feast', 'rareness', and 'solemnity' (or their adjectives). 'Pontifical' indicates that Shakespeare was indeed thinking of a Church feast. Beeching argued that an unusual association of words was often experienced for a short time and then dissipated; so it was a better test for pieces composed within a short time of each other than similarity of sentiment or of wording. He was sure sonnet 52 and that speech from *Henry IV*, Part I were composed within a few days of each other. (If so, we may now date this scene of the play to the second half of April 1598.) Certainly the speech has other echoes of the sonnets of te 7: 'Being daily swallowed by men's eyes' and 'Being with his presence glutted, gorged, and full' both recall the dominant image of *a* (75); 'and so my state' recalls *c*'s (29) 'and then my state' and 'my outcast state', each of the three at the end of a line; 'gaze, Such as is bent on sun-like majesty' recalls *d*'s image:

> Great princes' favourites their fair leaves spread
> But as the marigold at the sun's eye;
> And in themselves their pride lies burièd,
> For at a frown they in their glory die.

Shakespeare may have taken the marigold image for a courtier's life from Thomas Nashe's novel, *The Unfortunate Traveller* (1594), in which he had written of 'The Marigold, which opens and shuts with the sun'. In his book, *Shakespeare's Rival* (1960), Robert Gittings showed that Shakespeare had read Nashe's novel carefully for his revised version of *Love's Labours Lost* (1597–8) and that he quoted from it also in *King Henry IV*, Part 1.[54] So the metaphor would have been ready in Shakespeare's mind.

The first pair of te 7 has the shared theme of waiting and watching. In *a* we seem to be with Shakespeare, hungry and thirsty, in a place from which he can see Herbert with his family; like many experiences of looking this sonnet explores the alternating states of fullness and emptiness. In *b* the looking is rewarded and the images are of things possessed. The first two rhymes of *b* bind it to *a*, the first to *a*'s couplet, the second, *treasure/pleasure*, being *a*'s actual middle rhyme. The first

lines of both are of course intentionally similar – 'So are you as. . . .'
'So am I as . . .'.

The second pair of te 7 has the shared theme of envy of those who are
better off than the poet, but in *c* the envy brings dejection until the last
lines, when recovery begins, while in *d* the envy is shown to have been
based on an illusion. The rhymes of *c* 5–8 are the same as those of *b*'s
couplet (*hope/scope*, a rare rhyme) and *b*'s fifth rhyme, while *c*'s opening
quatrain and third quatrain have similar rhymes – *eyes/state/cries/fate*
and *despising/state/arising/gate*. This last feature suggests antiphony and
therefore was perhaps prompted by the anthem sung after the Mass,
like the image of the lark singing 'hymns at heaven's gate'.

Sonnet *d* has only one rhyme in common with an earlier sonnet of
the tetrad; *fight* (conjectured)/*quite* echo *a*'s *sight/delight*, but it looks as if
Shakespeare was later prepared to sacrifice this link to make a new link
with the opening of the next tetrad. What should be the fifth rhyme of *d*
stands in Q as *worth/quite*. I believe that Shakespeare wrote and recited
fight/quite, but while actually writing te 8 *a* about a week later:

> O how thy worth with manners may I sing . . . ?

thought of changing that rhyme to *worth/forth* and wrote 'worth',
crossing out 'fight', but being preoccupied with the new sonnet he was
writing, forgot to complete the change. If so, it is a most informative
lapse, because it tells us that Q was printed from Shakespeare's own
copy, not from Herbert's, and also that Shakespeare did not correct
the text.

The word *worth* was then used to denote *excellence*, but it was specially
associated with Sir Philip Sidney, the model of excellence, who had
been given the most magnificent state funeral of Queen Elizabeth's
reign on 16 February 1587, when he was re-interred in St Paul's. Hugh
Sanford's introduction to Sidney's *Arcadia*, published in 1593 with a
title page drawing of a pig smelling a bush of marjoram,[55] explains that
the pig denotes 'the worthless reader' who 'cannot worthily conceive of
so worthy a writing'. If the first eight lines of *d* are the fruit of
Shakespeare's watching the royal procession leave the cathedral after
the Easter service, the next four

> The painful warrior famousèd for fight,
> After a thousand victories once foiled,
> Is from the book of honour razèd quite
> And all the rest forgot for which he toiled

could not have been heard by Sidneys without reminding them of Sir Philip. We may imagine the family visiting his tomb after the Service and Lady Mary exclaiming, 'How soon the people forget their hero!'

The four sonnets of this tetrad are now seen to allude to the following: waiting for the service to begin, the Mass, the anthem, and the procession out followed by a visit to the tomb.

The next poem, as its last sonnet says, was written and sent, not recited:

> To thee I send this written ambassage.

Once more, the tetrad consists of two pairs (39, 36; 37, 26). The theme of the first pair is the need to live apart. Two reasons are given for this necessity: in *a* the opportunity for praising the absent one, in *b* the importance of not contaminating or diminishing his honour. We can now understand the second reason as a reference to the way in which Shakespeare's association with the Pembrokes had had to end abruptly in July, owing to the Order in Council which closed the theatres; he must have been warned then to stay away from Baynard's Castle because, as an actor, he would blemish the honour of the young man courting Burghley's granddaughter. Obviously there was no need in 1598, after the birthday and Easter celebrations, for Shakespeare to refer to that episode of July, unless it suited him. I think we can take it that it did suit him just by the way it offered the perfect excuse for continuing to live apart. So we may infer an invitation he received soon after Easter to take up his residence in Baynard's Castle. The Pembrokes seem to have made such offers fairly easily to poets, writers, and scientists whose work they valued. By referring to July and his residual blots Shakespeare could forstall the pressing of such an invitation, yet still do so 'with manners'.

The two reasons for living separately surround an invocation to Absence (*a* 9–14), which stands as a kind of musical trio to the minuet before and after. The opening of *a* and the ending of *b* also state or imply a close identification between poet and patron:

> thou art all the better part of me;

and

> thou being mine, mine is thy good report.

63

The links of rhyme between the two sonnets are that the actual rhyme words of *a*'s couplet (*twain/remain*) and of lines 6 and 8 (*one/alone*) are used again as the first two rhymes of *b* (also *me/thee* of *a* recurs as *thee/me* in *b*, but that is a common repetition). We found similar links between *a* and *b* of **te** 7.

The second pair defines the nature of the bond between poet and young patron: *c* says it resembles the father–son bond, *d* that it is like that of vassal and lord. In *c* Shakespeare seems to be strongly identified with his own father, John Shakespeare, who perhaps called himself 'decrepit', as an ageing melancholic is prone to do (S. Schoenbaum in his *Documentary Life* of Shakespeare gives the evidence for John's melancholy and makes the diagnosis),[56] but who also may actually have been lame; this would have offered William Shakespeare the metaphor for his own state, disadvantaged by birth and calling with respect to a noble family. Yet John in 1576 before his depression had sought, and in October 1596 – perhaps with William's help – had gained, the status of gentleman. His pride in his dramatist son, who only the year before had acquired the second biggest house in Stratford-upon-Avon, could have been expressed in the very words which in the last six lines of *c* the poet uses to his patron, ending

> Look-what is best, that best I wish in thee;
> This wish I have: then ten times happy me!

But the first two lines suggest the transference of another relationship onto that of poet and patron, not the relationship of John and William Shakespeare, father and son, but that of John and Hamnet Shakespeare, grandfather and grandson. Old John must have known Hamnet better than William, his father, had known him and, like many a grandfather, had probably enjoyed describing the boy's 'deeds of youth', and Hamnet had died a bare two months before the old man received his patent of gentility to match his wife, an Arden.[57]

Once again the opening rhyme of *c* – *delight/spite* – repeats the actual words of *b*'s middle rhyme. Also the sixth rhyme – *give/live* – repeats the words of *a*'s third rhyme (and we meet *thee/me* again in the couplet).

The last sonnet, *d* (26), is also linked by rhyme both to *c* and to *b*. The line in *c*

> For whether beauty, birth, or wealth, or wit,

is echoed by *d*'s line

To witness duty, not to show my wit.

And *b*'s third rhyme (*respect/effect*) occurs in *d*'s sixth – *aspect/respect*.
In *d* Shakespeare's duty to his patron,

bare in wanting words to show it,

is imaged as a foundling babe which Herbert's understanding

In (his) soul's thought all naked will bestow it,

and will apparel his 'tattered loving'. The last six lines of *d* hint at a journey on which the poet is about to go and from which he will return.

It is remarkable that *a* mentions three times the activity of the poet as *praise* of his patron and that this whole tetrad uses the word *love* more frequently than any other. According to the concept of 'reaction-formation' or of 'compensation' we may suppose that Shakespeare's emphasis covers something neither praiseworthy nor loving; before he left London he must have introduced William Herbert to the Dark Woman. He had put him in the way of temptation.

From the dates of Herbert's birthday and Easter[58] we get an approximate time interval between successive tetrads. We are lucky to get even one and if we use it to suppose that Shakespeare determined, when writing **te** 8 near the end of April, to compose three tetrads a month for six months, a tribute of eighteen tetrads for the year in which Herbert was eighteen, we shall find that it fits two other indications of date – a letter of 18 June and the usual pursuits of late summer, which will be pointed out as they arise. We shall not be far out if we imagine that a tetrad was recited or delivered on approximately the 8th, 18th, and 28th of each month.

There is one last question. If Shakespeare began **te** 8 by refusing an invitation to reside in Baynard's Castle, whose invitation was it? It may have been conveyed by William Herbert but it could have come only with the approval of the older generation. I believe that it was Lady Mary's idea for giving Shakespeare a better opportunity to be close to her son and to use the triads. But Shakespeare by then had formed the plan of sending them one at a time when he was absent. Even though his journey, as it will appear, was to Stratford, it was quite possibly a company tour that would include Stratford and so take much more than the two or three days of riding directly there.

Episode 2: The journey (tetrads 9–11)

Anybody who works backwards through the sonnets from 126 to 18 will have gathered up Q's 23, 32, and 38 to complete the rival-poet series, will have linked 75 and 52, and will have joined 48 and 49 with the two sets of three about the friend's relations with the woman, before he reaches the journey sonnets. He will therefore gain conviction by meeting nine sonnets all together (43–7, 50–1, 53–4) and will quickly add another pair on the same topic (27–8). The remarkable thing about these eleven sonnets is that they consist of five pairs and one unpaired (43) which will require and be found a fellow. One of the pairs, however, will prove to be much better when inverted – 54, 53.

The three tetrads which these sonnets go to form will all have been written and sent, not recited. 'Swift messengers' supply a metaphor in te 9 *d* (45) and we may suppose that messengers could and did move fast between Baynard's Castle and Shakespeare, for Rowland Whyte, Robert Sidney's agent, was Postmaster General in charge of the royal courier service, which conveyed letters and packets as safely and nearly as quickly as the post in Britain of the 1980s. The Sidneys and Pembrokes would have had a privileged facility for sending and receiving mail.

Tetrad 9 is united by the themes of travel and separation. It consists of two pairs (50, 51; 44, 45). The first pair has the theme of *riding* – riding away in *a* and some of *b*, but also (at least in imagination) riding back in *b*. From the last line of *a*

My grief lies onward and my joy behind

we may understand that Shakespeare rides towards Stratford, towards the place where Hamnet had lived and towards the two grieving families – his mother and sisters and his grandparents, uncles, and aunt.

The second pair is united by the metaphor of the four elements – earth, water, air, and fire – elements which signified very contrasting speeds of movement. For the pace of the poetry changes throughout these four sonnets, matching the elements mentioned in the second pair. The pace of *a* is slow; in *b* it quickens; *c* starts quick but slows down in the last six lines; *d* also starts quick, slows down in 7–8, quickens again in 9–13, but slows once more to end the tetrad in 13–14.

There is also a concept which holds the four sonnets together. That of *dullness*. In *a* the beast 'plods dully on' and is called in *b* 'my dull

66

bearer'; but later in *b* desire, given the image of a horse, has 'no dull flesh in *his* fiery race'; *c* opens

> If the dull substance of my flesh were thought . . .

a nice link between the pairs; and in *d* the dullness recurs in the phrase 'oppressed with melancholy', when air and fire are absent.

The rhyme links in these four sonnets are quite profuse, more so than in any other tetrad. The rhyme *-ee* and *-ow* (*-oe*) occur four times each, *-oan* (*-on(e)*) three times, and *-ay*, *-ide*, *-ind*, *-ade* (*-ad*), *-ought* twice each. It is worth noting that rhyme is less used to make intra-tetradic links after the journey series.

The various concepts of physical motion which are reflected in the changes of movement in the verse provide another means of linking the two pairs of this tetrad. The words for movement are: journeying, plodding, speeding, spurring, winging, running, going (walking), jumping, leaping, attending, abiding, sliding with swift motion, sinking down, swift return, sending back. The increasing frequency of change of pace corresponds with an ever more restless searching for some way to relieve pining. We may compare Vergil's line:

> First this way and then that dividing his swift mind.

A self divided by mortal war between eye and heart is therefore a most appropriate sequel to this tetrad, the only one to end in a minor key and restlessly. On the other hand the first line of *a*:

> How heavy do I journey on the way!

is a perfect opening to the whole poem. It sets the scene as accurately as any stage directions or as the first words of an act of a play.

Thoughts of the absent friend is the theme that unites the next tetrad – **te** 10. It again consists of two pairs (46, 47; 54, 53) both concerned with the contrast of outer and inner truth but slightly differently, *a* and *b* with the subjective opposition of eyes and heart, *c* and *d* with the objective contrast between show and essence. There are two obvious reasons for making 54 *c* and 53 *d*. The last line of 54 ends 'by verse distils your truth'. The first line of 53 begins 'What *is* your substance?' The then natural association of distillation and substance is the same as that in the couplet of **te** 1 *a* (5):

> But flowers distilled, though they with winter meet,
> Leese but their show; their substance still lives sweet.

Therefore *c* here is concerned with the inadequacy of show, *d* with substance.

The second reason is that the ending of 53 makes a better close to the tetrad:

> But you like none, none you for constant heart.

It contains no implied threat like 'When that shall vade (go, vanish)'. There is a third reason. The first pair of this tetrad has the same theme as the first of the triads addressing the Dark Woman (tr 2) – the opposition between eyes and heart. If it was composed as a covering letter to the triad, the tetrad's opening is explained; its ending – 'none you for constant heart' – had a dramatic irony, if it accompanied the first instalment of the temptation. We may even see those five words as Shakespeare's hope that Herbert will not yield to the temptation into which he was leading him.

The rhyme links between *a* and *b* are two, between *c* and *d* also two, between *a* and *c* one, and between *d* and *a* (or *b*) again one. But that last is a special one that helps to clinch the order. The last two rhymes of *a* are *heart/part*, *part/heart*; the fourth rhyme of *b* is *heart/part*; and the last of *d* *part/heart*, rounding off the group.

Tetrad 11 opens like the other two with a scene-setting line

> Weary with toil I haste me to my bed.

There were references in te 10 *b* to Herbert's picture –

> With my love's picture then my eye doth feast
> And to the painted banquet bids my heart.

– and again in lines 9 and 13; 10 *d* had indicated the representation of likenesses of Herbert in painting. It would seem that Shakespeare had received (perhaps as a present for *his* birthday) a miniature portrait of Herbert, maybe the very one which had *not* been given to Bridget Vere. It would have come by messenger. A framed miniature was sometimes called 'a jewel' and this adds point to Shakespeare's simile in 11 *a*:

> thy shadow . . . like a jewel hung in ghastly night
> Makes black night beauteous and her old face new.

We may imagine Shakespeare hanging the miniature near his bed's head.

The third tetrad of the journey consists of two pairs (27, 28; 43, ?).
The first pair is about the poet's inability to sleep. He is restless and
obsessed by his friend's image. The pining of te 10 has become more
acute. In *b* we note that although he asks

> How can I then return in happy plight?

he is still on his *outward* journey:

> How far I toil, still farther off from thee!

It has always been assumed that 'return' here means to London and his
friend, but if the journey was a tour including Stratford and this night
the last before arriving there, 'return' could mean 'to my home and
family', and the argumentative 'then' of the first line suggests that
Shakespeare had received a letter with the miniature, saying 'You will
be happy to return to your family'. This makes better sense of the in-
dignant question when a sleepless night torments him on his *outward*
journey.

The rhymes linking *a* and *b* are *thee/see* and *sight/night* (4th and 5th)
followed in *b* by *plight/night, me/thee*, and *bright/night* (1st, 4th and 5th).
The same rhymes occur in *c* – *see/thee, bright/light, thee/me* (1st, 4th and
7th) – and make convincing links. The theme is nearly the same but
there has been some sleep and the visions are no longer waking
hallucinations of Herbert's image but remembered dreams. The
day–night antagonism still obtains but with a hope of day's brightness
near.

To decide on *c*'s pair it is a good idea to repeat its last six lines:

> How would, I say, mine eyes be blessèd made
> By looking on thee in the living day,
> When in dead night thy fair imperfect shade
> Though heavy sleep on sightless eyes doth stay!
>   All days are nights to see till I see thee,
>   And nights bright days when dreams do show thee me.

Then pause – for breath or to get out of bed and draw the curtains –
and continue:

> Shall I compare thee to a summer's day?
> Thou art more lively and more temperate:

Rough winds do shake the darling buds of May
And summer's lease hath all too short a date.
. . .
But thy eternal summer shall not fade
Nor lose possession of that fair thou owest;
Nor shall Death brag thou wander'st in his shade,
When in eternal lines to time thou growest.
So long as men can breathe or eyes can see,
So long lives this and this gives life to thee.

Even if the last three rhymes of *c* did not recur as the first, fifth, and seventh rhymes of Q's 18, we should have the *d* that we needed. Day triumphs over night. Shakespeare looks out upon a May morning and accepts it as the image he requires for its two qualities of beauty and transience. Each of the next three tetrads (**te** 12 – **te** 14) will end with a promise of immortality through verse, and **te** 14, being the close of the next month's episode, is the nearest to this in the wording of its couplet:

You still shall live (such virtue hath my pen)
Where breath most breathes, even in the mouths of men.

Not all agree upon the perfection of **te** 11 *d*. The last six lines are elated in mood and breathe a confidence which for many people does deny the reality of loss; and its couplet promises the impossible. If this is the day on which Shakespeare will reach Stratford, he is about to meet again his wife and daughters, his parents and his sister and brothers, who have lived with the loss of Hamnet from among them (by chance? or by nature's changing course?) as he himself has not. The separation anxiety that has pervaded all the sonnets of the journey as far as **te** 11 *c* now proves to have another face; it has been a disguise for anticipation anxiety, the anticipation of depression, which poetic creation can deal with only incompletely. Mourning is not yet over and only the sharing of memories and feelings by talk in the family may help to finish it, and Shakespeare has still to face his family again.

Finding a substitute is one way to postpone mourning. So when, on return to the place where the dead boy lived, Shakespeare's renewal of mourning becomes inevitable, he is bound to experience the loss of his son afresh but also a sense that he will lose his substitute as well; for that, apparently, is what Herbert's image had become to him, at least for the period of the journey. The promises of immortality belong to

Stratford and tell of Shakespeare's sustained endeavours to keep his depression from becoming too acute.

In te 11 _d_ Death's brag of having in his shade the shade of the boy recalls to us the words at the end of te 9 _a_, with which this episode opened – 'My grief lies onward'. Shakespeare may have been back home in time for Susanna's fifteenth birthday (she had been baptized on the 26th), but with such intervals between returns he must have known the clear truth for himself and for all the members of his family, that absences prolonged are a kind of death:

> Thy bosom is endearèd with all hearts
> Which I by lacking have supposèd dead.

Even such effective ways to postpone mourning do not hold out against the familiar place and figures.[59]

A restless night as the major theme of this tetrad was probably suggested by the triad for which it will have been composed as covering letter. **Tr** 3 had closed with the image of a fever in which the poet is

> frantic-mad with evermore unrest.

Even its closing rhyme had been _bright/night_, the prominent rhyme of te 11 _a_, _b_, and _c_.

Reconstructing the three tetrads of this episode has made very vivid the two orders of reality with which we have to concern ourselves:[60]

(1) the sequence of events, including the times and places at which they probably happened in actuality. All we can say about this is that, although Shakespeare may have been composing the poems in his head as he rode, certain features of te 10 suggest that it did not acquire its shape and content until the messengers had come and brought the miniature and the letter; te 11 likewise not until Stratford had begun to work upon him.

(2) the dramatic reality; there are three scenes: setting out on the ride, the soliloquy over the portrait, and the night before arrival. That is the order that lives for us, which is what we should expect from Shakespeare.

At each stage of reviewing the order we are reminded of the question, Who changed it?, and this time, Who put 11 _d_ as Q's 18, first after the marriage sonnets? Its heightened tone at that point has suggested to many people that Shakespeare suddenly fell in love with the youth upon whom he had been urging marriage. Perhaps that was the very intention of the editors in placing it there. And they could have heightened the tone a little further by changing 'lively' of line 2 to 'lovely'. In his edition of the sonnets Tucker pointed out that the two qualities which a summer's day lacks – lastingness and equability – were not both represented in 'more *lovely* and more temperate'. He suggested 'more *lively*' in the sense of *long-living*. His argument seems right: line 3 confirms the 'more temperate' and line 4 ought to confirm 'more lovely' but does not; it would confirm 'more lasting'. Lines 5–6 confirm the 'more temperate' and lines 7–8 would confirm 'more lasting' but not 'more lovely.' And the next four lines confirm not the youth's loveliness but the *endurance* of his youth and beauty, his life sustained by the poet's immortal lines. The couplet asserts the life's continuance, ensured by the verse. Although the sense here required of 'lively' occurs nowhere in the plays, the modern sense of 'lively' does not either; 'life-like', 'vivid', 'full of life' are the meanings that Shakespeare mostly gives it, but 'that record is lively in my soul' (*Twelfth Night* V.i. 253) clearly has the double sense of 'vivid' and 'lasting' and is near to what we need; the only later use of it in the sonnets is at **te** 14*b* (67) 10:

> Beggared of blood to blush through lively veins.

There it means 'having abundant life, which uniquely has endured until now and still endures, life more real and lasting than that of its parasitic imitators'. This seems a double meaning near enough to justify Tucker's emendation; and the last line of our sonnet – with 'lives' and 'life' – is enhanced if we have had 'lively' in line 2. Earlier, in **pr** 1 *b* 6, the phrase, 'A dateless lively heat', gives the very meaning that is required – 'enduring for ever'.

Episode 3: Melancholy at Stratford (tetrads 12–14)

The title of this episode needs to be justified – not the melancholy, which pervades all three poems, but the place. It is of course an inference that, since the poems are an expansion of the last six lines of **te** 11 *d* (18), then, if the goal of the journey was Stratford (at least for Shakespeare, though Stratford may have been only one stopping place on his company's tour), the tone of these sonnets was set by the mourning which Shakespeare did again in his home there.[61] There is one other likely sign in this poetry of his being at home. As several scholars have pointed out – T. Tyler, Sir Sidney Lee, J. B. Leishman, and Dover Wilson are those whose work successively deepened the knowledge – these twelve sonnets are all strongly influenced in idea and in wording by one text, Arthur Golding's translation of Book XV of Ovid's *Metamorphoses*.[62] (These are not the only sonnets to be influenced by the Metamorphoses; for example, sonnets 71–4 (making up **te** 17) are as well and also 44–5 (**te** 9 *c* and *d*); but, whereas the latter pair employs the unusual image of the four elements of matter and therefore would naturally recall the passage where Shakespeare had first met the doctrine, **te** 17 could well have been written when Shakespeare was just leaving Stratford; this will be reasoned when examining the next episode.) That translation of Golding's had first been published when Shakespeare was a small boy and was complete by 1567. On psychological grounds we can ask how Shakespeare had come to be so deeply familiar with it (the plays as well show this) and also why his recall of its actual wording should have fluctuated so widely. We require some hypotheses to account for these two facts besides the particular vividness of his recall at the time of writing these twelve sonnets. I believe he had known the book as a boy, left it at Stratford for his own children to read, and on his intermittent returns home read it aloud to them; what more appropriate way for him to re-establish some closeness between himself and his children than by reading aloud with them the book on which he himself had been brought up, which had informed his imagination and stocked his vocabulary, and which he will have refound there on the family bookshelf, if not at 'his beddes head'? So Book XV on this occasion will have helped him and them to mourn their loss of Hamnet.

The themes of loss, destruction, decay, and death, which also unite these tetrads, are linked with promises of immortality through verse, all most fitting to the place of loss, where Hamnet had died at the age of eleven and a half and Shakespeare's sister Anne at seven and a half when he was fifteen. For a short time at least William Herbert in absence became strongly identified with Hamnet in Shakespeare's mind.[63]

For the first time the tetrads have a different and more complex structure than that of two linked pairs of sonnets. The whole set of three tetrads has a formal symmetry. The last sonnet, *d*, both of **te** 12 and of **te** 14 is and claims to be a kind of monument. With such weight attached to the *d*s, the *c*s cannot form pairs and so are more closely linked with their preceding *b*s. This is specially clear in the couplets. So the structure of the first and last tetrads of the group is *a bc d*; the middle one combines this structure in the couplets with the double-pair structure, *ab cd*, in theme.

Te 12 (60, 59, 62, 55) begins in *a* with a measured simile for the way

> our minutes hasten to their end.

The succession of waves going onward against resistance appears in the rhythms. In the next four lines the life of a child is told from birth to puberty, when fate destroys him:

> time that gave doth now his gift confound.

This quatrain can be read as an obituary of Hamnet. The next one widens and universalizes the ravages of time – upon the bloom of youth, the smooth forehead, the special creations of nature, and all that grows and stands:

> But yet to times in hope my verse shall stand
> Praising thy worth, despite his cruel hand.

In *b* the doubt about being able to produce any really new praise in verse is expressed by a compressed metaphor from pregnancy, child-bearing, miscarriage, and the replacement of one dead child by the bearing of another. Shakespeare had known this in the family from which he came. His mother had borne two daughters before him and at least one, probably both, died before his birth, so he himself was a replacement child. His sister Anne died at seven and a half and soon after that Edmund, his youngest brother, was born. Sonnet *b* continues with a longing actually to *see* the paragon of time past, portrayed in literature, surely a likeness of the living Herbert.

> But sure I am the wits of former days
> To subjects worse have given admiring praise.

The next sonnet, *c*, shows the poet losing his own wit in self-admiration, until he beholds the reality in his mirror. In self-love he gives admiring praise to a subject far far worse, but he recovers from his illusion:

> 'Tis thee, my self, that for myself I praise,
> Painting my age with beauty of thy days.

74

Finally, in *d*, he offers his verse as a more enduring, powerful, and shining monument than any material one:

> Gainst death and all oblivious enmity
> Shall you pace forth; your praise shall still find room
> Even in the eyes of all posterity
> That wear this world out to the ending doom.
> So till the judgment that yourself arise,
> You live in this and dwell in lovers' eyes.

In each sonnet the word *praise* recurs until in *d* it comes well before the couplet and seems to become the very process and activity which confers immortality upon the subject praised. The final couplet negates the losses to which *a* and *b* allude, and perhaps in the word-play of the last three words – not just *admirers'* eyes but *lovers'* – we may catch a hint of the baby they will make, a true replacement.

Along with this tetrad went off **tr** 4, the last third of the charm-to-bind. If, as I believe, Shakesepare re-read that triad to stimulate his thought for writing **te** 12, it was the sonnet of self-love that owed most to the account of how the poet then

> gave eyes to blindness
> Or made them swear against the thing they see.
> For I have sworn thee fair: more perjured eye,
> To swear against the truth so foul a lie.

The middle tetrad of the Stratford group may owe something to Giles Fletcher's sonnet no. 28 of *Licia*. Both describe the inevitability of change and decay but Fletcher uses the device of repeating in almost every line the phrase 'With Time'; Shakespeare uses the measured repetition of time clauses, beginning with 'When' in *a*, less measured and opening with 'Against' (='when') in *c*.

The structure of the whole poem is 3 against 2. That is to say, although the *couplet* linkage is *a bc d*, the *theme* linkage is *ab cd*. In *a* and *b* (64 and 65) the theme is mortality – the power of time to lessen, bring low, and remove the grandest, most solid, and most precious things, including the one beloved. In *c* (63) and *d* (19) the theme is of violence to the person of the one beloved – the violence of time. Only verse may have the power to preserve 'my love' and to keep the beauty of his face intact. It is worth considering simply the sequence of couplets:

75

This thought is as a death, which cannot choose
But weep to have that which it fears to lose.   (a)

O none; unless this miracle have might
That in black ink my love should still shine bright.   (b)

His beauty shall in these black lines be seen
And they shall live and he in them still green.   (c)

Yet do thy worst, old Time; whate'er thy wrong,
My love shall in my verse ever live young.   (d)

The pair *a* and *b* are linked by the way in which *b*'s first two lines summarize the first eight of *a*

Since brass nor stone nor earth nor boundless sea
But sad mortality o'er-sways their power . . .

It is remarkable how *c*, which stands before *a* and *b* in Q and has often been thought contrived and artificial, provokes pity and terror when heard or read just after them. It opens up the tetrad by admitting the idea of bodily damage *after* the ideas of loss and theft. The tension of *c* reaches a maximum in lines 9–10:

For such a time do I now fortify
Against confounding age's cruel knife.

Here 'For' has the meaning of 'Against' that began the sonnet (except that there it was a conjunction) and the new 'Against' directs the poetic power at the aggressive object itself and not just towards a future eventuality.

The sonnet (19) which the first editors brought forward to pair with the summer's-day comparison has place *d* and is the climax of the tetrad. Time is addressed in three vocatives – 'Devouring time', 'Swift-footed time', and 'Old time' – and the six imperative verbs of the opening convey the intensity to which sonnet *c* (63) has led. The climax of *d* is the two prohibitions – 'carve not' and 'draw no lines there'. The phrase 'with thine hours' is of course ambiguous in sense between the hours as characters incised on a dial and the hours as the instrument like the 'antique pen' – the 'cruel knife' once more.

Both *c* and *d* present the personal and facial 'spoil of beauty'. Whereas this had been suggested in *b* only in the metaphors of flower and jewel, it is now direct and specific and the instrument with which time inflicts it is the knife – and the pen! There is a crescendo throughout the tetrad and *d* has for main verbs ten imperatives and only two indicatives – 'I forbid' and, a prophecy of immortality, 'My love shall . . . ever live young', a gift surpassing Aurora's to Tithonus. Yet the confidence of the last line is belied by the very proverb it recalls: Whom the gods love, die young. That, after all, is the only way in which a human brow can escape being marked by time.

There is no thematic link between this tetrad and any of the triads, while there is a very strong link of theme between the *next* tetrad and the next triad (**tr** 5, the first of the last three triads). So we may assume that tetrad 13 went off to Herbert without a triad. This is an additional reason for thinking of the six triads (**tr** 2–7) as a double poem, each half an 'ennead' (three sets of three). By reckoning three tetrads a month from 8 April, we calculate that this one was due for delivery on or around 18 June. Now on 18 June a letter was sent from Herbert's father at Wilton to the Queen's secretary, Sir Robert Cecil, apologizing for his own return from service in south Wales on the ground of ill health and for his son's absence from the Court on the ground of bodily disorder – 'as it is, I must for a few days stay him, till he perfectly recover'.

William was subject to headaches, relieved by tobacco[64] (migrainous headache is relieved by sneezing), and later he was to have an attack of ague. But it is highly unlikely that he had ridden the ninety miles from London to Wilton because of migraine or ague. (In the winter of 1599–1600 he had to delay, later to stop on the way, and eventually to turn back from Newbury on his journey from Wilton to London, when he was ill, his chief symptom being headache.) He must have had an anxiety about his health, perhaps with physical symptoms which did not prevent such a long ride.

Panic that he had contracted syphilis is high on the list of possible reasons for William Herbert's sudden return home to his family and the doctor he knew best. An acute anxiety on that score commonly afflicts a young man after his first sexual intercourse, particularly after intercourse with a woman he believes to be either another man's mistress or generally promiscuous; from the sonnets of the first ennead (**tr** 2–4) William Herbert would have had strong reason to believe either or both to be true of the Dark Woman; moreover the prominent images of fever, physician, and madness, which set the tone of **tr** 3 *b* and *c*, following directly on the concept of sin rewarded by pain, which is explicit in $\text{tr}_{\wedge}^{2} b$ and *c*, were likely to arouse anxiety (at least retrospectively, once symptoms had appeared) in Herbert's mind.

There would have been a family crisis. A young man of eighteen absents himself from the Court suddenly without leave in the middle of his first season there, and for a reason that he could not give. What his parents knew, but he did not, was that they themselves had instigated the scheme that had effected his seduction. If it had been primarily the Earl's exasperation over his son's prim aversion to women – an aversion which had frustrated his father's insurance policy for his family – that had caused Lady Pembroke's second approach to Shakespeare, she now, made anxious by William's unexpected arrival at Wilton both on account of his health and also for his future career, would have summoned her husband at once. So the Earl returned from Wales and wrote the brief but cleverly worded letter to Sir Robert Cecil; he put first his own dereliction from duty on account of ill health, he smoothed the way for his son's return to Court, and he took responsibility for keeping him a bit longer at home.

If William had not actually contracted syphilis (and the facts that later his first child – by Mary Fitton – died within a day or two and that the only child born in his marriage also died in infancy do suggest that he may have), the chief consequence of the whole episode would have been that it turned him into the compulsive womanizer that Lord Clarendon was to describe.[65]

All in all it was probably no accident that Shakespeare unconsciously hit upon the destructive power – and pen – of Time for the theme of the first tetrad after he had sent the final instalment of the first ennead. It may account for the greater depression that underlies the themes of the next tetrad, a poem composed as covering letter for triad 5.

Giles Fletcher's sonnet on Time had been an enumeration.[66] This may have prompted an enumeration for te 14 *a*:

> Tired with all these for restful death I cry,
> As to . . .

and there follow eleven instances of the unfairness and wrongs of the world. After the enumeration, the couplet

> Tired with all these from these would I be gone,
> Save that to die I leave my love alone.

– another instance of dramatic irony, since the poet's two loves had just been solacing one another. This leads to the ambivalent cry:[67]

78

Ah, wherefore with infection should he live. . . ?

The structure of **te** 14 (66, 67, 68, 81) is once again *a bc d*, the middle
two sonnets sharing the theme of Herbert's unique, young, fresh
beauty contrasted with others' simulation of beauty through cosmetic
painting and the wearing of fair wigs. Also common to *b* and *c* is the
notion of robbing one who actually has or has had beauty, health, and
vigour. ('The golden tresses of the dead' may have come from a
memory of Anne, Shakespeare's younger sister.) The couplets make
the paring of *b* and *c* especially clear:

> And him she stores to show what wealth she had
> In days long since, before these last so bad.
>
> And him as for a map doth Nature store
> To show false Art what beauty was of yore.

The enumeration of *a* is balanced by the second monument sonnet, *d*,
which once more addresses Herbert and closes with six lines promising
immortality.

The symmetries of these three tetrads are striking. The pattern of
a bc d runs through them, more marked in **te** 12 and **te** 14. The pattern
of time as revealed in verbs is similarly marked:

te 12 : present; a wish to see the past; present; future.
te 13 : past; present; future; imperative.
te 14 : present (a wish to die); present; present; future.

The pattern of pronouns is also obvious. Throughout **te** 12 Herbert is
addressed (as 'thou', 'you', 'thou', 'you'); in the next seven sonnets he
is spoken of in the third person; he is addressed again (as 'you') only in
te 14 *d*.

In **te** 12 Shakespeare is at one level identified with the woman (wife
or mother) who goes through pregnancy and childbirth perhaps to
miscarry, perhaps to lose her baby or the older child she has nurtured.
Te 12 *a* describes the life of such a child in lines 5–9; 12 *b* alludes to the
miscarriage or neonatal death (it also records the 'wish to see', not only
the likeness of an ancestor or the recently dead but also the baby still
unborn). **Te** 12 *c* is the vivid experience of disidentification from the
baby (every mother goes through this, *as does every child who empathizes
with his mother in her later pregnancies*); in 12 *d* Shakespeare regains the

79

sense of his own power to create and to preserve; in the last line there is still another hint of a baby.

In te 13 we experience the ever more threatening power of the ogre. This too draws its force from childhood, reinforced perhaps by Ovid's picture of Polyphemus.[68] The ogre is the traditional figure of dread for a child whose bond to his mother is threatened and for whom separation holds terrors. His father plays, 'I'm coming to eat you up'.

Te 14 expresses the emptiness of life and the falseness and deceits of society. Adolescence knows this well but it may be increased by parents' disturbances or by the deaths of any close relatives. Only creative effort can be counted on to bring the dead to life.

So in the three poems of the episode there is a developmental sequence: early childhood and identification with mother; slightly later childhood facing fears away from mother; adolescence. This compound poem is the most complex of all the episodes. Its complexity is due to the way in which it weaves a pattern from such different strands, all irradiated by idealization of the person of William Herbert. The chief strands are: Shakespeare's power to love and to create for the future; his life ahead till death; the deaths in his life both recent and early; his living through family births; his father's melancholy and the emotional experiences his mother had shared with him. It is my private speculation that as a boy he had read the Ovid aloud to her and later to his younger siblings.

Triad 5, which te 14 was written to accompany, had as the main theme of *a* the devaluation of beauty by the fashion of make-up and the false fairing of darkness by the wearing of wigs. It had clearly suggested the main ideas of te 14 *b* and *c*. Discovery of the sexual offence will be the theme not only of tr 6 but also of te 15, which begins the next episode – of events after return to London.

Episode 4: Infidelities (tetrads 15–17)

The three scenes of this episode are quite distinct. Between the first and the second there has been an interview between Shakespeare and Herbert. At the end of the second Shakespeare anticipates the time when Herbert will not wish to know him; in the third he anticipates the time when he will be dead and asks Herbert then to forget him but to retain this, the best of his poetry.

The first two of these three tetrads were apparently covering letters to the last two triads, since their themes are linked. They are very closely interlocked with Herbert's seduction and probably for this reason they have been more dislocated from their original position than any of the other groups except one. They have also been disorganized; te 15's *a* and te 16's *d* have been removed, put together, and placed apart in Q as 48 and 49. Then the truncated second tetrad, as a group of three, has been placed very early (33–5) and the truncated first, as another group of three, has been placed nearly as early (40–2). The third tetrad has been left in its chronological place (71–4). But all three – the third tetrad and both the residual threes of the first two tetrads – have undergone the same disorganization: *the order of the first two sonnets has been reversed*. We may suppose the reason for these changes to be the same as the reason for the changes in the ordering of the triads – to hide the situations and to make it as hard as possible to link the triads with the tetrads and so to reconstruct the sequence of these particular events.

Tetrad 15 (48, 41; 40, 42) consists of two pairs. The first pair expresses a dread of loss and its realization; in *a* we have Shakespeare's anxiety that he would find on his return that his friend has been stolen from him; in *b* his anxiety proves justified, when he acknowledges his discovery; though the woman has wooed the youth, the youth has 'leaped into Shakespeare's seat', has tempted and seduced Shakespeare's mistress no less than he was tempted by her. The last line of *a*

> For truth proves thievish for a prize so dear

where Herbert looks as if he will passively be stolen, is translated into the last three lines of *b*

> thou art forced to break a two-fold truth:
> Hers by thy beauty tempting her to thee,
> Thine by thy beauty being false to me.

where Herbert's active share in the stealing is explicit. In either case the main meaning of 'truth' is *fidelity*.

Besides the fact that *a*'s apprehension is fulfilled in *b*, there are minor links between the sonnets: 'truth' has been mentioned and the repetition of 'gentle' is another. There are rhyme links of the usual kind: *a*'s sixth (*art/part*) is echoed in *b*'s second (*heart/art*) and *a*'s seventh (*fear/dear*) in *b*'s sixth (*forbear/there*).

The second pair explores the two kinds of loss, *c* the loss of the woman to the man and *d* the loss of the man to the woman. The tetrad ends with the unreal self-consolation that, since poet and friend are one, the woman loves only the poet. A strong link is that *c*'s sixth rhyme (*thief/grief*) is *d*'s first (*grief/chief*); this same rhyme binds the pair to *a*, in

81

which *grief/thief* had been the fourth. The concept of stealing is prominent in *a* and *c*.

The theme of the triad (**tr** 6) which this tetrad accompanied is *appropriation* – taking, imprisoning, and keeping; it had clearly prompted the chief image of the tetrad's first pair. One word in common, a word unusual for the sonnets, is 'ward':

> Prison my heart in thy steel bosom's ward   (**tr** 6 *a*)

and

> in sure wards of trust.   (**te** 15 *a*)

The repetition of 'use' is also obvious:

> Thou usurer that put'st forth all to use,   (**tr** 6 *b*)

and

> That to my use it might unusèd stay.   (**te** 15 *a*)

But perhaps the strongest link is the idea of bodily containment:

> Prison my heart in thy steel bosom's ward . . .
>   . . . I being pent in thee
> Perforce am thine and all that is in me.   (**tr** 6 *a*)

Te 15 *a* has

> Thee have I not locked up in any chest
> Save where thou art not, though I feel thou art,
> Within the gentle closure of my breast,
> From whence at pleasure thou may'st come and part.

It is a conceit that is used seldom in the sonnets and only in these two places to point the contrast between freedom and unfreedom, possessiveness and unpossessiveness.

Tetrad 16 (34, 33; 35, 49) is again of two pairs. It follows an interview between Herbert and Shakespeare and purports to reproduce it dramatically – *a* the expostulation and reproach, melting at the youth's tears, *b* Shakespeare's meditative soliloquy that if the fouling of sunshine by storms happens in cosmic terms, it can be tolerated in human terms:

> Yet him for this my love no whit disdaineth;
> Suns of the world may stain when heaven's sun staineth.

Then forgiveness follows in *c* with the recognition that 'staining' is universal and Shakespeare justifies the trespass against himself with his first statement of a legal metaphor. This metaphor is restated and expanded in *d*, which echoes *c*'s 'a lawful plea against myself' with 'the lawful reasons on thy part'. The two pairs contrast strongly in their dominant images – the weather in *a* and *b*, legal process and witness in *c* and *d*. The sun, one of the main images in the first pair, recurs in both sonnets of the second pair; *d*'s metaphor, 'that sun, thine eye', vividly recalls *b*.

It is remarkable how continuity is restored by inverting the order of Q's 33 and 34. In position *a*, 34 picks up two rhymes of **te** 15 *d* (42) with *grief/relief* and *loss/cross*; in position *b*, 33's last line, with its repetition of the verb *stain*, is brought next to the consolation in the first quatrain of *c* (35) with its examples of *staining* in nature. Also it is dramatically right that 34 should open the tetrad, making vivid, as it does, what had just passed between the man and the youth. The rhyme *face/disgrace* helps to bind together *a* and *b*. This had been a rhyme linking all three sonnets of **tr** 5; **tr** 7, which **te** 16 accompanied, has the rhyme *spacious/gracious*.

It was presumably the unkind mockery of the woman in the couplet of **tr** 7, with its hint that she might give the youth syphilis, which suggested to Shakespeare the dominant image of *staining* in **te** 16. Herbert could have told Shakespeare of his fear of infection and of his ride home to Wilton. A joke like that of 'firing out', however unpleasant, may even act as a reassurance after the panic is over and the symptoms have been cured or proved of no significance. Herbert himself could have enjoyed **tr** 7 *c* and quoted it to friends from memory. This may be the reason for its being passed to somebody else from whom Jaggard got hold of it with some minor alterations and printed it the next year in his anthology, *The Passionate Pilgrim*.

With **te** 16 the last of the triads has been conveyed and the episode of the Dark Woman is over – but not yet done with, not until **te** 17 closes the account, as we shall see. But it is worth looking at two things:

One is the thought of Hamnet, which must have returned with the third quatrain of **te** 16 *b*:

Even so my sun one early morn did shine
With all-triumphant splendour on my brow,
But out alack! he was but one hour mine;
The region cloud hath masked him from me now.

Even if the pun, *sun/son*, was not intended at the beginning, it was surely to mind while the third line was being written.

The other thing is the changed relationship in which Shakespeare stood to Herbert at the end of the Dark Woman affair. He could not in all conscience put the matter behind him without acknowledging somehow that Herbert was not solely to blame, and that, I believe, is the function of the second pair. The second quatrain of *c* makes a kind of admission which cannot properly state the case for him without giving away the whole plan which Shakespeare, on behalf of Herbert's parents, had elaborated and carried through.

Shakespeare states his own fault in one line:

> Authórizing thy trespass with compare,

Taken at its face value this meant 'giving your offence some justification by comparing it'. By comparing it with what? With the stains of nature and the faults that all men make, we answer immediately. And how is that a fault of the poet's? The next two lines are almost self-contradictory. The line

> Myself corrupting salving thy amiss,

in one meaning suggests that the offence is too serious to be extenuated, or that the extenuator shares in the guilt. The line

> Excusing thy sins more than thy sins are,

suddenly makes the offence seem trivial and Shakespeare to be at fault in dwelling on it. In the rest of the sonnet, whether or not there is a contrived pun in 'I bring *in sense/incense*', Shakespeare does admit himself 'an accessary' – on grounds which would ensure his acquittal! We reflect on the line

> Authórizing thy trespass with compare,

84

and recall the couplet that had closed **tr** 1 *b*, a sonnet of negative comparisons:

> And yet by heaven I think my love as rare
> As any she belied with false compare.

The very point of that sonnet in July of the year before had been to *prompt* Herbert's curiosity, and in April, when repeated, it was meant to *prompt* him to go and see for himself. And the next sonnet

> When my love swears that she is made of truth . . .

had underlined the poet's tolerance of his mistress's infidelities and thus far *permitted* Herbert's second visit to her, once he had been introduced. And the introduction that we have inferred had been part of Shakespeare's *script* for Herbert's initiation. So the three more meanings we can find in *authórized* – permitted, prompted, scripted – are all present in this admission of what Shakespeare had done, an admission which Herbert can hardly have been intended consciously to understand. But it is no wonder that in *d*, when Shakespeare continues the case against himself, in anticipation of the time when Herbert will pass him by he acknowledges that he will have no reason to protest:

> To leave poor me thou hast the strength of laws,
> Since why to love I can allege no cause.

The next poem will open

> O lest the world should task you to recite
> What merit lived in me that you should love . . .

– a perfect continuation, after an interval, from the sentiment of the final couplet of the preceding poem.

Tetrad 17 consists of two pairs (72, 71; 73, 74). Q's 71–4 has often been seen as a run of four, all sharing the theme of Shakespeare's coming death, but only the reversal of the first two sonnets restores the structure. Indeed it has been thought that there is a contradiction between the self-devaluation in 72

> For I am shamed by that which I bring forth

and the confidence of value in his poetry which 74 displays

> The best of that is that which it contains,
> And that is this, and this with thee remains.

The solution is that by taking 72 as *a*, the first element of the tetrad, we get the sonnet which depicts the burial *between* the shame and the confidence (i.e. the bad is disposed of in *b* – 71) and (even more important) the poet's shame over what he brings forth can now refer to what has just preceded **te** 17, namely the indecent triad (**tr** 7) sent along with **te** 16. But there is still greater reason for Shakespeare's expression of shame and concern over the verdict of 'the wise world', if what had more immediately preceded **te** 17 had been Herbert's intimation – by note of hand or by word of mouth – that he had shown **tr** 7 to some friends and they had all admired its wit and had particularly enjoyed the sonnet 'Two loves have I . . .'. Shakespeare's answer reveals his anxiety over the escape of these indecent verses of his and also administers a gentle reproof:

> For I am shamed by that which I bring forth,
> And so should you, to love things nothing worth.

'Things nothing worth' had an extra meaning for Herbert; along with the indecent triad it included the worthless woman.

The two lines before the couplet are

> My name be buried where my body is   (11)
> And live no more to shame nor me nor you.   (12)

It is entirely appropriate that *b* (71) should expand *a*'s line 11, the burial of the body and the name together; the wish of *a* 11 would be otiose if it followed the burial sonnet, as it does in Q. This means that mention of the world, the wise world, encloses the rest of the pair; it both begins and ends it. In Q's order the two mentions come together and form an apparent link; but the falsity of this juxtaposition can be realized from the inappropriateness of following the scrutiny and the mockery of 'the wise world' with an apparently innocent demand of the world for proof of the poet's merit.

The first pair of sonnets is united by the wish to be forgotten by his patron. The last words of *b* are 'after I am gone'. An unspoken question ties this to the second pair – 'When will that be?' And *c* answers in effect

86

'Very soon now'. Three deliberate similes for extreme old age take up the three quatrains of *c*, which ends

> This thou perceiv'st, which makes thy love more strong
> To love that well which thou must leave ere long.

Who is being addressed in this couplet? Herbert? – but he is not the one about to die. Shakespeare himself? – but what a wrench to have a different 'thou' from that in lines 1, 5, and 9! It would have been so easy for Shakespeare to write 'lose' or 'leese' instead of 'leave'. It is of course possible that Shakespeare did write 'leese' here (cf. **te** 1 *a* 14) but 'leave' can be explained by saying that he was strongly identified with his father, John Shakespeare, when he wrote this sonnet, as also when he wrote some of the other sonnets from Stratford. The lines

> Bated and chopped with tanned antiquity

and

> With time's injurious hand crushed and o'er-worn,

must both have described John far more accurately than William Shakespeare. Leave-taking from an aged, depressed father, each wondering whether he will see the other again, naturally leads to a son's temporary identification with him and to an emotional uncertainty over who is leaving whom. The last five words of this sonnet embody that uncertainty. If Shakespeare *is* addressing himself, he is doing so *in persona patris*; father is addressing son as well as son father, and Hamnet's shade hovers near again as *his* father leaves Stratford. For I believe that this sonnet and the next were written, or composed in thought, just then, probably before **te** 15 and **te** 16 or **te** 17 *a* and *b*.

The last sonnet is a recovery from the painful prospect of loss, whether loss of the world of nature or loss of the relative or friend. Once again the lastingness of the verse is compensation for loss of the person. The opening links the sonnet syntactically to the one before:

> But be contented . . .

The rhyme links afford some slight confirmation that *c* and *d* may have been composed as a pair before *a* and *b*. Unlike most other tetrads which consist of two pairs, of which the first is more closely wrought than the second, here the second is more carefully tied together; besides its link of syntax, it also has a prominent double rhyme to connect *d* with *c*. The third and fourth rhymes of *c* are *day/West/away/rest*; the first and second of *d* are *arrest/away/interest/stay*. The first pair's bonds are less elaborate; *a* and *b* have no rhymes in common with each other, though *a* shares one rhyme with *c* (*lie*) and one with *d* (*untrue*; review) and *b* shares one rhyme with *c* (*day*) and two with *d* (-*ay* and *dead*).

It is fitting that the whole of the Dark Woman episode should finish with a poem of depression that begins with disposal of the bad because of acknowledged shame and ends with preservation of the good.

Episode 5: Poets and patron (tetrads 18–20)

By the end of Episode 4 Shakespeare's job was done. He had created a real-life drama in which, all unknowing, Herbert had taken part, brought into a temptation (of stealing an older man's mistress) to which he had yielded, and had so been sexually initiated. Shakespeare had then freed him from the woman's clutches and could have signed off with tetrad 17, in which he acknowledges his own shame and, feeling old, imagines his own death and the survival of the best of his poetry. But his plan was for eighteen tetrads, beginning on the day on which Herbert had turned eighteen; so he had two more episodes to create and, as often to precipitate the ending of a play, the last act but one he staged as a contest.

Contests of various kinds have been shown by Professor Muriel Bradbrook to have been current in Elizabethan times, some surviving from the early middle ages. At least one society had been founded in the thirteenth century for the purpose of holding an annual festival, The Great Festival of the Pui (and by implication minor festivals), to encourage the writing, singing, and judging of songs.[69] The entry of poems without music, even in the correct metrical form of eight-line stanzas ('royal songs'), was expressly excluded in the redrafted statutes of the early fourteenth century, so presumably the practice *had* crept in of entering words without music.[70] Other occasions for poetic competition, including *ex tempore*, were likely and we need not suppose that the Festival of the Pui itself was in Shakespeare's mind. The calligraphic writing out of a winning entry (if that is what line 3 of Q's 85 – **te** 19 *a* – refers to rather than the individual style and fair copy of each entry) and the hanging of it up for all to read were the kinds of award that would have been made at any festivals when there were poetic contests.

I shall argue that a poetic competition was organized privately at

Baynard's Castle in August 1598 and that Shakespeare's entries reveal by their wording that it was spaced out over three occasions, tetrad 18 being composed for the first, at which only other poets actually recited and Shakespeare was chided by Herbert for holding back, tetrad 19 being composed for the second, at which George Chapman recited but Shakespeare again reserved his entry, and tetrad 20 being composed for the third, at which Shakespeare eventually recited all three of his tetrads.

Nine of the eleven sonnets (76–86) which immediately precede the 'farewell' in Q are about comparisons and rivalry in poetic composition (77 and 81 have found other places) and three more (23, 32, and 38) bring the total to twelve, the right number for the three tetrads of an episode. Q's 86 (te 20 c), not read as irony but taken at face value, has often been thought (even by Dover Wilson) to be Shakespeare's acknowledgement that he felt inferior as a poet to his chief rival; 87 (te 23 d), coming first of the farewell group in Q reinforces that impression. When the tetrads are reconstituted, 86 does not come last in its group but is followed by 80 (te 20 d) and the satirical tone is much clearer. Also 87 comes last instead of first in its group and so does not refer to Shakespeare's self-estimation as a poet.

By collecting the four sonnets which mention just *one* rival (Q's 23, 79, 80, and 86) we can reconstruct tetrad 20. The four sonnets which treat first with irony and then with scorn the deadly praises of Herbert uttered by *several* poets (Q's 82–5) can be arranged as tetrad 19; the last couplet of 83

> There lives more life in one of your fair eyes
> Than both your poets can in praise devise

not only makes a good final couplet for the whole tetrad but anticipates the rivalry with just one other which is the situation underlying tetrad 20. This is fortunate, since 82 must immediately precede 83 because of the word-link – 'painting' (i.e. exaggerated praise); so we can fix c and d of the tetrad at once.

The four remaining sonnets (Q's 32, 38, 76, and 78) are to be reordered to form tetrad 18. Q's 32 is the suitable d, because its irony, apparent in the phrases, 'the bett'ring of the time', 'outstripped by every pen', 'exceeded by the height of happier men', 'poets better prove', is a suitable anticipation of the irony in 84 and 85. What is more, three words in 32 – *re-survey*, *reserve*, and *ranks* – not only anticipate the words *reserve* and *rank* in 85 but clarify their use there. So 32 is the almost certain element d of tetrad 18 (and 85 the probable a of tetrad 19); Shakespeare's fore-imagined obituary put into Herbert's mouth in the last five lines of 32 make a perfect close to the tetrad and fix this sonnet as *d*.

The tetrad begins with Q's 78; the first four lines of *a*, besides repeating the rhymes of **te** 5 *a* (a reminder of their second meeting), announce the situation; Shakespeare has been imitated by many verse writers in addressing and dedicating poetry to Herbert but he still asks to come first in his patron's estimation:

> Yet be most proud of that which I compile . . .

In apparent doubt about his creativeness and freshness he then asks in 76(= *b*):

> Why is my verse so barren of new pride . . .?

A phrase in **pr** 2 *b* (151), 'proud of this pride', used there in a sexual sense, shows the same relationship between the words, *proud* and *pride*, as here in *a* and *b* of **te** 18. The unspoken thought sequence is: 'I have just begged Lord Herbert to be proudest of my compilation. Does my verse display the new pride to warrant my entreaty?'

The chief contrast which Shakespeare establishes in *a* is that between himself as untutored and ignorant but taught to sing by Herbert's eyes (another reminder of their first meeting and of the miniature) and the alien poets, learned and graced in Arts, who require no tutoring – merely the mending of their style. The contrast which he develops in *b* is that between his own verse, 'barren of new pride', 'still all one, ever the same', keeping 'invention in a noted weed' (i.e. in one garb or form – the tetrad?), and the fashionable variation, quick change, new-found methods, and strange compounds of the time – in short between the old and the new, until he points out

> all my best is dressing old words new,

and finds an image for his half-way couplet:

> For as the sun is daily new and old,
> So is my verse still telling what is told.

In *c* (38) he argues that his own verse *is* assured of 'invention' – i.e. of newness – by having for its subject Herbert's 'own sweet argument'; it cannot lack freshness as long as Herbert lives. The words of *b* 10

> you and love are still my argument

are taken up early in *c*

> (thou) pour'st into my verse
> Thine own sweet argument, too excellent
> For every vulgar paper to rehearse

and *b*'s sixth rhyme (*argument/spent*) is used as *c*'s first (*invent/argument too excellent*). By the end of *c* Shakespeare has issued a challenge to comparison by the test of lastingness; the novel inventions of the other poets have all dwindled to 'these curious days' and we are prepared for the ironical comparisons to be enumerated in *d* (32).

Whereas *a* and *b* are linked by the notion of birth, *c* and *d* are linked by the notions of eternity and death. Herbert's 'influence' unites *a* and *c*; the contrasting styles and ways of composition of Shakespeare and the modern poets provide a theme shared by *b* and *d*. The pairs are parallel and the whole tetrad is tightly knit.

The two halves of tetrad 19 also are closely linked. We have already fixed *c* and *d* (Q's 82 and 83) and 85's identity as *a*, suggested by its word links, is confirmed in several ways: by its formal opening of humble politeness to the scholar poets, whom Shakespeare had now actually heard – at the occasion for which he had written, but not recited, te 18; by its reiterated, deferential reasons for Shakespeare's own silence at the preceding session, marked, as it had been, by a profusion of elaborate praises from other pens; and lastly by the fact that lines 9–10

> Hearing you praised, I say, ' 'Tis so; 'tis true',
> And to the most of praise add something more

are just what we need to have heard if we are to catch at once the meaning of the opening of *b* (84):

> Who is it (that says most) which *can* say more
> Than this rich praise that you alone are you. . .?

So *b* is fixed by this as well as by its outspoken couplet

> You to your beauteous blessings add a curse,
> Being fond on praise, which makes your praises worse.

At the half-way point the couplet marks the end of the irony and the

91

transition to Shakespeare's open derogation of the learned poets in *c* and *d*.

In *c* Shakespeare acknowledges that he has no monopoly of Herbert, who is free to find elsewhere his more proper praise. In *d* we get franker reasons for his silence at the previous session: first, Herbert living proved the inadequacy of description; second, the deadly praises he received from the other poets were a kind of tomb, letting Shakespeare shine by his very muteness; being dumb *he* has done no such damage to Herbert's glory. It is admitted at last that Shakespeare's silence at the session before, which Herbert had reproved,

> This silence for my sin you did impute

had been deliberate. The closing couplet of the tetrad, quoted above, gives reason to suppose that the first session had concluded with an arrangement that the two special poets, who had *not* recited yet, should do so at a second session. If Shakespeare should be obliged to stick to that arrangement, here was his entry, closing with a claim that his rival's merit was no greater than his, and was derived, like his, from Herbert's own qualities. Tetrad 19 makes it plain that Shakespeare has not yet heard his chief rival's entry, although he had heard those of the other poets.

Tetrad 20 therefore begins with an admission of Shakespeare's new silence and finds a new reason for it – not this time a decision but a last-minute failure of nerve. We are free to suppose that his 'failure' was rather a tactical move than behaviour emotionally forced on him; it gave him the advantage of hearing his rival's entry at the second session so as to answer it at the third. However, Herbert's enthusiastic reception of the rival's verse could have reinforced Shakespeare's intention to hold his fire once more.

Various names have been suggested for the rival poet. The arguments for identifying him are discussed in many editions and books. Robert Gittings in *Shakespeare's Rival* (1960) gives a full account[71] and Dover Wilson's edition[72] took Gittings's ideas fully into consideration before settling for George Chapman, a name proposed by William Minto in 1874 and usually adopted by those who have identified 'Mr W. H.' as William Herbert and chosen the later dating for the sonnets.

Chapman's patron had been Sir Thomas Walsingham, cousin to the father-in-law of Sir Philip Sidney; so the family connection would have aroused Herbert's early interest in Chapman, an interest that would have grown when Chapman published his early work, *The*

Shadow of Night, when Herbert was up at Oxford. We have seen that te 5 *a* had very likely been one hit at Herbert's favourite poet and the Princess's comment in *L.L.L.* upon 'The base sale of chapmen's tongues' could have been another. But since the composition and presentation of those two (in 1597) Chapman had published two major works – on 2 March 1598 the two sestiads of Marlowe's *Hero and Leander*, continued and completed by himself in four more sestiads, and his own translation of Books 1–7 of Homer's *Iliad* on 10 April. In August 1598 his would have been the major name to compare with Shakespeare's and the first line of te 20 *c* (86) surely contains Shakespeare's compliment to his recent achievement. 'The proud full sail of his great verse' was apt for Chapman's alexandrines, as well as for an allusion to Marlowe, with whose verse Chapman had just associated his own. Dover Wilson pointed this out besides endorsing the powerful argument of J. A. K. Thomson in his *Shakespeare and the Classics* that Chapman had actually claimed to have been inspired twice by the ghost or spirit of Homer, and that the other allusions in sonnet 20 *c* (86) fit perfectly some lines of Chapman's. In *The Tears of Peace*, published in 1609, Chapman makes the claim, which Thomson and Wilson associate with a Stoic doctrine reported by the widely read Italian philosopher and doctor Jerome Cardan (translated into English and published in 1573 and 1576), that some genii (including 'souls of men departed') are 'desirous of men's company, very affable and familiar with them, as dogs are'.[73] I have nothing to add to Dover Wilson's magnificent statement of the arguments for identifying the rival poet as Chapman, except to speculate that in his poem of 1609, from which Thomson and Wilson quote, Chapman could have reworked an earlier account of Homer's first visitation and that earlier account could have been the verse he recited before Herbert in the presence of Sir Robert Sidney, Shakespeare, Daniel and others in mid August 1598. It would have been in character.

The order of the sonnets in tetrad 20 is soon fixed. Once more it has the form of two pairs. In *a* (Q's 23) Shakespeare excuses his failure by comparing himself to an actor who does not know his lines or to a fierce creature

> Whose strength's abundance weakens his own heart . . .
> (I) in my own love's strength seem to decay.

In *b* (79) he says

> But now my gracious numbers are decayed
> And my sick Muse doth give another place.

He closes *c* (86) by denying the power over him of the rival and 'his affable familiar ghost':

> I was not sick of any power from thence,
> But when your countenance filled up his line,
> Then lacked I matter – *that* enfeebled mine.

And *d* (80) begins

> O how I faint when I of you do write,
> Knowing a better spirit doth use your name,

and ends

> Then if he thrive and I be cast away,
> The worst was this – my love was my decay.

These are natural sequences – of weakening, enfeeblement, and faintness, of decay ('seems to decay', 'are decayed', 'was my decay' – an effective sequence of tenses), and of sickness ('I was not sick' implies just such a previous near use of 'sick'' as 'my sick Muse'). This indicates the order to be 23, 79, 86, 80. Q's 80 (*d*) must follow 86 (*c*) for several reasons:

(1) The 'saucy bark' of 80 (not as yet 'a worthless boat') makes a more potent appeal – like the little *Revenge* – than the marauding galleon of 86.1 (and of 80.6); it has, so to speak, wrecked the image of the greater vessel, which can thrive no more.

(2) 80.9–10 assert the far greater independence of Shakespeare (he can manage with the shallowest help; his rival needs abundant depth) and by a marvellous word-play on 'soundless' convey that all the wordy praise, on which the rival spends 'all his might to make (Shakespeare) tongue-tied', has amounted to – nothing at all.

(3) 'the proudest sail' of 80.6 is a suitable allusion to 'the proud full sail of his great verse' of 86.1 and the ten-line nautical image in 80 is a suitable expansion of that line of 86; the converse would read oddly and the opening of 86 be an anti-climax.

(4) The couplet of 80 is a good close to the pair of sonnets and to the tetrad – indeed to all three tetrads. It also makes fine symmetry with the final couplet of tetrad 18:

> 'But since he died and poets better prove,
> Theirs for their style I'll read, his for his love.'

Then if he thrive and I be cast away,
The worst was this – my love was my decay.

Chapman enters in *a* only at line 12, when Shakespeare admits that he looks for recompense

More than that tongue that more hath more expressed.

(The triple 'more' is enhanced by following the 'more's and the 'most's of praise in *a* and *b* of the previous tetrad.) In *b* Chapman becomes 'thy poet' and his praises of the patron he longs for are undermined in the last eight lines. In *c* his weighty verse is given its due but his claim to inspiration from 'an heavenly familiar' is ridiculed; his vain efforts to silence Shakespeare and his greater dependence upon help are made apparent in *d*.

Plainly Shakespeare has been made anything but tongue-tied and nobody who reads or recites these tetrads (18–20) as a triple poem and reflects upon their structure and sequential thought in context will ever again imagine that in his *rival-poet* series Shakespeare was making a confession of 'artistic failure'. No wonder he reserved his entry, and his triumph, till the last!

Episode 6: The ending (Tetrads 21–23 and 'envoi')

The thought of Shakespeare reciting te 18–20 all together at the last session of August makes us ask how he and his poetry were received. The next tetrad, when we find it, should tell us. This was the principle used in reconstructing the situations and events at the two occasions for which te 18 and te 19 had been composed; te 19 gave us information about the first occasion and te 20 about the second.

In Q the rival poet sonnets are followed by eight (87–94) which are two groups of four as long as we hold that there is a break after 94 and that 95 (te 26 *a*) is a reproach about something quite different from 94's reproach. It is easy to see the *two* groups, because 91 (te 21 *a*) begins with four lines of generalizations about men's differing pursuits and tastes, lines which are sheer bathos when taken immediately after the dread of loss which ends 90 (te 23 *c*). This gives a useful clue: *start* with 91 and the generalizations make a suitable opening to the first tetrad (91–4) of the Episode; then put 87, the Farewell sonnet, *after* 88–90, so that the sonnet of imminent loss (90) is followed by the one which actually says 'Farewell', and we have the Episode's third tetrad. Something is missing between them; 93–4 (te 21 *c–d*) are a pair of sonnets expressing deep uncertainty – What are Herbert's real feelings (if he does feel), his *real* attitude and intentions? Sonnet 88 (**te 23** *a*) opens by assuming Herbert's readiness to speak slightingly of Shakespeare and scornfully of his best work. Something has happened between the two groups and we can gather what it was by replacing the tetrad that will have originally stood between them.

Te 22 consists of a pair of sonnets about the poet's forced servitude (*a–b*), a sonnet of extreme jealousy (*c*), and one offering renewal of friendship and trust (*d*). If that final overture to reconciliation was ignored by Herbert, we can easily understand the opening of **te 23** (88):

> When thou shalt be disposed to set me light
> And place my merit in the eye of scorn . . .

The sonnets of servitude (57–8), jealousy (61), and return of love (56) have always, I believe, been associated by editors and critics with the sonnets of *sexual* offence (Q's 40–2 and 48, rearranged as **te** 15), to which they are closer in Q; or they have been assumed to imply a repetition of it, for which there is no other evidence. The trouble with that interpretation is that Shakespeare had not found it hard to forgive the sexual offence, nor had he expressed much jealousy over it (if it was part of his own script for Herbert, we know why). But if the jealousy concerns Herbert's intimacy with other *poets*

> From me far off, with others all too near

it is quite another matter.

Now we can reconstruct the three occasions of September. **Te 21** is the only one so far with the sonnets in their original order; indeed they follow one another so logically that it would be difficult to change their order, so the editors of Q used a different form of camouflage: they blurred the ending by placing straight after it 95–6 (**te 26** *a–b*), which by their reproof retrospectively suggested that 94's reproof was also for a sexual lapse. In fact 94 (*d*) follows 93 (*c*) just as closely as 93 follows 92 and 92 follows 91. **Te 21** *c* (93) establishes an all-too-possible dissociation between the unchanging sweetness and love in Herbert's face and the falseness, frowning moods, and even hatred that could be in his heart. Then *d* (94) starts with two lines of which the first implies that Herbert will not *do* any hurt (whatever his thoughts or his heart's workings be – *c* 11) and the second that he does not *do* what he most *shows* (that is, he doesn't act with the sweetness that his looks tell – *c* 13–14):

How like Eve's apple doth thy beauty grow,
If thy sweet virtue answer not thy show.   (*c* 13–14)

They that have power to hurt and will do none,
That do not do the thing they most do show . . . (*d* 1–2)

Editors who have failed to see 94 as running closely on from 93 have assumed that its line 2 is saying the same as line 1 or is explaining it, although it is more vague than what they say it explains and nowhere else in the sonnets is the friend represented as *showing* a will to hurt. In fact line 2 can only be antithetical to line 1, with the same kind of antithesis as that of the previous sonnet, between heart and face; the speaking voice (these are an actor's poems) marks the antithesis by putting an unspoken 'either' in the second line:

That do not (either) *do* the thing they most do *show*.

What had happened becomes clear if we imagine the situation in the few moments after Shakespeare had finished reciting te 18–20. Amid Herbert and his group of poets he had spoken with scorn of the learned ones and had slighted the claims of Chapman to be inspired by Homer's spirit. The poetic triumph had been a social solecism, probably intended. The best that Herbert could manage to face what he must have thought outrageous behaviour of Shakespeare's was a smile and silence, until he or somebody else started conversation by talking of the pursuits he and they were following that summer. (We know from the Sidney papers that the pursuits mentioned in te 21 *a* 1–4 were those of the late summer and that in subsequent years Herbert cut a figure with 200 horse from Wilton, away from Court 'swaggering it in London', wearing fine clothes and armour 'following the camp at Wanstead' (Aug.–Sept. 1599), and that he practised tilt at Greenwich for the Queen's birthday lists (Sept. 1600).)[74]

Shakespeare's new poem conveyed his response to the utter blankness which had greeted his brilliant performance last time. He knew that Herbert could hate him for putting down his rivals as he had, offending the poet whom Herbert had most favoured. (Chapman was a touchy person, who later rounded on Ben Jonson for pointing out that he had misunderstood Horace's Latin.)[75] But he had to discover what Herbert really thought and to remind him of his responsibility and power – including that of judge (Prince of the Feast). He could also remind him of their recent closeness by means of a quotation. The line he used was from a play, *Edward III*, published in 1596, in which Shakespeare just possibly may have had a hand.[76] The line is

Lilies that fester smell far worse than weeds.

Its aptness is simply not apparent, since in the play a king had used his royal power to attempt a rape of his loyal earl's wife; he had been restrained by her threat of suicide and by her reminder that villainy in a king is far worse than in a lowly man. But its aptness here is obvious if we suppose the previous use of the quotation *by Herbert himself*. If he had used it when he confessed to the sexual offence and wept (cf. **te 16 *a***), his use then would have been appropriate and Shakespeare is now reminding him indirectly of his previous contrition; the line's aptness would have been at once apparent to Herbert: he owed Shakespeare another apology for having pointedly ignored his verses and his performance, giving him neither award nor recognition, though obliged by the power he had as judge to pronounce a verdict.

So Shakespeare took **te 21** round to Baynard's Castle at the proper time early in September and found. . . **Te 22** tells us what he found: Herbert absent and no usual gathering. If a porter could tell him anything, it might have been that they were holding the gathering somewhere else; but perhaps Shakespeare just waited in vain, composed *a* and *b* and went home to sleep; couldn't sleep and composed *c*, adding *d* next day or soon after.

The order of the tetrad's sonnets *a–c* (58, 57, 61) is fixed by their wording as well as by the logical sequences. In *a* 1–8 there is the fact of Herbert's absence and Shakespeare's own first reaction to it; his decision follows in 9–14. Starting

That god forbid, that made me first your slave. . .!

he reaches his conclusion, 'I am to wait . . .', and continues

> Being your slave, what should I do but tend
> Upon the hours and times of your desire?
> I have no precious time at all to spend
> Nor services to do, till you require.   (*b* 1–4)

His irony may be manifest but he puts aside his helpless jealousy for a slave's thought:

. . . where you are, how happy you make those.

So true a fool is Love that in your will,
Though you do anything, he thinks no ill.   (*b* 12–14)

Is it thy will . . . ?   (*c* 1)

he asks, when, back at his own lodging, his jealousy develops. Can Herbert be jealous enough to spy in spirit upon his poet? No, it is his own jealousy, his 'own true love', that keeps him wakeful, wondering about the others with his patron friend.

Finally, in *d*, he apostrophizes Love and begs for a renewal of the closeness of the relationship, as the world is renewed after winter. Allusively he acknowledges *Hero and Leander*.

The contemptuous ill-manners with which Herbert had humiliated Shakespeare were perhaps the thing which ten years later he most wished to hide, from aristocratic shame if not from guilt. So this tetrad has been disorganized and embedded in the tetrad which most idealizes Herbert – te 12, disorganized itself in exactly the same way – D, B, A, C; so that we find (55–62) D, d, b, a, B, A, c, C. The metaphors of *c* were themselves of heterosexual love; so the tetrad was well camouflaged by being placed a little after the sonnets concerned with the sexual offence.

If Shakespeare went round to Baynard's Castle in mid September taking te 22 he was received distantly if received at all. That much we can gather from te 23, the eighteenth tetrad of the year and the one that brought the drama to an end. Once more, the sequence in *a–c* is logical: in *a* he anticipates the coming break; in *b* he says that after it he will behave with the utmost loyalty and discretion; in *c* he urges that the break be not delayed; finally, in *d* (87), he makes it himself. The only masculine rhyme in *d* –*estimate/determinate* – picks up the important rhyme word *hate* at the end of *b*, already picked up as the first strong syllable of *c*:

Then hate me when thou wilt. . . .

If we wish to know in what other way at this time Shakespeare was suffering 'the spite of Fortune', how else 'the world was bent (his) deeds to cross', we may recall that the Burbages' lease of the theatre was running out and that the Lord Chamberlain's company faced ruin, unless some desperate plan could save it. (It was saved at the last minute at the end of the year, when the theatre was dismantled and its timbers shipped across the Thames in one night for re-erection on the South Bank.)[77]

Like *Love's Labours Lost* in its second version and just as Costard would have wished,[78] this drama too has an 'envoi' – a poem of six rhyming couplets with which Shakespeare bows out by giving young Lord Herbert a new version of the warning he had sung him over eighteen months before:

> Thy end is Truth's and Beauty's doom and date.

But the editors of Q found a different use for the 'envoi'. By placing it last (126) of all the sonnets to the man they gave the whole series a different flavour of finality from the one we find in te 31, seven and a half years later.

It is pleasant to speculate that to close the 'envoi' Shakespeare perhaps took his metaphor of the *audite*, of rendering accounts, from his company's actual dealings with their ground landlord. A *quietus* is the final account paid; they may have enjoyed the joke, as they hatched their desperate scheme to save their theatre, that they were about to make him his *quietus*.

(v)   Tetrads for eight birthdays (1599–1606)

In Q all but one of the last eight tetrads have been disarranged internally and have had either their beginnings or their endings obscured, so that they have lost their shape; but there have been only three dislocations in the order of their sequence and we saw in section 5 (pp. 21–5) that the datable events suggested as allusions in four of them allowed us to assign them all, by working backwards, to the years 1599–1606. Once the shape of each of the eight tetrads is restored, not only are the beginnings and endings obvious but the substantial time intervals and changes of situation from one to the next become clear; also five of the eight have some indications of having been composed in the month or so leading up to Herbert's birthday, so it is a likely hypothesis that they were all annual tributes to him as patron.

1599 (te 24: 100, 101; 102, 103)

In *a* the poet invokes his absent Muse and bids her sing.

In *b* he suggests her probable excuse for silence, says it will not do, and tells her to proceed, under his tuition, with praising Herbert.

In *c* the Muse sings and insists that she loves no less and had good reason for her recent silence.

In *d* the poet judges her song and calls it inadequate.

We could imagine a brief scene: the poet's invocation; the appearance of the Muse, spotlighted and bidden to sing; her song; the spotlight fading and the poet's comment.

This is the second of the only two tetrads left by the editors of Q in their original order. One reason why it has not been recognized until now as a set of four – even by Dover Wilson, who actually suggested that those around it (97–9 + 104) were 'a linked quartet' – may be that Absence has been the theme of 97 and of 98 ('two separate absences', pronounced C. K. Pooler), so by the time we reach 100 the theme does not seem new. Another reason is that 102 has not been heard, or thought of, as the song demanded in *a* and *b* and judged in *d*. (Shakespeare has not always been allowed his dramatic technique when writing sonnets!)

This poem is a tentative approach to Herbert after the almost bitter 'farewell' and warning six months before. In the first pair the poet addresses his Muse; only in *d* does he address Herbert directly, though his Muse has done so in *c*. It is certainly the first poem after the ending of the Drama, because it is the only one which refers to the episode of the rival poets, which the Muse offers as her reason for having interrupted her song:

. . . wild singing burdens every bough
And sweets grown common lose their dear delight.

(That emphatic 'every' recalls five such 'every's in te 18–19.) So here is the poem for Herbert's nineteenth birthday, the first after the farewell.

1600 (te 25: 98, 99; 97, 104)

This is the only tetrad which bears signs of having been made at two quite different times; *d* (104) is the third anniversary sonnet and therefore belongs to early April; *a–c* belong to the late summer or autumn, but six months or so *after d*, as we have good astronomical reason to think. The chief image of the tetrad is the lapse of seasons, marked by flowers in *a* and *b* and by trees in *c* and *d*. .

In the late summer, when Shakespeare resumed at his own leisure the completion of te 25, he designed a pair of sonnets looking back upon the spring and recording the first April since they had met in which he had not attended Herbert:

From you I have been absent in the Spring,
When proud-pied April, dressed in all his trim,
Hath put a spirit of youth in everything –
That heavy Saturn laughed and leaped with him.

The year 1600 was the first since 1592 in which the planet Saturn rose in
April. (It did so again in the next two years but later and later in the
month, more and more obliquely, and *after* Herbert's birthday.) If we
imagine Shakespeare taking te 25 d to Baynard's Castle at sundown on
7 or 8 April, he could have looked along the Thames to the East and
seen the brilliant and abrupt rising of Saturn, a sight rare enough to be
'lively in his memory' five or six months later.

That Shakespeare should have written only one sonnet for Herbert's
twentieth birthday, the third anniversary of their meeting, requires an
explanation. The sonnet itself, in line 3, implies that he had recently
seen Herbert – 'Such seems your beauty still' – yet in the late summer
he can say 'From you I have been absent in the Spring.' A natural way
to reconcile the two statements is to suppose that he had called at
Baynard's Castle in March to enquire whether he was expected to recite
a poem for this fourth birthday in succession and had been told that he
was not – that there would be no ceremony that year, though perhaps
there could be a recitation in the autumn. Herbert himself had been at
Wilton for much of the winter and his father and mother had decided
to spend the whole summer there (so Whyte informs Sidney in a letter
of 12 April); moreover his uncle was no longer in England, so his
family was no more at Baynard's Castle. Herbert may have con-
templated returning to Wilton for his birthday (that same letter of
Whyte's enclosed letters to Sidney from Herbert and from his mother;
so perhaps they were together); but if he did go home, he was back in
London by 26 April.[79]

Shakespeare, although his presence was not required, could have
marked the anniversary by writing and leaving one sonnet at Baynard's
Castle on 7 or 8 April without having attended to perform on
Herbert's birthday; he had 'been absent from him'. The last lines of *a*
'and, you away, As with your shadow I with these did play' – suggest
that it was *Herbert* who had been absent.

Here is the first of the three *d* sonnets which have couplets ending in
(un-)bred/ dead. There must have been a reason in 1602 for the repetition of the rhyme; I suggest that it was meant as a reminder to Pembroke, who could have said at the birthday performance of 1601 that
there had been none the year before, thereby provoking Shakespeare

to give the next year a tactful jog to his memory. (Perhaps Shakespeare had not yet been rewarded.)

Herbert's social life had kept him busy during this time. In the autumn of 1599 he had had to get the Queen's leave to return to Wilton, where his father was again dangerously ill; but Goodrich had gone down there from London and saved the Earl's life by 'cutting' (i.e. probably removing a urinary stone). Pembroke had made a good recovery.[80] In the winter the young Earl of Southampton and Sir Charles Danvers had been given hospitality by the Herberts at Ramsbury in Wiltshire.[81] Herbert's own stay had been prolonged owing to an illness, apparently the ague, and the first time he had set off for London he had had to turn back at Newbury. He eventually returned on 12 March. He became popular at Court, and also renewed his contacts with Danvers and Southampton.[82] They might have turned out to be dangerous for him, since both were implicated in Essex's rebellion in February the next year, but his love-affair with a lady-in-waiting diverted his energies and kept him assiduous at Court throughout the summer.

On 16 June his cousin, Henry Somerset Lord Herbert, son of the Earl of Worcester, married Anne Russell, sister of one of the Ladies-in-Waiting; the Queen herself attended the ceremony, landing near Blackfriars and being carried in a canopied chair on the shoulders of six knights to Lord Cobham's residence there. She attended also the evening festivities, a masque and dancing, in which she joined.[83] There is a picture, probably by Marcus Gheeraerts, of the Queen being escorted after landing from the Thames. Dr Leslie Hotson has identified the leading Lady-in-Waiting and the courtier holding her hand, who are to be seen in the lower right-hand corner of the painting, as Mary Fitton and William Herbert.[84] They began a passionate affair that night, as a result of which a short-lived baby boy was born just after mid March 1601. It was a serious affair, for evidence was later given that Mary Fitton had been seen repeatedly that summer striding through the streets in a cloak to visit William Herbert, who could not have been so prominent at Court during the next two or three months if the affair had not lasted.[85]

In fact *two* copies of the picture are extant, both in collections in Dorset, at Sherborne Castle and at Melbury House. A reasonable explanation of this would be that it was Herbert who had commissioned two copies to be painted, one for his mistress and one for himself, but that by the time they were ready, say in September, there was already a rift caused by the news of Mary's pregnancy; so both pictures would have been taken to Wilton and later sold from there, a likely provenance for pictures surviving in Dorset.

Pregnancy is the underlying theme of *te* 25 *c* (97), which its wording shows to have been composed in the autumn. To take the sonnet *after* 98–9 allows the absence referred to in *a* and *c* to be one and the same:

> From you I have been absent in the Spring . . .

> How like a Winter hath my absence been
> From thee. . .!

It seems as if Shakespeare had not polished *b* (99) and, since he never had to recite it, he had perhaps put it aside to finish later. It has five lines, rhyming alternately, instead of the usual first four. Moreover in Q the first heavy punctuation is a question-mark *at the end of line 4*. It seems as if the first sentence had ended with line 4 and as if line 5 had been an immediate afterthought, Shakespeare's idea probably being to advance the question-mark to the middle of line 4 (where modern editors put it), if he could find a way to fuse lines 1 and 2 into one. But there can have been no urgency to finish the revision and, before it was done, Herbert will have summoned him for advice. Presumably he told him of Mary Fitton's pregnancy, of his doubts whether his parents could countenance his marriage to her, and of his own deep aversion to marriage; he was going to spend the last ten days of October practising tilt at Greenwich.[86]

In his book, *Conceitful Thought*, Alastair Fowler has a four-page discussion of the next sonnet, *c* (97), correcting the mistaken impression 'that autumn's husband is deceased . . . Shakespeare's meaning is different; namely that autumn's continuing fertility during the absence of the beloved is as heart-breakingly poignant *as if it were* the pregnancy of a widow' (p. 112; Fowler's own italics).[86] It adds to the poignancy to link this sonnet with Mary's actual pregnancy, especially when we learn of her touching faith next May, when her son has been born and has died and her father is taking her home to Cheshire, still weak, that if she could only have one interview with William Herbert in the presence of neutrals, he would return into love with her – and marry her.[88] In her early pregnancy how gently Shakespeare had hinted in *c* at the sadness there would be if Herbert did not play his supreme and natural part!

Given the relevance to *te* 25 *c* of this love-affair which ended sadly, we can use it also to explain the composition of *A Lover's Complaint*, printed in Q after the sonnets. It has a double message: on the one hand the irresistible youth who seduced the maiden is heartless and his fault unforgivable; on the other hand she would act no differently, even with hindsight, and his charms would 'new pervert a reconcilèd maid'. If the poem belonged like the sonnet to late 1600, it was a compliment to Herbert's attractiveness and potency but also a hint that he might still give the story a happy ending in reality. If J. C. Maxwell's dating (1601 or 1602) is followed closely, it could be Shakespeare's ambivalent consolation to his patron in his remorse, if he was capable of it, at having wronged the young woman.[89]

Having written *d* five or six months before the other three sonnets, Shakespeare took care to give it links of rhyme in the pair that was to open the tetrad; *b* therefore has two rhymes in common with *d*, *chide/pride/dyed* matching *eyed/pride*, and *hand/stand* matching *dial-hand/stand*; *c* has one, *been/seen* matching *seen/green*.

1601 (te 26: 95, 96; 69, 70)

The dénouement of the Mary Fitton affair is the inescapable background to the poem for Herbert's next birthday. But while it was proceeding to term, other crucial events occurred.

After another illness in September, from which he had recovered with the help of the Queen's own physician, Dr Gotherous, whom she sent down to Wilton, the second Earl of Pembroke died at last on 19 January.[90] This was eleven weeks before his son and heir, now the third Earl, became twenty-one and legally able to manage his fortunes. So for the rest of his minority – probably thanks to his parents' prior arrangement, he became the ward of Sir Robert Cecil, who was not only the Queen's secretary but almost a family friend.

One week later Mary Fitton's pregnancy was discovered and she was committed to the care of Lady Hawkins, a senior lady of the Court. On 5 February the new young Earl was arrested and examined about his responsibility for her condition.[91]

Three days later the malcontent Earl of Essex, kept in uncertainty since his return from his bungled command in Ireland, led a hopelessly bungled rising of impecunious nobles, knights, soldiers, and retainers; he surrendered to arrest. Young Pembroke had the sense to write a letter at once to Cecil, dissociating himself from the rebels – 'men I cannot call them'.[92] Although Danvers was among those of Essex's followers who were executed, Southampton, because of his youth, was only imprisoned.

Copies of a popular ballad with topical stanzas have survived.[93] One stanza laughs at the way Pembroke has worsted Sir William Knollys by stealing his girl; it 'names Pembroke's name' and 'tells the story of his days'. It runs

> Parti-beard was afeard,
> When they ran at the herd;
> The reindeer was imbost;
> The white doe she was lost;
> Pembroke struck her down
> And took her from the clown,
>   Lord for thy pity.
>   (*or* Like a good woodman.)

the herd = the ladies-in-waiting, looked after by the Controller; *parti-beard=the clown*=Sir William Knollys, Controller, protector and would-be lover of *the white doe*=Mary Fitton; *the reindeer* . . . *imbost*= the Earl of Essex (his crest a reindeer) . . . run to exhaustion; *woodman*=lecher.)

After mid March Mary's baby was born and died; Pembroke himself, who acknowledged his previous love-affair with her but absolutely refused to marry her, was imprisoned in the Fleet but was probably out and at home in Baynard's Castle for his coming-of-age.[94]

Letters from Pembroke to Cecil in February acknowledge how much his guardian has been doing for him, the first saying that his deeds have expressed his love and the second begging continuance of his love. A letter in March says the Lord Admiral has told him how much Cecil had favoured him lately.[95] Sir Edward Fitton's letter of 18 May to Cecil, which was mentioned above, describes his daughter's confidence in her case and in Pembroke, adding 'But for myself, I expect no good from him that in all this time has not showed any kindness'.[96] This implies that Pembroke had been enough at liberty to show kindness. The likeliest reconstruction is that ever since his arrest for examination Pembroke had been confined to his residence except for the week or so when he was in prison around the time of Mary's confinement.

In te 26 Shakespeare knows no more of Pembroke than what is publicly said of him. Its two pairs correspond to one another in so far as the first sonnet of each gives the poet's own statement of, and feeling about, the gossip or satire of which Pembroke has become the subject, while the second of each explores the significance of the various public opinions about him and ends with the poet's conditional reassurance. Sonnet 95 provides the better opening – an exclamation – and stands as *a*, 70 the more positive close and is therefore *d*. The first pair is clearly about Pembroke's sexual escapade and lines 5–8 are entirely appropriate as a comment on the lampoon quoted above; *b* ends by quoting the actual couplet of te 8 *b*, an earlier appeal to Herbert not to diminish his honour by base contacts, and the two lines before it may be paraphrased,

> How many admirers might you seduce
> If you should use the strength of your high rank!

– a tactful reminder of the fact that William Herbert has now become Earl. The second pair is a more general warning about the readiness of suspicion ('suspect' – a noun) and envy to seize upon and erode Pembroke's hitherto unblemished reputation. The pair is out of place in Q being the only sonnets of the series 55–74 which are *not* strongly influenced in wording and ideas by Book XV of Ovid's *Metamorphoses* in Golding's translation.[97] The final couplet is the nearest that Shakespeare comes to hinting at Pembroke's dangerous political contacts. He himself had recently known the danger, because his company had been hired by the Essex faction and on Saturday, 7 February, had publicly performed his play, *Richard II*, in which a sovereign of England is deposed; this was a piece of last-minute propaganda before the rebellion next day.[98]

1602 (te 27: 110, 109; 111, 112)

Once more we have to reconstruct Pembroke's movements in order to give the background to this poem for his twenty-second birthday.

In a letter to Cecil from Baynard's Castle on 19 June 1601 he complains of the burden of the bill for his wardship yet agrees to pay it, since it is the Queen's sacred will. He also equates with imprisonment the hardships of not being allowed to go abroad (*sc.* out of doors) to follow his own business and of being excluded from the Court and the Queen's presence.[99]

The next two letters of his to Cecil are from Wiltshire – 13 and 26 August – and concern his surrender of the patent of the Forest of Dean, because the Queen intends transferring it to 'sweet Sir Edward Fitton', whom she prefers before him. Pembroke is deeply irked by being banished to his estates in the country. He begs Cecil to assist him 'to get leave to go into some other land, that the change of climate may purge me of melancholy'.

On 2 September he writes from Ramsbury acknowledging the blow that he has failed to stop the transfer to Fitton of the Forest of Dean patent. He begs Cecil to get a promise that he 'should have leave to travel after the Parliament; it would make me more able to do her Majesty and my country service, and lessen if not wipe out the memory of my disgraces'. The four-yearly Parliament was held from October to December and during it the Queen clearly had some use for him in London. In October he writes to Cecil, 'I have written to my Lord Admiral to be earnest with her Majesty for my leave to travel . . . When the parliament is ended her Majesty will have no employment for me and I hope she will not so far extend her anger towards me, as, having herself no use for me, to confine me to a country now most hateful to me of all others, when my travel will enable me to do her service.' And, in another letter, 'yesternight I received a message from my Lord Admiral by my uncle, that, when his Lordship moved the Queen for me, she said she would have me go keep house in the country . . . I perceive her Majesty still continues in her wonted displeasure towards me, for when she was in the height of her anger, her answer was the very same.' Once more he begs only for the leave to travel.[101]

His last three letters to Cecil filed under 1601 (which could mean anything up to 24 March, since the new year began on 25 March) are two that concern a position he requests for a cousin and, last of all, a brief letter of joyful thanks to Cecil: 'I know not how to be sufficiently thankful for so great a favour bestowed on me, in getting the Queen's consent for my going beyond the seas . . . I beseech you, while her Majesty is in this good disposition, you will give order to Mr Lake to draw my licence, and procure her Majesty's gracious hand' (*sc.* signature).[102]

Te 27, one of the most beautiful tetrads, can be read as Shakespeare's compassionate answer to the young Earl's peevish summons: 'This year I shall expect and give you welcome here at Wilton. Fortune ever smiles on you, and you, as usual, have been free to range, to go here and there, a motley to the view of all and making new affections, false in your absence to your old, true friends. I am confined still to my house here in the country, most hateful to me now. But very soon I shall taste freedom, for I have at last the Queen's leave to travel, to go beyond the seas. So look to it that you arrive just to the time, for I shall set forth straight after my birthday.' This (imaginary) letter elicits comfort – Shakespeare too is confined, joyously to his patron on the one hand, ruefully to his actor's calling on the other. The first two sonnets have been transposed by Q's editors: *a* begins with an exclamation of agreement with a rebuke just received, *b* with a negation that limits the extent of his admitted offence; *a* ends with an acceptance of his welcome

> to thy pure and most most loving breast,

while *b* speaks of

> my soul which in thy breast doth lie;
> That is my home of love.

It continues

> If I have ranged,
> Like him that travels I return again.

Shakespeare's comparison here, if he had received Pembroke's news that he soon would travel, is at once a complimentary acknowledgement and an assurance of safe home-coming. Then *b* twice brings in the concept of *stain*, of *being stained*, which becomes the powerful image of *c*:

> my nature almost is subdued
> To what it works in, like the dyer's hand.

The brand received in *c* requires his friend's pity and *d* opens with the curative effect of pity granted:

> Your love and pity doth th'impression fill
> Which vulgar scandal stamped upon my brow.

The emphasis on 'staining' makes more likely the conjecture of 'o'er-grain' (='stain over') for 'o'er-green' (of doubtful sense).[103]

The tetrad ends with the same rhyme words as that of 1600, best taken as a tactful reminder that he *had* in fact made him a tetrad two years before, if Pembroke had reproached him the year before with neglecting to do so.

1603 (te 28: 106, 105, 107, 108)

If Queen Elizabeth did sign Pembroke's passport, it probably specified limited travel and perhaps no more than a visit to his uncle; for

Pembroke was certainly back in London by early July 1602. William Browne, Sidney's agent in Flushing, visited him in Baynard's Castle on 6 July to give him a letter from Sidney. Anne Herbert, his sister, was there but not seen because she was unwell.[104] Pembroke's banishment to his estates had clearly been relaxed but perhaps only temporarily for the period of his travel and return. The same may be true while he was supervised by his uncle, for he and his uncle were Sir John Harington's guests among others over the Christmas period at Exton, Rutland, Sidney being in England from mid October to mid January.[105]

The one feature that dates the tetrad to 1603 is the allusion in c (107) to the death of Queen Elizabeth, which, as we saw, alone makes sense of the *two* lines 5–6. It occurred at about 2 a.m. on 24 March, fifteen days before Pembroke's twenty-third birthday. There are two reasons for thinking that the tetrad was ready before her death and that the present c is a replacement for the original one.

The first reason is the theme of *sameness*, of 'no change', common to b and d. If Pembroke was still confined to his estates, which allows the double meaning to 'my love',

> Supposed as forfeit to a confined doom,

Shakespeare can assure him that his own verse is 'to constancy confined'. In b (105) he makes the repetition the focus:

> 'Fair, kind, and true' is all my argument,
> 'Fair, kind, and true' varying to other words;
> And in this change is my invention spent,
> Three themes in one, which wondrous scope affords.

In d (108) he asks, and answers his own question, about *change*:

> What's new to speak, what now to register,
> That may express my love or thy dear merit?
> Nothing, sweet boy; but yet, like prayers divine,
> I must each day say o'er the very same.

In a (106) there is a similar sense of things being just as they were, at least as far as poets and poetry are concerned, coming short of adequate praise – previously because poets had not eyes enough (they looked but into the future), now, since Pembroke's birth, because they have not tongue enough.

Given that it is set among those three sonnets, which all emphasize repetition, variation in sameness, c is powerfully dramatic in its announcement of change, of a new event which has transformed the whole situation. The sonnet is like a flashing jewel, all the more brilliant for the repetitious patterns of its setting. We almost forget, when we reach d (fixed as d by its couplet's bred/dead rhyme – the third instance), that its 'nothing new' does contradict the resounding news proclaimed in c.

A second reason for thinking that c was a later substitute is the use of rhymes. Shakespeare has grafted it to the other three sonnets by means of three of its last four rhymes, one being common to each of the others and at least one rhyme word being shared, age with d, time/rhyme with a, and spent with b. This is a master craftsman's splicing, and though by now there is little use of rhyme to bind the sonnets of a group together, the replacement of one sonnet by another may well have called out the old technique.

The order of a and b, reversed in Q, is settled by several points:

(1) A measured when-clause begins the whole tetrad and is answered by a four-line main clause beginning 'then'.

(2) The more insistent, negative opening of b

> Let not my love be called idolatry

comes well after the last six lines of a, in which the praises and prophecies of bygone poets are contrasted with the tongue-lacking praise of present ones; by contrast with others' lack of tongue, Shakespeare's love might be called idolatry:

> Since all alike my songs and praises be
> To one, of one, still such and ever so.

(3) Not only is the word 'praises' more effective just after 'praise' at the end of a, but the second rhyme of b (show/so) picks up the fourth of a (brow/now), a common type of link.

(4) Finally, the repeated 'fair, kind, and true' of b 9, 10, 13 come better after the fairness has been demonstrated fully in a, the kindness in b 5, and the truth ('constancy') in b 6. The formula sums up, binding the pair together.

1604 (te 29: 113, 114; 116, 115)

Again we find a tetrad of two pairs. The opening of a, announcing that

Shakespeare has just left Pembroke and been in an extraordinary state of mind ever since, leaves us wondering what can have caused it, but Pembroke himself can have been in no such uncertainty. It can only have been a surprise, a piece of news that he had told to Shakespeare at their recent meeting. From the opening of c (116) we can guess what it was – the news that he intended to marry. His wedding was to take place on 4 November 1604 and his bride was to be Mary Talbot, eldest of the three heiress daughters of Gilbert Talbot, seventh Earl of Shrewsbury.

Pembroke himself had made an overture to Shrewsbury by a letter dated 29 August 1603 and the progress of the negotiations and bargaining may be read in the published letters and in the catalogues of those unpublished in the Talbot collection.[106] The last item listed, after a letter dated 29 January 1604, is an undated paper of 'the Earl of Pembroke's objections to certain terms proposed by the Earl of Shrewsbury with regard to the Lady Mary's portion'. So we may gather that it took five or six months from 17 September (the date of the first proposal on Pembroke's behalf) to settle the terms of the marriage contract. The engagement could have been public knowledge from the spring onwards.

The preoccupation into which the news had temporarily cast Shakespeare may be interpreted variously, but his essential reply is 'it makes no difference; my love is even greater than before'. 'The marriage of true minds' has been understood as the friendship and that surely is the underlying meaning; but I take the overt meaning to be the marriage just announced. Shakespeare adopts the *persona* of parson and we hear the emphasis so that it brings out the contingency of 'true':

> Let *me* not to the marriage of *true* minds
> Ad*mit* impediments.

His implication is 'Only you and she know if you can be true to each other, true (that is) as you have known me to be'. The manner of Pembroke's telling will have affected Shakespeare as profoundly as the actual news.

Why *was* Pembroke to marry? Royal commands, no doubt, to the spoilt pair of brothers now taken to favour. (Philip also married – Susan Vere – at the end of 1604 and benefited handsomely from the new King's lavish gifts.) Perhaps his mother reminded him of an express wish of his father's; at any rate Pembroke had it as a Herbert tradition, if you needed a wife at short notice, to sue for one of the Talbot girls;

his father and grandfather had so acquired their second wives, the former when his sister, Anne, married Francis Talbot. In all likelihood Pembroke imparted the news to Shakespeare with some cynicism at his decision not to let his mother lose her prayers this time.

We have no reason to think that Shakespeare met Pembroke while negotiations for his marriage were in progress, or that he would have been told of them if he had. King James had paid a planned visit to Wilton on Saturday 27 August 1603, and spent the night there. It is possible, even likely, that Shakespeare's company, the King's Men (so entitled from 17 May 1603), played before him then, engaged for the entertainment he loved by the rehabilitated Pembroke and his mother, great patrons of poetry and drama; this they might well have arranged even had they not had their special bond with Shakespeare. That visit was to have been made during the King's first tour after his coronation in August, but his coronation had been postponed then and later owing to outbreaks of the plague. He and the Court returned to Wilton at least twice during the autumn.

On 15 March King James was crowned at last. This ceremony supplied the metaphor that dominates te 29 *b* (114) and recurs near the end of *d* (115). It is quite absent from *a* (113), which suggests that *a* was composed before 15 March and therefore that Shakespeare's call, during which Pembroke told him the news and which ended with Shakespeare's leaving as he describes in *a*, took place before the middle of March. In *b* we detect an effort to reimagine and reuse the earlier eye-mind dissociation which had underlain *a* but which was now recollected rather than re-experienced.

'Crowning' is quite absent from *c*; moreover *c* is a natural continuation of a dialogue between Pembroke and Shakespeare, e.g.

P. So it is fixed – November. I can level at your thoughts. You wonder I can be so worldly. You hear in your mind those other lovers' complaints – Mary Fitton's, those of your dark witch (I forget her name), and so many more; you miss in all I say one word of love. Well, play the parson; tell me to renounce the marriage for her good and for my own.

S. Sweet Lord,
These thoughts are not my thoughts; they are your own. Let me not to the marriage . . .

so it was perhaps composed first of the four, though later set as *c*.

We should consider here the whole structure of the tetrad. In the first pair *a* is about Shakespeare's unusual state of mind, called 'derealization' by psychiatrists, in which the external world has lost its reality.[107] He cannot rely upon his normal visual powers to perceive things around him properly. His eye delivers no forms or shapes of things to his heart; on the other hand, what his mind does catch, not of the eye's living objects but of fleeting images, it reshapes into the image of his friend. So the mind is more responsible than the eye for the untrue vision.

In *b* the same eye-mind dissociation continues, but the faulty perception finds a different explanation and the crowning of King James has supplied a new metaphor. Either Shakespeare's mind, crowned with the thought of Pembroke, behaves like a king and drinks up palatable untruths – flattery furnished by the courtier eye, or else his eye does pass on true images but his mind, taught by love, transforms everything, even bad, unwelcome objects, into the perfect picture of his friend. Shakespeare now opts for the first idea; his eye, not his mind, is at fault: the eye gives to the mind altered images, a cup prepared to his monarch's taste:

> If it be poisoned, 'tis the lesser sin
> That mine eye loves it and doth first begin.

That word 'begin' has two functions. It extends the metaphor, so that we sense the eye beginning to drink of the cup, but also, standing last word of the pair of sonnets, it points us on to the next pair with their shared theme of love and time; in their first words we begin to drink of the same cup ourselves.

The fact that Q's 115 and 116 have not been seen as a pair is due to their transposition; 116 is the *c* and 115 the *d*. As usual, the clearest indication of this is in their couplets, that of *d* being the proper close. The couplet of *c*

> If this be error and upon me proved,
> I never writ nor no man ever loved.

has been called weak in comparison with its three quatrains. Indeed it *is* weak if we isolate the sonnet, as is many a couplet in the series when we regard it as a full close instead of as a half-close and harbinger of the next sonnet. Here the final line is taken up at once in the first two lines of *d*:

> Those lines that I before have writ do lie,
> Even those that said I could not love you dearer.

114

Although *b*'s metaphor is not explicitly continued, the whole point of the courtier's tasting was to ensure that, had there been an error in the mixing, it should be proved upon him and not upon his sovereign. That is to say, we may take the three quatrains of 'the marriage of true minds' to be the cup-bearer's draught of the loving-cup and the couplet to be his assurance; the assurance is further strengthened by the opening of *d*, which in its first two lines comments on the inadequacy, the untruthfulness even, of the perfection and absoluteness of his love as told in the marvellous quatrains of *c*, now included in those lines which Shakespeare '*before* had writ'. In *d* both love and time come earlier than they did in *c* and love enters into a second, more creative relationship with time. Instead of encountering time only as the destructive reaper, love now finds in time the very condition for his growth, for passing from babyhood to maturity.

So **te** 29 *d* reverses the process of **te** 12*a*, in which the baby, the gift of time, had no sooner reached maturity than time struck him down. That sonnet could end but with the braving of time by verse; this one ends with enlargement through time. The 'crooked eclipses' and the 'millioned accidents' are left behind by the sweep of thought in which the uncompleted sentence breaks off to give way to the complex coda of the sestet, where the crowned present itself yields to the greater hope of the new generation. 'Love is a babe' looks back to the birth of every baby important in Shakespeare's life, and forward to the hope for Pembroke of a child to bless his newly announced marriage.

1605 (te 30: 119, 117, 118, 120)

This tetrad has grown out of an attitude of confession and a plea for mercy. It has two sonnets that imply return after absence and they form the first pair, *a* being identified by its dramatic opening – an exclamation for its first quatrain, two exclamations for the second, and still another for the third. The first two quatrains purport to be a vivid admission of how Shakespeare has been spending his time since he was last present (they could be his assent to an accusation). The couplet of *a*

> So I return rebuked to my content
> And gain by ills thrice more than I have spent.

by its financial language introduces the dominant metaphor of *b* – accounting and audit – and leads on to *b*'s opening – 'Accuse me thus . . .' In fact the first eight lines of *b* are Shakespeare's volunteered amplification of Pembroke's rebuke, mentioned in *a* 13, if we suppose that the actual rebuke for neglect had been made in a letter anticipating Shakespeare's annual visit or in an interview upon arrival.

The third quatrain encourages Pembroke to go further but to stop short of hate; the couplet explains:

> Since my appeal says I did strive to prove
> The constancy and virtue of your love.

The proof of his own constancy behind his inconstancy is in *c*, a sonnet of paradoxes. He represents his wilfulness and errors, in seeking relationships remote from his patron in distance, station, and quality, as attempts to get the excess of sweetness – Pembroke's – out of his system, or as drugs to purge himself:

> But thence I learn, and find the lesson true,
> Drugs poison him who so fell sick of you.

'That you were once *un*kind' (*d*) is a fine continuation and a salutary reminder that Shakespeare's judgement and memory had erred; Pembroke's sweetness had not been quite so consistent as it had appeared in *c* and he was also capable of being shaken by feelings over inconstancy no less than Shakespeare had been once:

> But that your trespass now becomes a fee;
> Mine ransomes yours and yours must ransome me.

The close of *c* and the opening of *d* have bound these into a convincing pair and now *d*'s couplet ends the tetrad positively and realistically. Shakespeare treats on equal terms for all his wilful wretched errors and his need for forgiveness. We may see here the beginning of his refusal to be dominated, a refusal that will become more explicit the next year, when he declines to join the ranks of those who

> Lose all, and more, by paying too much rent.

There is no other obvious indication of date for this tetrad, but if we bear in mind that *Measure for Measure* was first performed on 26 December 1604 (the day before Philip Herbert's wedding, which followed his brother's in under eight weeks), a parallel of unusual thought may be significant. Te 30*a* 9–10 are

O benefit of ill, now I find true
That better is by evil still made better!

Measure for Measure (V.i.435–7) has this:

They say best men are moulded out of faults
And, for the most, become much more the better
For being a little bad.

What is called in *d* 'our night of woe' was almost certainly a quarrel that lasted longer than it might have if Shakespeare had remembered 'how hard true sorrow hits' and had offered sooner 'the humble salve', such salve as Pembroke had given him in te 16 *a* and perhaps also over his 'infidelity' with Chapman, when they met again for the birthday of 1599. The quarrel would have occurred upon the evening of Shakespeare's arrival, following the rebuke. If a cause of it has to be suggested out of the fragments of information that we possess of the two men, the most plausible one might be that Shakespeare had excused himself from attending Pembroke's wedding on Sunday 4 November.

1606 (te: 121, 125; 124, 123)

Two pairs make up the last tetrad of all. The theme uniting the first pair is Shakespeare's independence; in *a* (121) he asserts it in the face of baseless ill reports from worthless men about his sexual life; in *b* (125) it is his independence from observing outward conformity; it is enough that he is inwardly compliant. The corrupt informer returns at the end of *b*, powerless over 'true soul'. The true soul of *b*'s couplet sets the theme for the second pair: *c* (124) spells out what truth means in contrast with social, political, and religious inconstancy (we recall that Guy Fawkes had been a Protestant before he became a Catholic); *d* (123) defines the poet's truth as a quality beyond the power of time to change it.

There is a nice confirmation of the order in the sequence of dramatic 'Noes'. 'No!' begins lines 9 of *a* and of *b*, line 5 of *c*, and line 1 of *d*, a fine crescendo.

We saw above that the execution of the Gunpowder Plot conspirators on 31 January 1606 was a likely allusion in *c*'s couplet. Their reported scheme to destroy by explosion the King, Lords, and Commons during the opening of Parliament may be glanced at in the words of line 7, 'the blow of thrallèd discontent'.

> This I do vow and this will ever be:
> I will be true despite thy scythe and thee.

is the only couplet of the four which could end the tetrad; it alone gives strong, positive assurance. But G. Wilson Knight (quoted by Martin Seymour-Smith) said of *d* that it was written by 'a man who knows that his love *is* changing but who refuses to believe that the essence of it is lost'. If that is true of *d*, it is true of the whole tetrad. To have been in the previous year upbraided for neglect and this year to be accused, upon information received, of sexual perversions must have made it evident to Shakespeare that the relationship, as it had existed, could not long survive, and that in the face of these accusations from his patron there was little he could do but deny the charges and insist upon his constancy.

The manner in which a relationship ends may tell us more about its nature than did its previous steady continuance. Pembroke, as we later learn from Clarendon, became compulsively promiscuous with women. Psychoanalysis recognizes behind such behaviour a strong *unconscious* homosexual urge. The year and a half which followed his wedding we might expect to be the period of increasing strain until he could no longer bear to be restricted to one woman. Such a strain may make a man accuse another of the sexual licence he consciously misses or of the sexual perversity for which he unconsciously longs.

Pembroke's father had died five years before and Shakespeare had been for perhaps eight years *in loco parentis* to William Herbert after the emotional fashion that Falstaff is to Prince Hal. It was therefore natural that the younger man, now married, should turn upon him the brunt of any sexual resentments, especially as his younger brother, Philip, had become preferred before himself by their new father figure, King James. Moreover, James was becoming known for the very sexual perversions hinted at in **te** 31 *a*; early in the morning after Philip's wedding night he had got into bed with the newly weds and insisted on putting a garter on the bride's leg with his own hands. The story is told by Chamberlain.[109] Philip became the royal favourite for some years.

Te 31 gives more ground for speculation about the pressure to do something which Shakespeare feels to be incompatible with his self-respect (this is apparent in *b*). For the present we may restate Wilson Knight's verdict and say that the tetrad is written by a man who knows that his patron has changed towards him yet leaves the door open for him to recognize his poet's independence, although he no longer has any real hope that he will do so.

Next year and in subsequent years there were to be no more birthday recitations, no more sonnets. In fact the patron-poet bond was ended; yet Shakespeare made one more gesture to the person he had perhaps known all along to be his real patron – Pembroke's mother. In 1607 (this is held to be the likeliest date) he wrote *Antony and Cleopatra*, and paid thereby a double compliment to the Dowager Lady Pembroke. She had translated into English, with the title *Antonie*, the play *Marc-Antoine* by Robert Garnier. Garnier's play had been written and produced in 1578 and had been republished in a collected edition of his works in 1585. Her version had been published in 1592 and again in 1595. So she was the first person to publish in English a play upon a subject that was to become so popular. Shakespeare in at least five places uses words and phrases from her Argument in his play; he must have read, or re-read, her *Antonie* in the winter of 1606–7.[110]

8 *The publication of Q in 1609*

There is an immense probability against there being any second way of arranging 124 sonnets in sets of four; that is the degree of certainty that the man who wrote the sonnets designed and made the tetrads. Any critic determined to discount the probability would have to show at least a few tetrads as good as, or better than, those found here. Failing that, we can – we must – now assume 'Shakespeare's order' and begin by comparing it with the order in Q.

There are several questions to which the comparison may suggest answers:

(1) What were the principles of reordering from Shakespeare's order to Q's?

(2) What did the editors (those who changed Shakespeare's order) most try to conceal?

(3) Does this give useful clues to the identity of the editors of Q?

(4) If so, can we ascribe various other motives to them?

(5) What does this imply concerning their relationship with Thorpe, Q's publisher?

(6) How does all this affect the elucidation of Q's vexed dedication?

(7) Can we tell, by comparison or by any other means, whether Q was printed from Shakespeare's copy or from copies given or sent to the persons addressed in the sonnets, and if so, can we explain how the editors might have obtained their copy?

The first part of question 7 is a useful preliminary to the others; the second part belongs at the end. There are two particular indications that Q's editors worked from Shakespeare's own personal copy or from a copy of it. The first is the non-rhyme, the half-altered rhyme, in te 7 *d* 9 and 11; it indicates Shakespeare's change of mind *after* he had recited, and perhaps delivered a copy of, te 7 and *while* he was just beginning to compose, or revise, te 8. (This change of mind may have caught the moment when he conceived and designed the Drama.) The second is the unfinished state of te 25 *b*. One single quintain (to coin a usage) in place of a quatrain is very unlikely in 154 sonnets, far more so when there is a surviving question-mark in the place appropriate to a quatrain and not yet re-positioned to make sense of the fifth line. These are two irregularities of a kind to be expected in Shakespeare's own copy and in no other.

There is a general indication that the copy was a good one (capitals and italics are used consistently) but that the printing was rather careless and the correcting of it more so. Shakespeare would never have passed the mistake of pr 3 *b* 2 or the indication of two supposedly missing lines at the end of the 'envoi,' never mind the punctuation, the frequent confusion of 'their' and 'thy', etc., etc., various evidences of his own hand but not his own eye. This general indication of Shakespeare's handwriting does not differentiate his own copy from any made from it.

(1) The principles of reordering could be worked out in great detail. Here it is enough to point to:

(a) the disordering of all the tetrads except two and the effective camouflaging of those two;

(b) the disordering of every one of the triads, and especially the transposition of te 2–4 and te 5–7 (enneads I and II);

(c) the leaving together of pairs in which the second sonnet obviously runs on from the first;

(d) the leaving together, but the inversion where possible, of nearly all pairs which do not run on but which, if separated, would have been detected as belonging together (the separation of te 6 *a* and *b* and of 7 *a* and *b* are exceptional and may indicate a different editor at the beginning from later on);

(e) the leaving of as much of a story as possible while breaking up the chronology and all indications of pattern other than pairs and occasional runs of three (Q's 71–4 are an exception);

(f) the suggestion of false clues – e.g. putting the epilogue (8) just before te 2 c (9) to make the word 'single' appear a link between them; putting te 6 b (122) near the end of the series to the man so as to suggest that Shakespeare might have been responsible for the whole publication of Q by giving away *all* his notebooks; putting 126 last of the series to the man, and seeding the *ex tempore* sonnets among the seven triads at the end to suggest that the musician and the Dark Woman were one and the same person;

(g) the advancement of the two infidelity tetrads to before the main journey sonnets;

(h) an effective rearrangement of the poetic-contest tetrads to suggest Shakespeare's chagrin rather than his triumph;

(i) the scrupulous maintenance of Shakespeare's text apart from three probable single-word (two of them single-letter) changes in Q's 18, 20, and 23 (i.e. early on)=te 12 d, 5 b, and 20 a;

(j) the suggestion of Shakespeare's emotional instability by massing several d sonnets, with their heightened tone, immediately after the seventeen marriage sonnets (Q's 18, 19, 22, 25, 26, 31, 32 even heighten the tone of the others now mixed with them).

(2) Q's editors have most tried to conceal the chronology, the sequence of the triads and their relationships to the corresponding tetrads, i.e. the story of Herbert's seduction; Herbert's dishonourable behaviour and the events behind Episode 6 of the Drama are well hidden; the poetic triumph of te 18–20 has been expertly reallocated away from Shakespeare. The destruction of all major patterning has been a secondary aim but one necessary to prevent the reconstruction of the whole story, which follows, given the fact of the tetrads and triads.

(3) The reputation of William Herbert and his family has been protected, according to the standards set by aristocratic tradition in the late Renaissance. Sexual escapades did not of themselves diminish it but to entrust family confidences and secrets to an actor and dramatist was most unconventional.

We have strong pointers to the Sidney–Herbert families. As we saw above, Sir Philip Sidney and Sir Robert Sidney[111] both arranged and rearranged their own sonnets and their sister reworded and revised obsessively her own and her eldest brother's translations of the Psalms. Poetic rearrangement could be looked on as a family trait of that generation of Sidneys. Lady Mary Pembroke is the likeliest editor-in-chief of Q.

The main motive for publishing from young Pembroke's point of view must have been to use registration at the Stationers' Office to prevent other publication of the same poems; he is not likely to have done the editing himself, being too impatient and high-handed and too dependent on others' ideas (*cf.* the likelihood that he would accept some 'pedantic invention' of Sanford's for a shield device at the Queen's birthday tilt in 1600 if his uncle did not propose one). Lady Pembroke may have used her secretaries' help in editing.

(4) Sanford died in 1607, two years before Q was published. If he had any hand in editing Q, it would have been at the beginning; he may have been the one to protect his own dignity by changing *maiden* to *man in* in te 5 *b* 7, since the original line jokes upon his enslavement to his master's feminine beauty. In that case the more thoroughgoing reordering of Q from its 18 to at least its 32 may also have been Sanford's doing since one effect of it has been to suggest that it was Shakespeare who had the crush on Herbert. (The inclusion of *A Lover's Complaint* tended the same way.) It could have been Sanford or somebody like Daniel who rearranged the poetic-contest tetrads – somebody with an envy of Shakespeare's supremacy.[112]

The general characteristics of the editors must have been obsessionality, piety (putting in *everything*, even what would have been conveniently omitted), and vicarious ambition, ambition on behalf of the poet praising as well as on behalf of the beautiful youth praised. These fit the Lady Pembroke–Hugh Sanford team, who had worked together so much on Sir Philip Sidney's texts. Lady Pembroke must have taken an especial pleasure over the fact that she had produced (in different ways) both the youth and the poet. If the males of the family had to be overruled, she was capable of doing it; she had the intellect, the enthusiasm, the persistence, and the personal investment in poetry and in beauty to prevail against any possible objections. The fact that it was in 1609 that she came up from Wilton to live in London, in Bishopsgate Street, her home for the next six years, may be connected with the publication of the *Sonnets* in that year.[113]

(5) Given the careful editing, Thomas Thorpe, the publisher, must have been supplied with the material and required to publish it as it was. He would have been grateful for the copy and have won the gratitude of Pembroke for doing exactly what he was told and keeping mum. The fact that he published another book with a dedication,

signed by himself, to Pembroke in 1610 indicates that he was on good terms with Pembroke in the year after Q came out.[114]

We saw earlier, in section 3 (pp. 14–16) that when George Wither published *Epigrams* (his first book) in 1613, his dedication, 'G.W. to himself wisheth all happiness', was an obvious allusion to the dedication of the sonnets in Q and hinted that he had heard a rumour that 'Mr W. H.' had in effect caused the sonnets to be dedicated to himself. Both Thorpe and Pembroke would have wished to scotch the rumour, Thorpe by assuring Pembroke that *he* was not the source of it and getting permission to dedicate yet another book to him in 1616, Pembroke by getting Ben Jonson, his pensioner, to dedicate to him *his* book of epigrams (in 1616) and to open the long dedication by hinting that Somebody Else (i.e. Thorpe) *had* been responsible for the dedication, and for the solecism of changing Pembroke's title.

(6) The straighforward meaning of Q's dedication of the sonnets becomes more apparent. 'The only begetter' of the sonnets that followed could obviously, by a natural metaphor seeing that the poet's brain wherein they grew was called the womb, be their inspirer. It is unnecessary to argue that the phrase could *not* mean 'the person who procured the copy of their text' (actually the same person!); even those who have maintained that that is its meaning have not shown that it could not mean 'their inspirer'. 'Only' can of course mean 'peerless' (as in te 1 c 10) as well as 'sole'. 'Mr W. H.' is a typically obsessional solution; it both conceals and reveals the identity. Only the family could here decide to use 'Mr' instead of 'Lord', and even they not without his consent.

So Boaden, who originally argued in 1832[115] that 'Mr W. H.' stood for William Herbert, and Thomas Tyler, who in 1890 made the case much stronger (even though he spoiled it by trying to prove that Mary Fitton was the Dark Lady), were both right in pointing to the simple solution of the mystery and in suggesting that Pembroke himself or somebody in his household had given Thomas Thorpe the material to publish.

The signature 'T.T.' appended to the dedication has no more force or validity than the 'Mr'. It would have been no less subject to dictation, just as the 'H. S.' that indicates Hugh Sanford at the end of the introduction to Sidney's *Arcadia* of 1593 and 1598 is no guarantee that some or all of it had not been dictated by Lady Pembroke.

(7) There is one exception to the statement of the hypothesis that Q's text was edited from Shakespeare's own copy. **Pr** 3, I have argued, was

never written down by Shakespeare but taken down as he improvised it, by Lady Mary, or perhaps by Sanford. If so, the text of those two sonnets (and possibily the text of the rest of the *ex tempore* – it depends on whether or not Shakespeare gathered up and took away his papers after his written and spoken performance) was added to the text of the rest after the Pembrokes obtained it.

Just how Pembroke did obtain it we shall never be sure. There were two possible immediate sources – from Shakespeare himself, by persuasion or coercion, or from somebody else who might have had access to Shakespeare's chest, which he probably kept locked (cf. te 15 *a* 9), or who could have persuaded him to lend him the sonnets to read; this could only have been somebody very close, say Edmund, his youngest brother, now an actor in London, whose bastard son Edward had been born around or before the time when the last tetrad was written (if this had prompted the wording in te 31 *c* = 124). Edward died and was buried early in August 1607 and Edmund his father at the end of 1607. The fact that Edmund's funeral, at which the great bell was tolled, was ten times as costly as it need have been could point to William's generosity or to Edmund's affluence, if he had recently sold his brother's sonnets.[116] If William had become bitter or angry towards his young brother (just three weeks younger than Pembroke), it might explain why he chose, or did not avoid, the name 'Edmund' for one of the nastiest villains he created just then – in *King Lear* – a brother doing a brother down.

The first hypothesis would suggest that Pembroke had put pressure on Shakespeare to surrender his personal copy of the sonnets; that could be the thing he demurs at in te 31 *b* (125). Possibly Pembroke overruled him, or possibly Shakespeare agreed in the end provided that *every* sonnet was published, not foreseeing that they would split up his delicate structures, reorder the sonnets in such a way as to suggest the *canard* that he had been hopelessly in love with young 'Mr. W. H.', and exhibit his 'passions' (= 'sonnets') for Jacobean ridicule. It would be nice to think that he had protested when Q was published and that Pembroke had had the edition withdrawn as soon as possible.

9 *Reconstructing the real relationships*

What inspired Shakespeare to the sonnets? Can we be sure that any person, any thing, or any situation did in fact inspire him? If he wrote them, or many of them, to commission, it could be argued that they were nothing more than a professional job. In April 1598, after the Easter service and his second recitation that month, he apparently made an excuse not to reside in Baynard's Castle and tellingly alluded to the Order in Council which had closed the theatres in the previous summer, or at least to the certainty at that time that public acknowledgement from him would diminish Herbert's honour. Did he then really mean it when he said – in the same two sonnets in which he makes the excuse (**te** 8 *a* and *b*) – 'You and I are one'? The very conventions of patronage seem to conflict with sincerity and with inspired utterance.

In discussing Episode 2 of the Drama I distinguished two orders of reality in the journey, the actual lived events and the dramatic reality. The dramatic reality, which now lives for us, in no way negates the actuality of the events lived by Shakespeare, even if it presents them rearranged. (Just so Shakespeare selected and rearranged the historical events of the fifteenth century to make his four plays, *King Henry VI, Parts 1, 2, and 3* and *King Richard III*, but their dramatic reality in no way negates the historical reality of those events, although there is, and always has been, a tension between the two orders of reality.) The dramatic reality even convinces us of the actual reality – not that the events happened exactly as presented but that actual events, of which we receive a version from Shakespeare, did happen like that. Shakespeare has made his poems out of what he lived through (out of what he *read* in the sources for his historical plays) – made them live again for us – for us and for his patron; for it was a convention, but also the very condition of their shared reality, that he would *invent* – i.e. *find and make* – something out of his experience for the benefit of his hearers. Patronage itself involved the poet in two orders of reality.

That was the nature of the tension between the conventions of patronage and the reality of private feelings. At points they conflicted but they needed each other in order to develop the intensity of experience. William Herbert, I have argued, used ˙the fact of this tension to tease Shakespeare about the sixteen sonnets he had written:

Stirred by a painted beauty to his verse.

Like Volodya in Tolstoy's *Childhood*, who undermined the conventions of his brothers' and sisters' play or spoiled it by joining in their pretence half-heartedly, Herbert would have undermined by his teasing the conventions of Shakespeare's performance on 8 April 1597 – but only after the performance was over; and in July Shakespeare could make a new poem out of the renewed teasing and out of the new situation of Herbert's coutship. Hamlet, struck by the tension between the conventions of a dramatic speech and the reality of feeling which the First Player is capable of using and he himself is not ('What's Hecuba to him or he to Hecuba?'), then reflects upon the power of a play to affect men's lives.

Recent critical insights have stressed the dramatic qualities of the sonnets. Professor G. K. Hunter in an essay of 1953,[117] republished in 1977, emphasized that those who 'ignore the biograpical approach miss a valuable clue to the bias of Shakespeare's technique'. He went on to argue that in the sonnets Shakespeare was writing as *a dramatist*. His final summing up is that we have in the sonnets a dramatist's description of 'a series of emotional situations between persons (real or fictitious) in a series of separate short poems'. Over a quarter of a century later we can pay tribute to Hunter's insistence upon 'the dramatically expressive way of writing' and upon the necessity of distinguishing it from other genres, especially from other sonnet genres (e.g. lyrical, metaphysical). But we must qualify his résumé: the sonnets are less a description than the actual text of a drama, and the poems are not so short as he says nor so discrete as he implies; his parenthesis, 'real or fictitious', itself especially demands restatement; he is after all pleading for the biographical approach and might more appropriately have said 'real, however dramatically shown'.

Professor Jan Kott in a book of 1964[118] wrote that the sonnets could be interpreted as a drama of which the characters were three – a man (the poet), a youth, and a woman; to these he added a fourth character, Time. Kott's insight is important even if we disagree about the level of consciousness at which it was true for the poet. The theme of the drama which Kott discerns in the sonnets – the impossibility for the man of choosing between the youth and the woman as love partners – is far from the theme of the *lived* drama we have found, even if it might be true of the *unconscious* experience of the poet. Shakespeare's drama was far more elaborately patterned than could be imagined from the sequence in Q and it had involved the development of new poetic structures, the tetrad and the triad, which could themselves be multiplied in combination. Moreover, the drama was written as a poetic text, commentary, and prompt book for a once-only performance of which one of the protagonists was at most half aware; the very patron-poet relationship had something of a dramatic quality, which would have served to lead Herbert on.

Professor M. M. Mahood in an essay of 1962[119] found both for the sonnets and for several of the middle-period plays a theme of selfless devotion discovered to have been shamefully misplaced and the theme of 'a fear of trust' preceding the discovery, in the time when the poet (or the character) is reluctant to face the truth he suspects – that the object of his devotion is unworthy of it. In the final section of her essay she draws back from 'the risk . . . of appearing to be a biographical speculator'. She nevertheless considers 'the fear of trust' to be 'a very strong element in the sonnets and middle plays' and a potential aid to criticism, 'even if it throws no clear light on Shakespeare's biography'. The parallels she finds between various characters in plays and that of the poet in the sonnets (as well as in the language in which the attitudes are expressed in those plays and in the sonnets) are convincing enough to give strong support to the idea that most of the sonnets belong to the same period of time as *The Merchant of Venice*, both parts of *King Henry IV*, *King Henry V*, and *Twelfth Night*, i.e. 1597–1601.

All three – Hunter, Kott, and Mahood – add to our knowledge of Shakespeare the man because they employ psychological speculation in adding to our knowledge of Shakespeare the writer.

Hunter says that the biographical approach is a necessary clue to the bias of his technique – a dramatist's. But if the biographical approach helps us to appreciate that technique, the technique is founded in his personality, and we have to say that Shakespeare wrote as a dramatist because he perceived and thought as a dramatist; the situations he described were biographically real, however dramatically presented. That is precisely the conclusion that most people reach who come to know the sonnets.

Kott attaches significance to Shakespeare's choice of dramatic theme – the poet's conflict. That is to say, the choice is a significant clue to Shakespeare's personality, even if the choice was deliberately made and the theme more constructed than Kott supposed.

Mahood is both a psychological and a biographical speculator; she is ultimately insisting upon some reason in the middle years of Shakespeare's professional life for the sequence she discerns, for a psychological attitude he maintained over at least four years, even if we do not know the events which might account for his 'fear of trust'.

Sir Sidney Lee changed his mind about the sonnets but eventually maintained that there was nothing in their sentiments or their wording that was inconsistent with the idea that they had all been written to a patron, been written therefore for reward. I wish here to put it on record that this was the last theory about the sonnets that I ever expected to hold myself but that I have been gradually compelled, by the events which the tetrads and triads imply and by the chronology which they entail, to the same conclusion. But, granted that they were the fruit of patronage, we still have to interpret the human relationships which the sonnets portray and imply, and the poems themselves can teach us better than any other literature how to do this; they teach us the range of patronage and its full potential meaning as a human relationsip.

Not knowing in the modern world the reality of patronage as it once was, we may assume lightly that either party, the bestower or the recipient, regarded it as commercial and coercive, or at least as incompatible with deep devotion. Lady Pembroke knew otherwise; for her it included some of the most real and meaningful relationships of her life, and at least one of the writers whom she patronized has testified to that and to the liberating experience which it was for him.[120] No wonder if she wished her son to learn to practise it and to learn on whom to rely.

So the Pembrokes engaged Shakespeare to compose the seventeen sonnets for their son's seventeenth birthday and heard as well the *ex tempore* performance which William probably did not. I have pointed out that Ben Jonson's first surviving play, *Every Man in his Own Humour*, has a character, Matheo, who pretends to have done just what Shakespeare had really done – written ten or a dozen sonnets at a sitting. How did Jonson know it? I suggest that Shakespeare, feeling that he owed it to Jonson, had told him his presumptive explanation of why he and Nashe had been put in prison for writing *The Isle of Dogs* and some of the actors among the Earl of Pembroke's Men for acting in it. Burghley must have been furiously offended that an actor had taken his granddaughter's suitor to see the play at the Swan. But Shakespeare could not have said so much without also revealing, probably confidentially, how he had first come to know the Pembrokes and how he had performed at Wilton in April. When Jonson's play was put on the next year by Shakespeare's company, it must have provoked curiosity among the *literati*. 'Who ever heard of a poet composing at that speed? Is even Shakespeare, as Jonson says, capable of *ex tempore* at that pitch?' Jonson, with his admiring wonder at Shakespeare's facility, had his justification; he *knew* that Shakespeare had really done it. 'Where?' And Jonson, preserving enough of Shakespeare's confidence, could have answered 'Among his private friends'.

Francis Meres used that last phrase in a book which he was commissioned to write and which was published in that same year, 1598.

Besides naming most of the plays of Shakespeare produced to date, Meres says: 'The sweet witty soul of Ovid lives in mellifluous and honey-tongued Shakespeare, witness his *Venus and Adonis*, his *Lucrece*, his sugared sonnets among his private friends.'[121]

It has always been assumed that 'among his private friends' implies 'passed round in writing' but it could just as well imply 'performed' or 'spoken'. It could mean 'recited among his friends in private' quite as naturally as 'shown around among his personal friends'; indeed, if the sonnets had been passed from hand to hand in written form, there could have been no natural way of restricting their circulation, whereas Shakespeare would in reality have kept an even tighter hold on the text of his sonnets than his company kept on the texts of his plays; privacy was essential for honouring the patronage of the Pembrokes and Jonson had gone quite far enough if he had hinted at Shakespeare's sonneteering.

The sequence of events and situations which I have reconstructed – from early April 1597 to the summer of 1598 – shows Shakespeare fully in the confidence of William Herbert's parents but concealing from Herbert himself the extent to which he was carrying out their wishes. They were his patrons and Herbert not, or not yet. Shakespeare had not so far established the basis of confidence; he had even made it harder for himself to do so, if he had poked fun at Hugh Sanford, whom Herbert trusted, and at George Chapman, whose verse he apparently appreciated. So we need to ask where Shakespeare could have found the enthusiasm and the devotion that shine through the sonnets. We need to know in an emotional sense what Herbert was to him or he to Herbert.

The sonnets addressed to William Herbert, arranged in tetrads and spaced at the intervals proposed, give no support to the idea that there was an intimate relationship between him and Shakespeare, or that Shakespeare was sexually attracted to him. For one thing, they seldom met; for another, from the day when they first did meet they seem to have been together outside Herbert's family only four times in the first year and a half – twice in late July 1597 (if at Lady Pembroke's wish Shakespeare escorted her son to Hilliard's studio and to a performance of *The Isle of Dogs*), once in the second half of April 1598 (if he introduced him to the Dark Woman), and once in late June or early July, when Herbert shed tears and said he was sorry for his offence of stealing the woman he believed to be Shakespeare's mistress. Except for the tetrads which were sent in written form (te 8–te 14 or 16, and te 21–te 23 with the 'envoi'), the tetrads appear to have been performed in Baynard's Castle (or at Wilton for some birthdays) probably before a small audience. The two early tetrads which most express love and devotion (te 6 and te 7) were recited in all likelihood when the family audience included Lady Pembroke.

The attraction recorded was certainly to Herbert's beauty, but first of all as told by his mother and as shown by Hilliard's earlier portrait, to which Shakespeare's pen was pupil. The words 'thou are thy mother's glass' were a compliment to Lady Pembroke and therefore all other compliments to Herbert's beauty were also compliments to her. She may have been present for most of the birthday tetrads and there can be little doubt of her pride in her son's good looks.

The only sonnets which suggest an attitude of abject devotion are in te 22, part of the 'farewell' episode; by then it is impossible to forget that we have Shakespeare's response to being let down and kept waiting without a message and therefore that there is a potential irony in the lines:

> I have no precious time at all to spend
> Nor services to do till you require.

Besides, it is part of my case that Shakespeare was teaching Herbert his manners as a patron and indicating the strains he imposed upon devotion.

We have now three paradoxes to resolve:

The first is that the sonnets express warmth, devotion, and admiration (which many have taken to indicate that the poet was in love), yet they were a professional job.

The second is that they breathe sincerity (all the tetrads to Herbert sound as if they were intended for one ear alone), yet at the same time as he was writing the central episodes Shakespeare was practising on Herbert a flagrant deception.

The third is that they express Shakespeare's humility and readiness to bear all wrong for Herbert's sake (all but the last two tetrads), yet they have signs enough that he knew Herbert's self-sufficiency, vanity, and coldness for what they were.

These paradoxes can, I believe, be resolved if we maintain, first of all, that it was Shakespeare's nature to perceive, think, and present dramatically, and that he could draw upon the same reserves of feeling as the First Player in *Hamlet*; secondly that the tetrads were written to be recited or performed; and thirdly that he was doing something important on behalf of Lady Pembroke, something that she believed to be in her son's — and her family's — best interests, even if it began with deception. Primarily Shakespeare was teaching Herbert how to be a patron and teaching him the mutual consideration which was its basis. In effect this meant accepting his narcissism and by enlargement transforming his pride in his beauty (his 'show') into a pride in his virtue (his 'essence'). Nowadays it would be a psychotherapeutic undertaking.

Besides all this, there was Shakespeare's excitement on his own behalf. Patronage was a prize and he was acquiring the most munificent patronage then going and the reliable appreciation of the woman most distinguished in the literary world – Sidney's sister. Inevitably this would have predisposed him to gratitude and to a sense of dependence – to what C. L. Barber called 'the perspective of early childhood', with its attendant fears of separation and loss.[122]

Lady Pembroke was inviting Shakespeare to be to her son both father- (or brother-) figure and vassal, to be to him what several poets were to her; most of all she must have compared his poetic facility with that of her own late brother, who had taught her the power of poetry and handed on to her the patronage of Edmund Spenser. But in doing something akin to match-making between her son and Shakespeare, she must have failed to realize how awkward an obstacle to the transfer of patronage would be her own confidential understanding with Shakespeare. Her son would be wary of a poet and man for whom she showed enthusiasm; he preferred Ben Jonson anyway.[123]

In the first century of the life of psychoanalysis it is appropriate to ask whether Shakespeare's emotional reactions, as the sonnets reveal them, can be called *transference*. It is not a clearly defined term and most experiences in which strong feeling is aroused are assumed to be in part transferential, particularly when the feeling is directed towards an 'unworthy' figure. But I suggest that Shakespeare's feeling had as its object not Herbert's person (except when at Stratford he stood in his absence for Shakespeare's dead son, 'found' in the renewal of mourning) but *the mother/son pair*, a mother wanting something done for her son. Onto the Lady Pembroke–William Herbert relationship Shakespeare could have transferred the mother – Edmund and also the mother–infant-self relationships. In Shakespeare's case the 'transference' would have had the content of helping a mother who was trying to make her son into what she seemed to think he needed to be, to give him what he needed to have, especially experience with another woman.

The tendency to place the pair rather than the single person as the central object of transference is, I believe, much increased by the state of mind of the mother during the infancy and early childhood of the subject and during any succeeding pregnancies. Mary Shakespeare must have been depressed after the deaths of her first two children and in reaction would have overvalued the health and early achievements of her first surviving child; he could have meant too much to her. All that the child can do in such a situation is to divide himself: he meets his mother's needs for reassurance, seeing himself with her eyes, and simultaneously he fixes his attention upon himself and his mother *as a pair* and upon the transactions between them, trying to facilitate her aims, which will often include the aim of getting him to accept a surrogate for herself as supplier of his needs. His tendency may be reinforced, until it becomes a habit, during the mothering of her next children, when he subjectively replaces the primary pair of mother-and-self with the pair of mother-and-other-child.

A depressed and mourning mother could have had a strong formative influence upon her son's habits of expression. To discover that his own power to dramatize roused her interest and brought animation into her face and bearing would have given the boy, William Shakespeare, a tremendous incentive to read, recite, and describe dramatically; add Golding's *Ovid* and he was furnished with a nearly inexhaustible repertoire from which to entertain his mother and the rest of his family.[124]

Lady Pembroke was in mourning when Shakespeare met her, mourning for her brother. He had died over ten years before, in the same year as both their parents. But she had known death before that. She had lost her second child at the age of three and in childhood herself had lost all her sisters. She was saved from the bad airs of the Welsh Marches by Queen Elizabeth's thought for her and her family; the Queen had urged her parents to let her come to Court at the age of thirteen, when her last sister died. Her sadness would have recalled to Shakespeare his mother's, and would have matched his own when they met, for Hamnet's death was still only eight months gone.

A disordered text, deliberately disordered, is like a jigsaw puzzle. So also are the scraps of historical information, reminiscences, files of letters, documents of various kinds, a vellum manuscript of psalms, and two copies of a painting in Dorset collections. When reordered the two puzzles make two pictures which require to be tested independently but which match each other at enough points to give mutual corroboration. Art and reality here throw light on one another and each supports the restoration of the other, but the artistic whole, the poetry, comes first and is the more certain of the two.

Bibliography

Aubrey, John: *Brief Lives* (second half of seventeenth century, pub. 1813)

Barber, C. L.: 'Full to overflowing', a review of Stephen Booth's edition of Shakespeare's sonnets in *New York Review of Books* (6 April 1978), pp. 32–8

Bartlett, Phyliss B. (ed.): *The Poems of George Chapman* (1941)

Beeching, H. C. (ed.): *The Sonnets of Shakespeare* (1904)

Bloom, E. A. (ed.): *Shakespeare 1564–1964*, Providence R.I. (1964)

Boaden, J.: *On the Sonnets of Shakespeare, identifying the Person to whom they were addressed* (1837)

Booth, Stephen: *An Essay on Shakespeare's Sonnets* (1969)

Booth, Stephen (ed.): *Shakespeare's Sonnets* (1977)

Bowlby, John: *Attachment and Loss* (vol. II, *Separation. Anxiety and Anger*, 1973, and vol. III, *Loss, Sadness, and Depression*, 1980)

Bradbrook, Muriel: *Shakespeare the Craftsman* (1969)

Bray, Sir Denys: *The Original Order of Shakespeare's Sonnets* (1925)

Brooke, Tucker (ed.): *The Shakespeare Apocrypha* (1908)

Burton, R: *The Anatomy of Melancholy* (first ed. 1621)

Butler, C., and Fowler, A.: 'Time-beguiling sport', in Bloom (ed.) (1964)

Chamberlain, J.: *Letters during the Reign of Queen Elizabeth* (ed. S. Williams, 1868)

Chambers, Sir Edmund K: *Shakespearean Gleanings* (1944)

Chapman, G.: (see Bartlett)

Culler, Jonathan: *Structuralist Poetics* (1975)

Daniel, Samuel: *Delia* (1592)

D.N.B.: *Dictionary of National Biography*

Edwards, P., Ewbank, I–S., and Hunter, G. K. (edd.): *Shakespeare's Styles* (1980)

Fowler, Alastair: *Conceitful Thought* (1975)

Fowler, A.: (see Butler)

Gardner, Helen (ed.): *The New Oxford Book of English Verse* (1978)

Gittings, Robert: *Shakespeare's Rival* (1960)

Golding, Arthur: *The Metamorphoses of Ovid*, trans. and ed. W. H. D. Rouse (1904)

Gurr, Andrew: 'Shakespeare's first poem: sonnet 145', in *Essays in Criticism* XXI (July 1971), pp. 221–6

H.M.C. Salisbury, vols. 7–11: Historical Manuscripts Commission, *Salisbury*, a publication of papers, 7–11 nearly all letters written to or for Sir Robert Cecil, the Queen's secretary

H.M.C. De L'Isle and Dudley, vol. 2 = *Penshurst Papers*, pub. 1933

Hotson, J. Leslie: *Shakespeare's Sonnets Dated* (1949)

Hotson, J. Leslie: *The First Night of Twelfth Night* (1954)

Hotson, J. Leslie: '*Mr. W.H.*' (1964)

Hunter, G. K.: 'The dramatic technique of Shakespeare's sonnets' (1953), reprinted in Jones (ed.), (1977)

Hutton, James: Paper in *Modern Philology* XXXVIII (1941), pp. 385–403

Ingram, W. G., and Redpath, Theo. (edd.): *Shakespeare's Sonnets* (1964)

Jones, Peter (ed.): *Shakespeare: the Sonnets* (1977), Casebook Series

Kelliher, Hilton: 'A manuscript of poems by Robert Sidney', in *Brit. Mus. Soc. Bulletin* 19 (July, p. 15, 1975)

Knight, G. Wilson: *The Mutual Flame* (1955)

Kott, Jan: *Shakespeare's Bitter Arcadia* (1964), extracts reprinted in Jones (ed.) (1977)

Lees-Milne, J.: *The Age of Inigo Jones* (1953)

Leishman, J. B.: *Themes and Variations in Shakespeare's Sonnets* (1961)

Lever, Tresham: *The Herberts of Wilton* (1967)

Lodge, E.: *Illustrations of British History* vol. 3 (1838)

Mahood, M. M.: *Shakespeare's Wordplay* (1957)

Mahood, M. M.: 'Love's confined doom' (1962), reprinted in Jones (ed.) (1977)

Maxwell, J. C. (ed.): *The Poems*, New Cambridge Shakespeare (1966)

Muir, K.: *Shakespeare's Sonnets* (1979)

Newdigate-Newdegate, Lady: *Gossip from a Muniment Room* (1898)

Nowottny, Winifred: 'Formal elements in Shakespeare's sonnets I–VI', in *Essays in Criticism* ii (1952), reprinted in Jones (ed.) (1977)

Padel, John H.: 'That the thought of hearts can mend', in *T.L.S.* 19 Dec. 1975

Parkes, Colin M.: *Bereavement* (1972)

P.P.: Penshurst Papers (see H.M.C. De L'Isle and Dudley)

Pui, The Great Feste of the: in *Liber Custumarum* vol. 2, part 2 (ed. H. T. Riley, 1860) pp. 216–8

Ringler, William A., Jnr.: *The Poems of Sir Philip Sidney* (1962)

Rollins, Hyder E. (ed.): *A New Variorum Edition of Shakespeare: the Sonnets* (1944)

Schoenbaum, S.: *William Shakespeare: a Documentary Life* (1975)

Schoenbaum, S.: *William Shakespeare: a compact Documentary Life* (1977)

Schoenbaum, S.: 'Shakespeare's Dark Lady: a question of identity', in Edwards, Ewbank and Hunter (edd.) (1980), pp. 221–39.

Seymour-Smith, Martin (ed.): *Shakespeare's Sonnets* (1963), Poetry Bookshelf

S.P.: *Sidney Papers* (two vols., ed. Arthur Collins, 1746)

Stirling, Brents: *The Shakespeare Sonnet Order* (1969)

Stopes, C. C.: *The Life of Henry Wriothesley, The Third Earl of Southampton* (1922)

Thomson, J. A. K.: *Shakespeare and the Classics* (1952)

T.L.S.: *The Times Literary Supplement*

Tucker, T. G. (ed.): *The Sonnets of Shakespeare* (1924)

Tyler, T. (ed.): *Shakespeare's Sonnets* (1890)

Tyler, T.: *The Herbert-Fitton Theory of Shakespeare's Sonnets: a Reply* (1898) (disproves the alleged fairness of Mary Fitton and gives useful bibliography on Thorpe)

Wickham, Glynne: *Early English Stages* vol. II, parts 1 and 2 (1963–1972)

Wilson, J. Dover (ed.): *Antony and Cleopatra*, New Cambridge Shakespeare (1950)

Wilson, J. Dover (ed.): *The Sonnets*, New Cambridge Shakespeare (1966)

Wyndham, Sir George: *The Poems of Shakespeare* (1898)

Young, Frances Berkeley: *Mary Sidney, Countess of Pembroke* (1912)

Notes

1   The expressions are C. L. Barber's (1978).

2   Brents Stirling also published (1969) the sonnets reordered on the principle of a compromise between the recovery of *literary* sequences and the hypothesis that individual sonnets had originally been written on opposite sides of single sheets of paper and that their dis-ordering before their first publication had been due to the sheets getting mixed. The application of the hypothesis led him to literary sacrifices.

3   *T.L.S.*, 18 Apr. 1975.

4   Clarendon Press, Oxford, 1962 and (corrected) 1967.

5   *T.L.S.*, 19 Dec. 1975.

6   By James Boaden in an article (1832) and a book (1837), but earlier by B. H. Bright in conversation (1819): see Rollins (1944), ii. 195.

7   *Shakespeare's Sonnets Dated* (1949) was the first of the books in which Hotson argued his case for the identification of 'Mr. W. H.' with William Hatcliffe and for the early dating of the sonnets. '*Mr. W. H.*' (1964) was his most systematic exposition of the case.

8   Mrs C. C. Stopes (1922), p. 34, made this point of a guardian's right to a ward's 'marriage'.

9   Both letters are quoted in full by Stopes, pp. 36–7 and pp. 37–8.

10   The information is given in a letter written by Henry Garnett, a priest. Although its truth has been questioned, yet the other piece of information with it – that the Earl of Derby's widow was pregnant and therefore the title of his brother insecure until the sex of the baby was known – was correct; the baby, a girl, was born 26 January 1596 (Stopes, p. 86).

11   *S.P.* I p. 348, letter of 23 Sept. 1595, 'My Lord of Southampton doth with too much familiarity court the fair Mistress Vernon'.

12   Letters quoted by Stopes (1922); p. 123 Sir R. Cecil to Southampton and to Sir Thomas Edmondes (both 3 Sept.) and, p. 131, Chamberlain to Carleton (11 and 22 Nov.).

13   'Time-beguiling sport: number-symbolism in Shakespeare's *Venus and Adonis*', in Bloom (ed.) (1964), pp. 125–33.

14   John Aubrey, *Brief Lives*, 'William Herbert, First Lord of Pembroke'. Aubrey's information is more to be entertained than trusted.

15   Bath/Bristol – H.M.C. *Salisbury* 9, p. 142 (Letter of 19 Apr. 1599); Goodrich – *S.P.* II, pp. 120, 121, 123 (letters of 8, 12, 13 Sept, 1599); Gotherous – H.M.C., *Salisbury* 9, p. 351, letter of 19 September 1599.

16   *S.P.* I, letter of 22 Nov. 1595 (p. 363).

17   *S.P.* I, letters of 22 Nov. (p. 363), 29 Nov. and 5 Dec. (pp. 370 and 372).

18   *S.P.* II, p. 43, letter of 19 Apr. and, p. 46, letter of 27 Apr. 1598.

19   Epilogue (= Q's 8), following te 4.

20   H.M.C. *Salisbury* 7, p. 354, letter from Earl of Pembroke, 16 Aug. 1597.
       H.M.C. *Salisbury* 7, p. 374, letter from Lord Herbert, Aug. 1597.
       H.M.C. *Salisbury* 7, p. 375, letter from Countess of Pembroke, Aug. 1597.
       Letters of Earl and Countess to Lord Burghley, dated 16 Aug. express their delight and thanks; letter to Burghley from the Earl of Oxford, dated 8 Sept., gives his approval and discusses Pembroke's motivation (all in Record Office and quoted by Tyler pp. 45–7).

21   Letter of 3 Sept. 1597 (Cal. State Papers Dom. Eliz. 1595–7, p. 497, printed by Tyler (pp. 45–7) and by F. B. Young (1912) pp. 64–6).

22   H.M.C. *Salisbury* 7, p. 405.

23   *P.P.* 2, p. 294, 8 Oct. Pembroke resolved to accept Burghley's offer.
       P.P. 2, p. 297, 22 Oct.: Pembroke has angered Burghley by demanding more.
       P.P. 2, p. 302, 5 Nov.: Matters of Herbert broken off. Herbert has not come to London.
       P.P. 2, p. 305, 20 Dec.: Burghley will offer no more.
       These four references are given by Chambers (1944) p. 127 (with quotations). They are all in letters from R. Whyte to Sidney that were omitted from the *S.P.*

24   *S.P.*, p. 94 and p. 95.

25   H.M.C. *Salisbury* 8, pp. 219–20.

26   Hotson (1964) suggested numerical correspondences between some sonnets and some Psalms; see Muir (1979), pp. 11–12.

27   E. Lodge (1838).

28   The division of a sonnet between octave and sestet is much commoner with *d* sonnets.

29   Sir George Wyndham discovered the facts about Saturn's rising from the Royal Observatory, Edinburgh, for his edition (1898). See Dover Wilson (1966), p. lxxxiv.

30   Miss Enid Lake, librarian of the Royal Astronomical Society, kindly supplied the dates of Easter from 1597 onwards.

31   Facts in the narrative are supported by documentary evidence that is quoted. None of Shakespeare's movements is known. For the sake of the story I avoid too frequent use of the potential constructions.

32   Letters of Pembroke, an endorsement by Burghley, and the later report of Philip Massinger attest the part played by Arthur

Massinger, Philip's father. Philip the dramatist was brought up at Wilton.

33   Ringler (1967), p. 140.

34   John Aubrey's 'Mary Herbert: Countess of Pembroke'.

35   Ringler (1962), p. 140.

36   Rollins (1944), i. 392–4 gives the reference to James Hutton's valuable paper, which discusses the sources for these two sonnets in detail.

37   The two sonnets by Sidney are on p. 58 of *The New Oxford Book of English Verse*, ed. Helen Gardner. Ringler (1962) has bibliographical notes on pp. 424–5 and p. 535.

38   Rollins, i. 374–8 enumerates the verbs suggested: 'rebuke', 'defeat', 'cast forth'.

39   Stephen Booth, *An Essay on Shakespeare's Sonnets* (1969), ch. 4, has a section on 'Phonetic unity and division' (pp. 87–90) and more information and discussion of the principle in his supplementary note 5 (pp. 199–204). The combinations of certain letters recur in this sonnet. We get -rs- in **Poor soul**, **Disperse**, **powers**, **worms**, **inheritor**s, **terms**, **hours**, **dross**, **there**'s. Also we get -t/d/th + s- in the **centre**, **disperse**, these, **dost**, **Dost**, **inheritors**, this, **servant**'s, **thy store**, **dross**, **feeds**, **there**'s. The two combinations occurring in one order in 'Poor soul, the centre', recur reversed in order in line 2 both in 'Disperse' and in 'these . . . powers'; finally they fuse in 'dross' and in 'there's'.

40   The relevant passages of *Every Man in his Own Humour* are in: (a) Act 3, sc. 1 (2.3 of 1598 version) – half-a-score or a dozen sonnets at a sitting; (b) Act 4, sc. 1 (3.4 of 1598 version) – Wellbred's surprise at *ex tempore*; (c) Act 5 – Dr. Clement challenges Mathew at oral *ex tempore*.

41   The brackets, which many editors remove from this line, preserve an important clue to Shakespeare's sense and to the twofold reality he is pointing to.

42   Schoenbaum (1977), p. 207, gives an outline of the episode; Glynne Wickham, *Early English Stages* vol. II, pt 2, ch. X, discusses it in detail. Significant features of the Order in Council are: (a) that it calls *The Isle of Dogs* 'a lewd play, containing seditious and slanderous matter'; (b) that it orders the (internal) dismantling of some theatres, naming them and including the theatre, where the Lord Chamberlain's Men and Shakespeare played; (c) that it banned plays for three months and its ban expired on 1 November 1597.
Further information given by Wickham includes the following: (a) Ben Jonson and other actors of Pembroke's Men were released by warrant on 8 October; (b) some companies risked putting on plays in mid October, before the ban expired; (c) on 19 February 1598 a licence was drawn for the Lord Admiral's and the Lord Chamberlain's companies and for a third (probably Lord Derby's).

The private motive of Burghley's, suggested in the text, would explain both the specific naming of the theatre, where Shakespeare's plays were performed, and the releasing of Ben Jonson and the actors just when Burghley had heard that Pembroke was going to accept the dowry he offered.

43 R. Gittings, *Shakespeare's Rival* (1960), pp. 99–100.

44 Hilliard clearly had tremendous respect for Dürer's work. Ringler (1967), p. xxvii, records Sidney's interest in Hilliard and Dee.

45 Schoenbaum (1977), p. 229. The documents are reproduced in Schoenbaum (1975), pp. 168, 169, 170.

46 Schoenbaum (1977) pp. 231–2.

47 There is no clue to her identity, see Schoenbaum (1980).

48 See letters cited in notes 20 and 21 above.

49 The editor who put te 4 c where it stands in Q and put tr 1 a just before it forged two false links of rhyme: the *bright/night* of tr 3 c (147)'s couplet seems to be picked up by the second rhyme of tr 1 a (*sight/aright*) instead of by the first of tr 4 a (150) – *might/sight*; also the couplet of tr 1 a (148), rhyming *blind/find*, is apparently echoed by the couplet of tr 4 c (149), rhyming *mind/blind*.

50 *S.P.* II, pp. 96–7: Whyte's last two letters to Sidney before he came are dated 22 Mar.

51 Yvor Winters is quoted in Peter Jones (ed.), *Shakespeare: the Sonnets*, pp. 161–3.

52 Ringler (1967), p. 268.

53 Ringler (1967), p. 502, p. 509, p. 547.

54 Gittings (1960), p. 83.

55 The title page of the *Arcadia* (1598) was reproduced in *T.L.S.* 19 Dec. 1975, p. 1520.

56 Schoenbaum (1975), p. xi mentions his 'melancholy eclipse'; whether or not he intended that diagnostically, it is a good presumptive diagnosis based on the facts given on his pp. 36–40.

57 The psychoanalytic term 'transference' has not yet been clearly defined by the nature of that which is transferred. A minor aim of my *T.L.S.* article of 1975 was to propose that what is transferred is always a relationship.

58 See note 30 above.

59 See J. Bowlby (1980).

60 The two orders of reality correspond, of course, to Shakespeare the man and to his persona as poet of these three poems; cf. Culler (1975) – the reader creates 'a meditative persona' for the poet and also a 'referential context' such as the poem's coherence demands.

61   Colin Murray Parkes in his book, *Bereavement* (1972 and 1975), gives an account of the anniversary reaction; see especially his ch. 4 'Searching'.

62   J. Dover Wilson (1966), pp. cxiv–cxix, gives the references and an account of the work on them. Golding's translation was published in parts but was complete by 1567, before Shakespeare was four years old.

63   The 'finding' of the deceased in a living person, which Colin Parkes and others have shown to be a frequent episode in mourning, need not be the finding of him in a person newly met. The essential feature of such 'finding' is the identification of a living person with the dead one. It is a particular instance of 'transference'.

64   Later the Countess of Pembroke and Herbert each got Whyte to write to Sidney for some of his excellent tobacco to relieve Herbert's headaches (*S.P.* II pp. 162 and 165; letters of 19 and 26 Jan. 1600).

65   Clarendon's description is quoted by Dover Wilson (1966), pp. cxxi–ii.

66   *Licia* no. 28.

67   In 1975, when I gave the substance of my *T.L.S.* article at a metting of the British Psychoanalytical Society, I was asked whether there were in the sonnets any indication of Shakespeare's unconscious aggression towards Herbert to match the idealization of him, since according to psychoanalytic theory the one does not occur without the other. I would point to this tetrad for the extremity of such aggression, and to the next one for its aftermath – depression. Depression is at the heart of te 17 also, but I believe on other grounds that it too was composed at, or just after leaving, Stratford. (In 1975 I had not formulated the theory that Shakespeare had been employed to get William Herbert sexually initiated. However different the sexual *mores* were nearly four centuries ago, there is aggression in such deception.)

68   *Metamorphoses* Books XIII and XIV. Coming just before Book XV, which has most affected the thought and wording of te 12–te 14 and te 17, the Polyphemus episodes (the wooing of Galatea and the warning of Telemachus in XIII and the blinding in XIV) may have contributed much to the way in which Shakespeare thought and wrote of Time the destroyer. They are passages that would horribly fascinate children.

69   Bradbrook (1969), p. 31.

70   'The Great Feste of the Pui' is one of the rolls collected in the early fourteenth century. It includes an earlier and a later draft of the regulations of the society. Considering the changes that had occurred, which are described and implied in the new regulations, it is clear that some decades had intervened.

71   Gittings (1960), pp. 99–101.

72   Dover Wilson (1966), pp. lxiii–lxxi.

73   R. Burton, in *The Anatomy of Melancholy*, pt 1, sec. II, mem. 1, subs. 2, quotes the Cardan. Chapman's lines are in *Euthymiae Raptus: the Tears of Peace*, Induct. 75–85.

74   *S.P.* II, pp. 113, 115, 118, 120 (letters of 4, 11 and 18 Aug. and 8 Sept. 1599); pp. 216, 218 and 220 (letters of 26 Sept. and 18, 24 and 30 Oct. 1600).

75   Bartlett (1941), Introd. p. 10 and p. 13.

76   *The Shakespeare Apocrypha*, Tucker Brook (ed.) 1908, Act 2, Sc. 1, 451. (In 4.4.60 of *Edward III* occurs the earliest use of 'extemporal' to mean 'who improvises'.)

77   Schoenbaum (1977), pp. 206–9, tells the story.

78   See *L.L.L.*, 3. 1. 71–123 for play upon the concept of *l'envoy*.

79   *S.P.* II, pp. 186–7: 'This morning I delivered Mr. Dericke a packet of letters for your Lordship, with some enclosed from my Lady Pembroke and my Lord Herbert, who promises to be with you before this post.' [The last clause must qualify Mr. D., not Lord H., since there is no other reference to Herbert's going to Flushing.] 'My Lord and Lady Pembroke go not to Wales but stay all this summer at Wilton.'
        S.P. II, p. 187 (letter of 26 Apr.).

80   *S.P.* II, pp. 121–3 (letter of 12 Sept. 1599) and pp. 123–4 (13 Sept.), p. 124 (15 Sept.), p. 128 (29 Sept.) and p. 13 (2 Oct.).

81   *S.P.* II, p. 158 (letter of 12 Jan. 1600).

82   *S.P.* II, p. 187 (letter of 26 Apr. 1600).

83   *S.P.* II, pp. 201–3 (letters of 14 and 23 June 1600): another account is given in Chamberlain's letters to Dudley Carleton.

84   Hotson (1954), p. 105, facing a photograph of the picture.

85   T. Tyler (1890), p. 57, quotes the evidence of Mrs Martin given *c*. Oct. 1602 (Record Office).

86   *S.P.* II, pp. 216 (26 Sept. 1600), pp. 218 (18 Oct.), p. 220 (24 Oct.) and p. 22 (30 Oct.). The last letter suggests an elated mood of Herbert's: 'he leaps, he dances, he sings, he gives counterbuffs, he makes his horse run with more speed; he thanks me and means to be exceeding merry with you this Winter in Baynard's Castle, where you must take physic.' (Not an unknown sort of reaction in a youth of twenty who has recently learnt that he has made his girl-friend pregnant!)

87   Fowler (1975), pp. 109–13.

88   H.M.C. *Salisbury* 11, p. 202, letter of Sir Edward Fitton (18 May 1601).

89   J. C. Maxwell (1966), p. xxxv.

90   H.M.C. *Salisbury* 11, p. 14.

91   A letter of Sir Robert Cecil to Sir Geo. Carew, Lord President of Munster: The Earl of Pembroke confesses . . . but renounces marriage . . . he may be sent to the Tower.

92   H.M.C. *Salisbury* 11, p. 40. Pembroke says he would have volunteered to help suppress the rebels. (His uncle has helped negotiate their surrender.)

93   The ballad is discussed by Hotson (1954) p. 107. He had found a second version. His interpretation of *reindeer . . . imbost* as referring to Essex seems better than a punning allusion to the Queen. Hotson (1964) gives an account of Sir William Knollys, 'Malvoglio', who managed the ladies-in-waiting, and of his hopeless love for Mary Fitton. Lady Newdigate-Newdegate, in her book *Gossip from a Muniment Room*, was the first to print the fascinating correspondence between Knollys and Mary Fitton's elder sister, Anne Newdegate, to whom he confided his passion for Mary.

94   A letter of 25 Mar. 1601 from Sir Toby Matthew to Dudley Carleton: 'The Earl of Pembroke is committed to the Fleet; his cause is delivered of a boy who is dead.'

95   H.M.C. *Salisbury* 11, pp. 91 and 91–2 two letters of Feb.; p. 119, letter of 11 Mar.

96   H.M.C. *Salisbury* 11, p. 202, letter of 18 May from Sir Edward Fitton.

97   te 22 (58, 57, 61, 56) of course excepted.

98   Glynne Wickham, vol. II pt. 1, p. 90.

99   H.M.C. *Salisbury* 11, p. 340 and p. 361.

100   H.M.C. *Salisbury* 11, pp. 375–6.

101   H.M.C. *Salisbury* 11, p. 464, both letters *c.* Oct. 1601.

102   H.M.C. *Salisbury*, p. 561, the last filed in 1601 (old style). It is highly unlikely that Pembroke could have gained the Queen's permission to leave the country before the end of 1601 or (probably) before his birthday, 8 April 1602. This means that the tradition that Inigo Jones travelled abroad in the company of Pembroke is wrong (James Lees-Milne, *The Age of Inigo Jones*, pp. 20–1). Lees-Milne anyway reckons that the tradition is wrong that records Inigo Jones being brought up at the expense of the third Earl of Pembroke, who was younger than he was.

103   'O'er-grain' was Tucker's conjecture, it meant 're-dye' or 'dye anew'. 'Th' are' (= they are) occurs in T. Middleton, *The Changeling*, at II.ii.5 and V. i. 18; 'All the world besides' in *S.P.* I, p. 353, letter of 8 Oct. 1595, and in Stanhope's letter referred to in note 9.

104   *S.P.* II, p. 257, letter of 7 July 1602, and p. 231, P.S. of 12 Aug. 1602.

105   Letters of J. Chamberlain to Dudley Carleton 15 Oct. and 23 Dec. 1602 and of 17 Jan. 1603.

106   See note 27 above.

107   *Derealization* is the objective correlate of *depersonalization*. Usually they are alternative experiences since one (the outside world or the self) is judged unreal by the standard of the other.

108   In *The Mutual Flame* (1955).

109   In a letter to Dudley Carleton.

110   Dover Wilson (ed.) Shakespeare's *Antony and Cleopatra*, p. x fn. 2 lists the five passages.

111   The autograph of Sir Robert Sidney's *Sonnets* was discovered and placed in the British (Museum) Library in 1975. Hilton Kelliher, who reported on it in the *British Museum Society Bulletin* (19), considered that it showed the signs of at least three attempts to arrange the series.

112   Samuel Daniel had been tutor to the young Herberts before Hugh Sanford. His connection with the Pembrokes was maintained on both sides.

113   *D.N.B.*, Mary Herbert.

114   Tyler (1898) showed this, pp. 7 (for 1610) and 9 (for 1616).

115   See note 6 above.

116   Schoenbaum (1975), p. 26 gives the parish register entries for the burials of Edward and Edmund and the facts of Edmund's funeral also in (1977), p. 29.

117   Hunter (1953), reprinted in Jones (ed.) (1977) pp. 120–33.

118   Kott (1964), extracts reprinted in Jones (ed.) (1977) pp. 219–33.

119   Mahood (1962), reprinted in Jones (ed.) (1977) pp. 200–18.

120   Nicholas Breton; see Young (1912) pp. 154–61.

121   Francis Meres' book was *Palladis Tamia*: *Wit's Treasury* (1598 Sept,). It was commissioned as the second of a series, digests of philosophy, theology, and literature, for use in schools and colleges.

122   C. L. Barber (1978) p. 37.

123   The dedication of the First Folio of Shakespeare's plays to Pembroke and his brother in 1623 is so worded that it appears a dedication to them as members of a family rather than as individuals. Shakespeare's actor colleagues who made the dedication would have known of his association with the family; if Lady Pembroke, mother of the 'incomparable pair of brethren', had not died two years before, her name might have stood there.

124   Colin Parkes (1972) worked out a sequence of subjective experiences in mourning. John Bowlby in *Separation* and in *Loss* (vols. II and III of his *Attachment and Loss*) gives a full account with clinical examples of the effects upon a child of the mother's own experience of loss.

Part II:
The Sonnets in their poems

TO . THE . ONLIE . BEGETTER . OF .
THESE . INSVING . SONNETS .
M^r. W. H.   ALL . HAPPINESSE .
AND . THAT . ETERNITIE .
PROMISED .

BY .

OVR . EVER-LIVING . POET .

WISHETH .

THE . WELL-WISHING .
ADVENTVRER . IN .
SETTING .
FORTH .

T. T.

Extempore Performance

GIVEN BEFORE THE EARL AND COUNTESS OF PEMBROKE ON OR ABOUT APRIL 1597
∧

Proëm

a sonnet to close Shakespeare's speech at his own wedding-feast
(Thursday, St Andrew's Day, 30 November 1582 at the earliest)
by telling the company how his bride had consented

Those lips that Love's own hand did make
Breathed forth the sound that said 'I hate'
To me that languished for her sake;
But when she saw my woeful state,   4
Straight in her heart did mercy come,
Chiding that tongue that ever sweet
Was used in giving gentle doom,
And taught it thus anew to greet: 8
'I hate' she altered with an end
That followed it as gentle day
Doth follow night, who like a fiend
From heaven to hell is flown away;   12
   'I hate' from hate away she threw,
   And saved my life saying 'not you'.

Proëm – notes (Q 145)

7 *giving gentle doom*   saying 'No' to suitors
12 *heaven* (one syllable, as usually in the sonnets)
13 *hate away* (w-p on 'Hathaway', as Andrew Gurr suggested in 1971)
14 *And savèd* (w-p on 'Anne saved', as Stephen Booth suggested in 1977, since the 'd' of 'and' was commonly not pronounced. Anne Hathaway was the name of Shakespeare's bride)

As Andrew Gurr saw, what requires explanation is the presence of this sonnet in the series. One way to account for this is to suppose that the Pembrokes began the occasion in early April 1597 by asking Shakespeare what was his very first sonnet, and when he told them asked to see or hear it; if they heard it, somebody present was good at taking down speech.

The Countess may already have shown Shakespeare her brother's unpublished MS. of *Certain Sonnets*. In that case the main extempore performance could have followed immediately; it consists of three pairs of sonnets, each pair composed upon a theme given impromptu:

  Pair 1 (written for the Countess): versions of a Greek epigram
  Pair 2 (written for the Earl): upon the virginalist who played during the writing
  Pair 3 (composed orally): transformations of *Certain Sonnets* 31 and 32

a

The little Love-god lying once asleep,
Laid by his side his heart-inflaming brand,
Whilst many nymphs that vowed chaste life to keep
Came tripping by; but in her maiden hand   4
The fairest votary took up that fire,
Which many legions of true hearts had warmed,
And so the general of hot desire
Was sleeping by a virgin hand disarmed.   8
This brand she quenchèd in a cool well by,
Which from Love's fire took heat perpetual,
Growing a bath and healthful remedy
For men diseased; but I, my mistress' thrall   12
    Came there for cure and this by that I prove –
    Love's fire heats water, water cools not love.

b

Cupid laid by his brand and fell asleep;
A maid of Dian's this advantage found
And his love-kindling fire did quickly steep
In a cold valley-fountain of that ground;   4
Which borrowed from this holy fire of Love
A dateless-lively heat still to endure
And grew a seething bath which yet men prove
Against strange maladies a sovereign cure.   8
But at my mistress' eye Love's brand new-fired
The boy for trial needs would touch my breast;
I sick withal the help of bath desired
And thither hied, a sad distempered guest,   12
    But found no cure; the bath for my help lies
    Where Cupid got new fire – my mistress' eyes.

a

How oft when thou, my music, music play'st
Upon that blessèd wood whose motion sounds
With thy sweet fingers when thou gently sway'st
The wiry concord that mine ear confounds, 4
Do I envy those jacks that nimble leap
To kiss the tender inward of thy hand,
Whilst my poor lips, which should that harvest reap,
At the wood's boldness by thee blushing stand; 8
To be so tickled they would change their state
And situation with those dancing chips,
O'er whom thy fingers walk with gentle gait,
Making dead wood more blest than living lips. 12
  Since saucy jacks so happy are in this,
  Give them thy fingers, me thy lips, to kiss.

b

Love is too young to know what conscience is,
Yet who knows not conscience is born of love?
Then, gentle cheater, urge not my amiss,
Lest guilty of my faults thy sweet self prove. 4
For thou betraying me I do betray
My nobler part to my gross body's treason –
My soul doth tell my body that he may
Triumph in love, flesh stays no farther reason 8
But rising at thy name doth point out thee
As his triumphant prize; proud of this pride,
He is contented thy poor drudge to be,
To stand in thy affairs, fall by thy side. 12
  No want of conscience hold it that I call
  Her 'love' for whose dear love I rise and fall.

Extempore – notes to Pairs 1 and 2 (Q 154, 153; 128, 151)

pr 1 *a* 2 *brand* lighted torch
    5 *votary* one who had taken the vow of line 3
    6–8 *legions . . . general . . . disarmed* a military metaphor

pr 1 *b* 6 *dateless-lively* living without end *still* ever
    8 (A virgin was supposed to be a cure for venereal disease)
    10 *for trial needs would touch* as a test would go and touch
    11 *withal* from that
    12 *sad distempered* (w–p) sad and sick, sorely sick
    7, 11, 13 *bath* (mentioned once in *a*, occurs three times in *b*, probably as w–p on
      the name of Bath, the city where the Earl of Pembroke took the waters for his ill
      health)

Wilton House library was probably the source of the Greek epigram which is adapted in the
first part of each sonnet of **pr** 1. A Giles Fletcher sonnet provided the idea for their endings; it
also provided the idea for the couplet of **pr** 2 *a*.

pr 2 *a* 2 *wood* 10 *chips* 5, 13 *jacks* (all denote the keys of the virginals, though 'jacks'
      had also a technical meaning – the levers that actually struck the wire strings; the
      word seems to be used for the sake of the (perhaps indecent) w-p, being derogatory
      for 'men')
    3 *sway'st* control
    4 *wiry concord* harmonious strings *confounds* ravishes, overwhelms

pr 2 *b* 3 *urge not my amiss* do not argue my wrong-doing
    5 *betraying me* undermining my resolution
    6 *my nobler part* my soul
    8–12 *flesh . . . rising . . . pride . . . stand* (words used for sexual erection, their
      metaphor all being apposite in a sonnet written for the son of an old general of the
      Queen (cf. **pr** 1 *a* 6–8))
    8 *stays* waits for, needs *reason* encouragement

The virginalist who seems to be addressed in **pr** 2 would have played during the writing of **pr**
1; *cf. M. of V.* 3.2 43, 'Let music sound while he doth make his choice.' There are several
indications of a display of extempore composition, in fashion just then. If the subjects of the
three pairs of extempore were suggested by the Countess, the Earl, and Shakespeare himself
respectively, it accounts for the presence of the six sonnets which, besides the Proëm, have no
obvious connection with all the rest.

Extempore – notes to Pair 3 (Q 129, 146)

pr 3 *a*   1   *expense of spirit*   (w–p)   pouring out of vital energy, waste of semen
6, 7   *Past reason*   beyond all sense
9   *Made . . . so*   made as follows (in lines 10–12)
14   *heaven . . . hell*   (w–p)   the experience, the female genital

pr 3 *b*   1   *my sinful earth*   my corrupt flesh
2   *Disperse*   (conjectural emendation of 'My sinful earth', repeated in Q from line 1 – a mistake most easily made in taking down from oral composition, especially given the assonance with 'sin . . . earth'); w–p on 'dis-purse'   *rebel powers*   (metaphor for sexual erection and all lusts of the flesh and of display)   *array*   (w-p)   attire showily, afflict, defile
4, 5, 6   *walls . . . large cost . . . short lease . . . fading mansion*   (metaphors for the body, its life-span, and its maintenance. In early April 1597 Shakespeare would have been negotiating for the purchase of New Place, Stratford, the date of the registration being 4 May)
7   *excess*   (w–p)   all that I spend on my body, its bulk of flesh
8   *charge*   (w–p)   the sum spent, the ward to the soul as guardian
9   *thy servant*   your drudge (body)
10   *let that pine*   let your body go hungry   *aggravate*   increase
11   *terms divine*   centuries of extra bliss in heaven   *hours of dross*   short spells of drudgery (including the writing of sonnets on commission to get the money to pay for his mansion!)

Sir Philip Sidney's *Certain Sonnets* 31 and 32 (*The New Oxford Book of English Verse*, p. 58) had not yet been published. There is one more manuscript copy of 31, otherwise both are known from no other MS than the one at Wilton House and not published till 1598 (Ringler 1962, pp. 424–5). So we may infer that Sidney's sister had just shown them to Shakespeare and would at once recognise his feat of extempore emulation.

a

Th' expense of spirit in a waste of shame
Is lust in action, and till action lust
Is perjured, murd'rous, bloody, full of blame,
Savage, extreme, rude, cruel, not to trust,   4
Enjoyed no sooner but despised straight,
Past reason hunted and no sooner had
Past reason hated as a swallowed bait
On purpose laid to make the taker mad.   8
Made in pursuit and in possession so –
Had, having, and in quest to have extreme,
A bliss in proof and – proved – a very woe,
Before – a joy proposed, behind – a dream.   12
　　All this the world well knows yet none knows well
　　To shun the heaven that leads men to this hell.

b

Poor soul the centre of my sinful earth,
Disperse these rebel powers that thee array.
Why dost thou pine within and suffer dearth
Painting thy outward walls so costly gay?   4
Why so large cost having so short a lease
Dost thou upon thy fading mansion spend?
Shall worms inheritors of this excess
Eat up thy charge? is this thy body's end?   8
Then, soul, live thou upon thy servant's loss
And let that pine to aggravate thy store;
Buy terms divine in selling hours of dross;
Within be fed, without be rich no more.   12
　　So shalt thou feed on death, that feeds on men,
　　And death once dead there's no more dying then.

6–7 April 1597 Persuasion to marry

(FOUR TETRADS AND EPILOGUE)

Tetrad 1 : the waste of self-love
Tetrad 2 : to pass on beauty – the debt to mother
Tetrad 3 : to continue the male line – the duty to father
Tetrad 4 : progeny – the proof that portrait and poems require

8 April Epilogue: family counterpoint

Tetrad 1

a

Those hours that with gentle work did frame
The lovely gaze where every eye doth dwell
Will play the tyrants to the very same
And that unfair which fairly doth excel;   4
For never-resting time leads summer on
To hideous winter and confounds him there,
Sap checked with frost and lusty leaves quite gone,
Beauty o'er-snowed and bareness everywhere.   8
Then were not summer's distillation left
A liquid prisoner pent in walls of glass,
Beauty's effect with beauty were bereft,
Nor it nor no remembrance what it was;   12
   But flowers distilled, though they with winter meet,
   Leese but their show, their substance still lives sweet.

b

Then let not winter's ragged hand deface
In thee thy summer ere thou be distilled;
Make sweet some vial; treasure thou some place
With beauty's treasure ere it be self-killed.   4
That use is not forbidden usury
Which happies those that pay the willing loan;
That's for thyself to breed another thee,
Or ten times happier be it ten for one.   8
Ten times thyself were happier than thou art,
If ten of thine ten times refigured thee;
Then what could death do if thou shouldst depart,
Leaving thee living in posterity?   12
   Be not self-willed, for thou art much too fair
   To be death's conquest and make worms thine heir.

c

From fairest creatures we desire increase,
That thereby beauty's rose might never die,
But, as the riper should by time decease,
His tender heir might bear his memory;   4
But thou contracted to thine own bright eyes
Feed'st thy light's flame with self-substantial fuel,
Making a famine where abundance lies,
Thyself thy foe, to thy sweet self too cruel.   8
Thou, that art now the world's fresh ornament
And only herald to the gaudy spring,
Within thine own bud buriest thy content,
And tender churl mak'st waste in niggarding;   12
   Pity the world, or else this glutton be –
   To eat the world's due, by the grave and thee.

d

Unthrifty loveliness, why dost thou spend
Upon thyself thy beauty's legacy?
Nature's bequest gives nothing but doth lend,
And being frank she lends to those are free;   4
Then, beauteous niggard, why dost thou abuse
The bounteous largess given thee to give?
Profitless usurer, why dost thou use
So great a sum of sums yet canst not live?   8
For, having traffic with thy self alone,
Thou of thyself thy sweet self dost deceive;
Then how when nature calls thee to be gone,
What acceptable audit canst thou leave?   12
   Thy unused beauty must be tombed with thee,
   Which usèd lives th' executor to be.

Tetrad 1

te 1 *a* 1 *hours* (two syllables here) . . . *frame* (w–p) (Shakespeare seems to have written Tetrads 1–4 to a miniature portrait of William Herbert, shown at age 15½ as standing in a garden with an inscription such as HORAE FELICES on the frame at the bottom; see notes on **te** 4 *b* and epilogue)

      2 *gaze . . . eye . . . dwell* (Herbert seems to have used this line to tease Shakespeare; see notes on **te** 5 and **te** 25 *d*) *gaze* eyes (cf. **te** 4 *d* 5)

      4 'and make unlovely that which now excels in loveliness'

      5 *confounds* overwhelms, defeats

      9 *distillation* essence (e.g. the perfume made from rose-petals – cf. **te** 10 *c* 11–12)

     11 *were bereft* would be snatched away

     12 '(leaving) neither it (i.e. the beauty) nor any recollection of what it was like'

     14 *leese* lose *show* visible appearance

te 1 *b* 1 *ragged* harsh, ravaging

      3 *vial* vessel (i.e. womb, woman) *treasure* make rich

      5 *use* (w–p) sexual intercourse, money-lending and -borrowing at interest

      6 *happies* fulfils, pleasures *pay . . . loan* pay the interest on, accept the consequences of, the 'use'

   8, 9 *happier* more fortunate, fulfilled

    10 *refigured* reproduced your image

    11 *self-willed* (perhaps sexual w–p on 'self-satisfying' as well as 'obstinate')

te 1 *c* 3 *riper* older *by time* through lapse of time

      5 *contracted to* (w–p) concentrated into, betrothed to

      6 *self-substantial* of your own substance

    10 *only* peerless *gaudy* gay in colour

    11 *content* (w–p) sperm, power to reproduce, satisfaction

    12 *churl* (w–p) miser, boor *niggarding* grudging to spend, over-thriftiness

    14 *due* entitlement (i.e. off-spring from you) *by the grave and thee* by your choosing to die childless

te 1 *d* 1 *beauty's legacy* the beauty you have inherited

      4 *frank . . . free* open-handed, liberal

      5 *niggard* hoarder *largess* bequest

      7 *use* make outlay of, exhaust (w-p – money, sexual vitality)

      8 *live* (w-p) make a living, live to the full

      9 *traffic* (w-p) sexual activity, commerce

  11–12 *how when* (the 'when'- clause does double duty – with 'how?' and with 'what?')

    12 *audit* statement of accounts

    14 *lives* (i.e. as beauty in a child)

The economic and financial metaphors for sexual activity and breeding come to a climax in **te** 1 *d* but are resumed in **te** 2 *a* 5–12 and in **te** 2 *c* 9–12.

Tetrad 2 – notes (Q 2, 3, 9, 10)

te 2 a   1   *forty*   (William Herbert's mother was still five years off forty, his father was about 64)

        2   *trenches*   wrinkles

        3   *livery*   apparel (as if the body-surface were a garment)

        4   *tottered weed*   ragged clothing

        8   *thriftless*   wasteful

        9   *use*   (emphatic – w-p)

      11   *sum my count*   show the final profit of my activity   *my old excuse*   (w-p)   the justification of my long life, my excuse for withdrawal on the ground of age

te 2 b   3   *fresh repair*   young condition

        4   *beguile*   defraud   *unbless*   leave unblessed (by any child)

        5   *uneared*   never sown or cropped

        6   *husbandry*   (w-p)

        7   *so fond*   (w-p)   so silly, so doting on himself

        8   *to stop posterity*   as to prevent off-spring

        9   *glass*   mirror

      13   *rememb'red not to be*   to be no more spoken of

te 2 c   3   *issueless*   without offspring

        4   *like a makeless wife*   (the world would wail) like a wife who has lost her mate

        5   *still*   continually

        6   *form*   image

        7   *private*   individual

        9   *Look-what*   whatever   *unthrift*   wastrel, spendthrift

      10   *his*   its ('its' does not occur in the Sonnets, 'his' doing duty for it)

      12   *kept*   if it is kept

te 2 d   6   *stick'st not to*   do not shrink from

        7   *roof* = 'house', (w-p) body, family

        8   *repair*   renew

      14   *still*   continually

a

When forty winters shall besiege thy brow
And dig deep trenches in thy beauty's field,
Thy youth's proud livery so gazed on now
Will be a tattered weed of small worth held.   4
Then being asked, where all thy beauty lies,
Where all the treasure of thy lusty days,
To say, within thine own deep sunken eyes,
Were an all-eating shame and thriftless praise.   8
How much more praise deserved thy beauty's use,
If thou couldst answer, 'This fair child of mine
Shall sum my count, and make my old excuse',
Proving his beauty by succession thine.   12
    This were to be new made when thou art old
    And see thy blood warm when thou feel'st it cold.

b

Look in thy glass and tell the face thou viewest,
Now is the time that face should form another,
Whose fresh repair if now thou not renewest,
Thou dost beguile the world, unbless some mother.   4
For where is she so fair whose uneared womb
Disdains the tillage of thy husbandry?
Or who is he so fond will be the tomb
Of his self-love to stop posterity?   8
Thou art thy mother's glass and she in thee
Calls back the lovely April of her prime;
So thou through windows of thine age shalt see
Despite of wrinkles this thy golden time;   12
    But if thou live rememb'red not to be,
    Die single and thine image dies with thee.

c

Is it for fear to wet a widow's eye
That thou consum'st thyself in single life?
Ah, if thou issueless shalt hap to die,
The world will wail thee like a makeless wife;   4
The world will be thy widow and still weep
That thou no form of thee hast left behind,
When every private widow well may keep,
By children's eyes, her husband's shape in mind.   8
Look-what an unthrift in the world doth spend
Shifts but his place, for still the world enjoys it;
But beauty's waste hath in the world an end,
And, kept unused, the user so destroys it.   12
   No love toward others in that bosom sits
   That on himself such murd'rous shame commits.

d

For shame deny that thou bear'st love to any,
Who for thy self art so unprovident.
Grant if thou wilt, thou art beloved of many,
But that thou none lov'st is most evident.   4
For thou art so possessed with murd'rous hate
That 'gainst thyself thou stick'st not to conspire,
Seeking that beauteous roof to ruinate
Which to repair should by thy chief desire.   8
O change thy thought, that I may change my mind;
Shall hate be fairer lodged than gentle love?
Be as thy presence is, gracious and kind,
Or to thyself at least kind-hearted prove;   12
   Make thee another self for love of me,
   That beauty still may live in thine or thee.

a

Lo in the orient when the gracious light
Lifts up his burning head, each under eye
Doth homage to his new-appearing sight,
Serving with looks his sacred majesty;   4
And having climbed the steep-up heavenly hill,
Resembling strong youth in his middle age,
Yet mortal looks adore his beauty still,
Attending on his golden pilgrimage;   8
But when from highmost pitch with weary car
Like feeble age he reeleth from the day,
The eyes (fore duteous) now converted are
From his low tract and look another way;   12
    So thou, thyself out-going in thy noon,
    Unlooked on diest unless thou get a son.

b

Not from the stars do I my judgement pluck,
And yet methinks I have astronomy,
But not to tell of good, or evil luck,
Of plagues, of dearths, or seasons' quality;   4
Nor can I fortune to brief minutes tell,
Pointing to each his thunder, rain and wind,
Or say with princes if it shall go well
By oft predict that I in heaven find;   8
But from thine eyes my knowledge I derive,
And constant stars in them I read such art
As, truth and beauty shall together thrive
If from thyself to store thou wouldst convert;   12
    Or else of thee this I prognosticate –
    Thy end is truth's and beauty's doom and date.

c

As fast as thou shalt wane so fast thou grow'st,
In one of thine, from that which thou departest,
And that fresh blood which youngly thou bestow'st
Thou mayst call thine, when thou from youth convertest; 4
Herein lives wisdom, beauty, and increase;
Without this folly, age and cold decay;
If all were minded so, the times should cease,
And threescore year would make the world away. 8
Let those whom nature hath not made for store,
Harsh, featureless, and rude, barrenly perish;
Look-whom she best endowed, she gave thee more;
Which bounteous gift thou shouldst in bounty cherish; 12
    She carved thee for her seal and meant thereby,
    Thou shouldst print more, not let that copy die.

d

When I do count the clock that tells the time
And see the brave day sunk in hideous night,
When I behold the violet past prime,
And sable curls o'er-silvered all with white; 4
When lofty trees I see barren of leaves,
Which erst from heat did canopy the herd,
And summer's green all girded up in sheaves,
Borne on the bier with white and bristly beard; 8
Then of thy beauty do I question make
That thou among the wastes of time must go,
Since sweets and beauties do themselves forsake
And die as fast as they see others grow, 12
    And nothing 'gainst Time's scythe can make defence
    Save breed to brave him, when he takes thee hence.

Tetrad 3

te 3 a
1 *the gracious light*   the sun
2 *each under eye*   each eye here below
5 *steep-up . . . hill*   to the zenith
7 *mortal looks*   men's gaze
9 *pitch*   elevation of his course   *car*   (Apollo's) chariot
11 *converted*   turned aside ('convert' is a key-word in this tetrad – cf. *b* 12, *c* 4)
12 *tract*   course
14 *get*   beget

The Second Earl of Pembroke was recurrently ill as well as being in his mid 60s. This sonnet may have reproduced his briefing of Shakespeare.

te 3 b
1 *pluck*   take
2 *have astronomy*   am proficient in astrology
5 *fortune to brief minutes tell*   foretell the future precisely as to time
6 *pointing to each*   assigning to each minute   *his*   its
8 *by oft predict*   by frequent foreknowledge
10–11 *such art As*   such a prediction as
12 *store*   seed for reproduction   *convert*   turn, apply
14 *doom and date*   utter extinction, as at the end of the world

te 3 c
3 *youngly*   in young manhood
4 *from youth convertest*   make the turning from youth (to middle age)
6 *without this*   aside from this provision
7 *the times*   human history
9 *for store*   for reproduction
10 *featureless and rude*   unbecoming and rough   *barrenly*   without offspring
11 *Look-whom*   whomsoever   *thee*   (Q has 'the')
12 *in bounty*   by being bounteous yourself

te 3 d
2 *brave*   glorious
4 *sable*   black   *o'er-silvered all*   (Q has 'or silvered ore'; the usual emendation is to *start* with 'all' but that seems less euphonious than to start with 'o'er-' – Tucker's idea first; Shakespeare uses many verbs and participles compounded with 'o'er-')
6 *erst*   previously
8 *bier*   stretcher for carrying (loads or bodies)
9 *question make*   reflect
14 *breed to brave him*   offspring so as to challenge him with some glory

Tetrad 4 – notes (Q 15, 16, 13, 17)

te 4 a   4   *in secret influence comment* 'influence' here has only two syllables) both 'affect with their unseen power' and 'give information to those that know and "have astronomy"'

6   *cheerèd and checked*   helped and hindered   *even*   (one syllable as usually in the Sonnets)   *sky* climate, starry influence

7   *vaunt* exult, show off their pride   *sap* vigour

8   *out of memory* till no more recalled

9   *conceit* thought   *inconstant stay* brief and uncertain life-span

10   *Sets* (w-p) puts, plants

11   *debateth* competes

14   *engraft* propagate, reproduce (in poetry)

te 4 b   5   *stand . . . on the top* (w-p) are at your peak, are shown in the miniature ('this – time's pencil') as standing above the words – e.g. HORAE FELICES – on the frame

6   *yet unset* not yet planted

8   *counterfeit* limned portrait

9   *lines of life* (w-p) living reality, lines of personal descent, lines of form   *repair* renew

10   *this* (i.e. 'neither the miniature I have before me nor the pen I use instructed by the portrait')

11   *fair* loveliness

12   *make* (emphatic) *yourself* (emphatic) as you really are

13   *give away* pass on (to offspring) *keeps* (w-p) holds, preserves

    The three 'yourself's of lines 12–13 will be echoed in *c*.

te 4 c   1   *yourself* yourself's (in meaning, if not written – Tucker)

3   *against* to provide for

5   *in lease* for a period, (almost) in trust

6   *determination* ending

8   *issue* child, children

9   *house* (w-p) body, family

10   *husbandry* (w-p as in te 2 *b* 6)

13   *unthrifts* wastrels, spendthrifts

14   *you had a father* (an encouragement to 'get weaving', as in *M.W. of W.* 3.4.36–41, not necessarily implying the father's death, though Slender so construes it and provides the laugh)

te 4 d   2   *deserts* ('desarts' in Q) attributes, praises

4   *parts* qualities of worth

5   (sc. as the miniature before me has them painted)

6   *numbers* verses

8   *touches* (w-p) the limner's brush-strokes, physical items of face and form

11   *true rights* due praises   *rage* madness, inspiration

12   *stretchèd metre* poetic licence

This tetrad supplies three of the five indications that tetrads 1–4 were written to a miniature portrait of Herbert: *b* 5–6, (w-p) *b* 10, the parenthesis pointing to the two tools of art, the one that had fixed and the one that was fixing Herbert's lines; *d* 5–8, the equation of the verse-writing with the limner's touches, an equation the Epilogue will undo. The other two indications are the w-p of te 1 *a* 1 and the emphasis on painting in te 5 *a* 1–2, 5 *b* 1, and 5 *c* 1–2 (especially the denial of 5 *a* 1–2).

a

When I consider every thing that grows
Hold in perfection but a little moment,
That this huge stage presenteth nought but shows
Whereon the stars in secret influence comment,   4
When I perceive that men as plants increase,
Cheerèd and checked even by the self-same sky,
Vaunt in their youthful sap, at height decrease,
And wear their brave state out of memory;   8
Then the conceit of this inconstant stay
Sets you most rich in youth before my sight,
Where wasteful time debateth with decay
To change your day of youth to sullied night,   12
    And all in war with Time for love of you,
    As he takes from you, I engraft you new.

b

But wherefore do not you a mightier way
Make war upon this bloody tyrant Time?
And fortify yourself in your decay
With means more blessèd than my barren rhyme?   4
Now stand you on the top of happy hours,
And many maiden gardens yet unset
With virtuous wish would bear your living flowers,
Much liker than your painted counterfeit.   8
So should the lines of life that life repair
Which this (Time's pencil or my pupil pen)
Neither in inward worth nor outward fair
Can make you live yourself in eyes of men;   12
    To give away yourself keeps your self still,
    And you must live drawn by your own sweet skill.

c

O that you were yourself! but (love) you are
No longer yours than you yourself here live;
Against this coming end you should prepare
And your sweet semblance to some other give;   4
So should that beauty which you hold in lease
Find no determination; then you were
Yourself again after your self's decease,
When your sweet issue your sweet form should bear.   8
Who lets so fair a house fall to decay,
Which husbandry in honour might uphold
Against the stormy gusts of winter's day
And barren rage of death's eternal cold?   12
    O none but unthrifts, dear my love, you know;
    You had a father, let your son say so.

d

Who will believe my verse in time to come
If it were filled with your most high deserts?
Though yet, heaven knows, it is but as a tomb
Which hides your life and shows not half your parts. 4
If I could write the beauty of your eyes
And in fresh numbers number all your graces,
The age to come would say, 'This poet lies –
Such heavenly touches ne'er touched earthly faces'.   8
So should my papers (yellowed with their age)
Be scorned, like old men of less truth than tongue,
And your true rights be termed 'a poet's rage'
And 'stretchèd metre of an antique song'.   12
    But were some child of yours alive that time,
    You should live twice – in it and in my rhyme.

Epilogue

Music to hear, why hear'st thou music sadly?
Sweets with sweets war not, joy delights in joy:
Why lov'st thou that which thou receiv'st not gladly,
Or else receiv'st with pleasure thine annoy?   4
If the true concord of well-tunèd sounds
By unions married do offend thine ear,
They do but sweetly chide thee, who confounds
In singleness the parts that thou shouldst bear.   8
Mark how one string sweet husband to another
Strikes each in each by mutual ordering,
Resembling sire, and child, and happy mother,
Who all in one, one pleasing note do sing;   12
    Whose speechless song being many, seeming one,
    Sings this to thee, 'Thou single wilt prove none'.

Epilogue – notes (Q 8)

1   *Music to hear*   (This vocative, addressing and describing William Herbert, along with the imagery of the whole sonnet emphasizes that Shakespeare has now met him and attends to his living person, no longer to his portrait. They have spoken and listened to music together; verse can record the living reality as painting cannot.)

6   *unions*   consonant unisons (but probably also the concords of the perfect intervals – fourth, fifth, and octave)

7–8   *who confounds In singleness*   who destroy (spoil) by playing not in consort but solo

8   *parts*   (w-p)   parts of the counterpoint, roles of husband and father as well as brother and son, qualities to be used

9   *husband to*   in harmony with

10   *strikes*   (this word implies a key-board instrument, e.g. the virginals of **pr 2 a**, but possibly a lute)

July 1597 (FOURTH WEEK)

Tetrad 5: painting and truth
(TO TEASE A YOUNG MAN COME A-COURTING)

a

So is it not with me as with that muse
Stirred by a painted beauty to his verse,
Who heaven itself for ornament doth use
And every fair with his fair doth rehearse,   4
Making a couplement of proud compare –
With sun and moon, with earth and sea's rich gems,
With April's first-born flowers and all things rare
That heaven's air in this huge rondure hems.   8
O let me true in love but truly write
And then believe me; my love is as fair
As any mother's child, though not so bright
As those gold candles fixed in heaven's air.   12
    Let them say more that like of hearsay well;
    I will not praise that purpose not to sell.

b

A woman's face with nature's own hand painted
Hast thou the master mistress of my passion,
A woman's gentle heart but not acquainted
With shifting change as is false women's fashion,   4
An eye more bright than theirs, less false in rolling,
Gilding the object whereupon it gazeth;
A maiden hue all Hues in his controlling,
Which steals men's eyes and women's souls amazeth.   8
And for a woman wert thou first created,
Till nature as she wrought thee fell a-doting
And by addition me of thee defeated –
By adding one thing to my purpose nothing.   12
    But since she pricked thee out for women's pleasure,
    Mine by thy love and thy love's use their treasure.

c

Mine eye hath played the painter and hath stelled
Thy beauty's form in table – of my heart,
My body is the frame wherein 'tis held
And perspective it is – best painter's art.   4
For through the painter must you see his skill,
To find where your true image pictured lies,
Which in my bosom's shop is hanging still,
That hath his windows glazèd with thine eyes.   8
Now see what good turns eyes for eyes have done –
Mine eyes have drawn thy shape, and thine for me
Are windows to my breast, where-through the sun
Delights to peep to gaze therein on thee;   12
    Yet eyes this cunning want to grace their art –
    They draw but what they see, know not the heart.

d

My glass shall not persuade me I am old
So long as youth and thou are of one date,
But when in thee time's furrows I behold,
Then look I death my days should expiate.   4
For all that beauty that doth cover thee
Is but the seemly raiment of my heart,
Which in thy breast doth live, as thine in me –
How can I then be elder than thou art?   8
O therefore, love, be of thyself so wary
As I, not for myself, but for thee will,
Bearing thy heart, which I will keep so chary
As tender nurse her babe from faring ill.   12
    Presume not on thy heart when mine is slain;
    Thou gav'st me thine not to give back again.

Tetrad 5

Tetrad 5 – notes (Q 21, 20, 24, 22)

te 5 a 1–2 *that muse Stirred* Shakespeare's professional past self, who had written tetrads 1–4 stimulated by a painted miniature of William Herbert

4 *rehearse* recite, enumerate for comparison

8 *rondure* the vault of heaven and circle of the horizon *hems* encloses

9–11 (a different tone – of ordinariness – followed in 12 by renewed extravagance)

13 *like of hearsay well* (w-p) enjoy descriptions, take to from mere description

14 *that* since I *to sell* (Whether or not this was an allusion to Chapman – his name meaning 'huckster' or 'pedlar' – would depend on whether or not the extravagant lines in the sonnet were recognizably in his style and on whether or not he had just been talked of – perhaps just met – by Herbert and Shakespeare together.)

te 5 b 2 *passion* (w-p) poem in tribute, feeling

5 *rolling* giving encouraging, sidelong glances

7 *maiden* (conjectural emendation of Q's 'man in', which would have been an editorial alteration) *hue* (w-p) colour, complexion (with a tease on 'shape' – a very Spenserian use) *Hues* (w-p) Hughs (Hugh Sanford was the former tutor of Herbert and still in the Pembroke household; later he may have begun the editing of the sonnets) *in his* in its (sc. 'hue') *controlling* (w-p) swaying, surpassing (a participle agreeing with 'hue' and governing 'all Hues')

9 (The tone is of mock heartiness)

10 *a-doting* (w-p) crazy, fond

12 *no-thing* (Q 'no thing') a thing nothing to my purpose

13 *pricked out* (w-p) selected, furnished with a penis (the 'addition' of line 11)

te 5 c 1–2 *stelled . . . in table* (w-p) represented in two dimensions by drawing (Q's spelling 'steeled' may be Shakespeare's w-p; 'steeled' occurs twice in the coat-of-arms grant to his father – autumn 1596 – in which it means 'The (spear's) steel tip represented (silver)'), made durable

3 *frame* (w-p) probably the lattice frame an artist looked through to fix proportion and perspective (some of Dürer's prints show an artist using one; Dürer wrote on perspective and is much quoted by Hilliard)

4 *perspective* (w-p) done in perspective, a see-through instrument

5–6 *you, your* (the sonnet otherwise has 'Thy', 'Thine') one, one's (Dover Wilson suggested this. These two lines are probably parodying the artist's explanation of the use of his frame to fix true perspective and proportion)

7 *shop* e.g. an artist's studio

8 *his* its

11 *sun* (w-p on 'son', peeping at the new baby or the pregnant body)

13 *cunning* skill *want* do not possess

te 5 d 2 *are of one date* look equal in age

4 *expiate* close

11 *chary* careful(-ly)

13 *presume not on* do not think you can have

The tone of this tetrad (especially of *a* and *b*) is gently teasing. William Herbert had come up to London with his mother in the second half of July 1597 to be presented at Court by Sir Robert Cecil and to court his niece, Bridget Vere, Lord Burghley's second granddaughter, aged 13. On their renewing acquaintance with Shakespeare he could have met any compliment by teasing – 'How can I believe the poet who wrote 16 sonnets to my painted beauty?' – and Shakespeare have teased back, beginning *a*, *b*, *c*, with allusions to painting and *d* with w-p on mirroring; but before *c* and *d* were written they seem to have visited together an artist's studio – presumably for Herbert to have an up-to-date miniature portrait painted by Hilliard for presentation to his future bride.

July 1597 (FOURTH WEEK)

   Triad 1 : faults and flattery
            (TO PROVOKE CURIOSITY)

a

O me! what eyes hath love put in my head,
Which have no correspondence with true sight!
Or if they have, where is my judgement fled,
That censures falsely what they see aright?   4
If that be fair whereon my false eyes dote,
What means the world to say it is not so?
If it be not, then love doth well denote
Love's eye is not so true as all men's No.   8
How can it? O how can love's eye be true,
That is so vexed with watching and with tears?
No marvel then though I mistake my view;
The sun itself sees not till heaven clears.
    O cunning love, with tears thou keep'st me blind,
    Lest eyes well-seeing thy foul faults should find.

b

My mistress' eyes are nothing like the sun;
Coral is far more red than her lips red;
If snow be white, why then her breasts are dun;
If hairs be wires, black wires grow on her head.   4
I have seen roses damasked red and white
But no such roses see I in her cheeks,
And in some perfumes is there more delight
Than in the breath that from my mistress reeks.   8
I love to hear her speak yet well I know
That music hath a far more pleasing sound;
I grant I never saw a goddess go —
My mistress when she walks treads on the ground.   12
    And yet by heaven I think my love as rare
    As any she belied with false compare.

c

When my love swears that she is made of truth,
I do believe her though I know she lies,
That she might think me some untutored youth,
Unlearnèd in the world's false subtleties.   4
Thus vainly thinking that she thinks me young,
Although she knows my days are past the best,
Simply I credit her false-speaking tongue;
On both sides thus is simple truth suppressed.   8
But wherefore says she not she is unjust?
And wherefore say not I that I am old?.
O love's best habit is in seeming trust
And age in love loves not to have years told.   12
　Therefore I lie with her and she with me,
　And in our faults by lies we flattered be.

Triad 1 – notes (Q 148, 130, 138)

tr 1 *a*　　4　*censures falsely*　classifies or interprets wrongly
　　　　　5　*dote*　(w-p)　go stupid, become fond
　　　　　8　*eye*　(w-p)　'Aye' (yes)
　　　　10　*watching*　staying awake
　　　　11　*though I mistake my view*　if my vision is faulty

tr 1 *b*　　5　*damasked*　variegated
　　　　　8　*reeks*　is exhaled
　　　　11　*go*　walk
　　　　12　*treads*　i.e. not lightly
　　　　14　*belied*　mis-represented　*compare*　(cf. te 5 *a* 4)

tr 1 *c*　　1　*made of truth*　(w-p)　maid who is truthful and faithful
　　　　　5　*vainly*　pointlessly, wrongly
　　　　　7　*simply*　(w-p)　straightforwardly, stupidly
　　　　　9　*unjust*　false
　　　　11　*habit*　(w-p)　dress, way of behaving
　　　　12　*told*　(w-p)　counted, admitted
　　　　13　*lie*　(w-p)
　　　　14　*faults*　(w-p)　defects, wrongs

　　The unifying idea of this triad is – personal faults. It is likely that it was shown (or recited) with te 5 before 28 July 1597, when an Order in Council prescribed the closing and dismantling of all theatres in and near London; from that date William Herbert, suing as he was for the hand of Lord Burghley's granddaughter, could no more be seen in Shakespeare's company nor Shakespeare be seen visiting at Baynard's Castle, the Herberts' London residence.

　　The function of the triad appears to have been to arouse Herbert's curiosity while overtly saying, 'She is – and has – nothing to interest *you*.' It prepared the way for the next six triads, a double poem which would lead Herbert into deep waters if he went back this time on his undertaking to marry.

Autumn 1597: Two Enneads

First Ennead: winding up a charm: a spell to bind

    Triad 2: held by a roving eye
    Triad 3: warnings of desperation
    Triad 4: the perversity of each

a

Thou blind fool Love, what dost thou to mine eyes,
That they behold and see not what they see?
They know what beauty is, see where it lies,
Yet what the best is take the worst to be.   4
If eyes, corrupt by over-partial looks,
Be anchored in the bay where all men ride,
Why of eyes' falsehood hast thou forgèd hooks
Whereto the judgment of my heart is tied?   8
Why should my heart think that a several plot
Which my heart knows the wide world's common place?
Or mine eyes seeing this say, 'This is not' –
To put fair truth upon so foul a face?   12
   In things right true my heart and eyes have erred
   And to this false plague are they now transferred.

b

In faith I do not love thee with mine eyes,
For they in thee a thousand errors note,
But 'tis my heart that loves what they despise,
Who in despite of view is pleased to dote.   4
Nor are mine ears with thy tongue's tune delighted,
Nor tender feeling (to base touches prone),
Nor taste, nor smell, desire to be invited
To any sensual feast with thee alone.   8
But my five wits, nor my five senses can
Dissuade one foolish heart from serving thee,
Who leaves unswayed the likeness of a man
Thy proud heart's slave and vassal wretch to be.   12
   Only my plague thus far I count my gain,
   That she that makes me sin awards me pain.

c

Love is my sin and thy dear virtue hate,
Hate of my sin, grounded on sinful loving;
O but with mine compare thou thine own state
And thou shalt find it merits not reproving –   4
Or if it do, not from those lips of thine,
That have profaned their scarlet ornaments
And sealed false bonds of love as oft as mine,
Robbed others' beds' revenues of their rents.   8
Be it lawful I love thee as thou lov'st those
Whom thine eyes woo as mine importune thee;
Root pity in thy heart, that when it grows
Thy pity may deserve to pitied be.   12
    If thou dost seek to have what thou dost hide,
    By self-example mayst thou be denied.

Triad 2 – notes (Q 137, 141, 142)

tr 2 *a*   3   *lies* actually is, dwells
            5   *corrupt* misled, biassed   *ride* (w-p – ships ride at anchor, men ride women)
            7   *eyes' falsehood* the mistaken judgment by appearance, eyes' error
            9   *several plot* separate and private holding of land
         10   *common place* (w-p) a piece of land used in common, a woman used by many men
         12   *To* and so *fair truth* (w-p) opinion of loveliness (of being fair), good truth
              foul (w-p) unlovely, morally corrupt
         13   *In things right true* where reality and fidelity are concerned
         14   *false plague* (w-p) the curse of error, the unfaithful woman

tr 2 *b*   4   *Who* (i.e. my heart) *view* the eyes' evidence *dote* (w-p) be foolish, be fond
            6   *base* sexual *prone* (w-p) open, liable
            9   *But my five wits* but neither my five wits (common sense, imagination, fantasy, true estimation, and memory)
         10   *serving* (w-p) being devoted to, having sexual intercourse with
         11   *unswayed* (agrees with 'who' – i.e. my heart, which, if not dominated by you, leaves me a man in mere outward appearance)
         13   *plague* (w-p, referring to *a* 14) error, woman
         14   *sin . . . pain* i.e. the sin is paid for in the suffering of knowing the error and of being hated and rejected

tr 2 *c*   1   *dear* most essential
            4   *it* i.e. my state
            6   *scarlet ornaments* (w-p) red appendages (seals), lovely redness
            7   *mine* my lips
            8   (i.e. stolen from other women their conjugal rights – 'revénues')
            9   *Be it lawful I* ('Be it' one syllable) let me be allowed to
         10   *importune* beseech, woo
         13   *hide* withhold

a

O call not me to justify the wrong
That thy unkindess lays upon my heart;
Wound me not with thine eye but with thy tongue,
Use power with power and slay me not by art;   4
Tell me thou lov'st elsewhere but in my sight,
Dear heart, forbear to glance thine eye aside;
What need'st thou wound with cunning when thy might
Is more than my o'erpressed defence can bide?   8
Let me excuse thee: 'Ah, my love well knows
Her pretty looks have been mine enemies
And therefore from my face she turns my foes
That they elsewhere might dart their injuries.'   12
    Yet do not so, but since I am near slain,
    Kill me outright with looks and rid my pain.

b

Be wise as thou art cruel, do not press
My tongue-tied patience with too much disdain,
Lest sorrow lend me words and words express
The manner of my pity-wanting pain.   4
If I might teach thee wit, better it were,
Though not to love, yet (love) to tell me so,
As testy sick men, when their deaths be near,
No news but health from their physicians know.   8
For if I should despair, I should grow mad
And in my madness might speak ill of thee;
Now this ill-wresting world is grown so bad,
Mad slanderers by mad ears believèd be.   12
    That I may not be so, nor thou belied,
    Bear thine eyes straight, though thy proud heart go wide.

c

My love is as a fever longing still
For that which longer nurseth the disease,
Feeding on that which doth preserve the ill,
Th' uncertain sickly appetite to please.   4
My reason, the physician to my love,
Angry that his prescriptions are not kept,
Hath left me and I desperate now approve
Desire is death, which physic did except.   8
Past cure I am, now reason is past care,
And frantic-mad with evermore unrest;
My thoughts and my discourse as madmen's are,
At random from the truth vainly expressed.   12
   For I have sworn thee fair and thought thee bright,
   Who art as black as hell, as dark as night.

Triad 3 – notes (Q 139, 140, 147)

tr 3 *a*   4   *with power* with manifest power   *art* (w-p) skill, deceit
           8   *bide* withstand
         11 *my foes* (i.e. her pretty looks)

tr 3 *b* 1–2 *press My tongue-tied patience* strain my dumb patience
          2 *disdain* rejection, contempt
          4 *pity-wanting* (w-p) lacking your pity, requiring your pity
          6 *yet (love)* yet, my love (brackets added. In Q vocatives are marked off by
             commas, by brackets, or – as here – by nothing. There may be w-p: 'yet enjoy
             telling me that you do.')
        11 *ill-wresting* putting bad constructions on things
        13 *so* (w-p) mad, believed in my slandering *belied* slandered
        14 *wide* far off from me.

tr 3 *c*   1 *still* continually
          2 *nurseth* nourishes
          7 *approve* verify that
          8 *Desire is . . . except* desire which rejected medicine is deadly
        12 *vainly* (w-p) uselessly, wrongly

Triad 4

a

O from what power hast thou this powerful might
With insufficiency my heart to sway,
To make me give the lie to my true sight
And swear that brightness doth not grace the day?   4
Whence hast thou this becoming of things ill,
That in the very refuse of thy deeds
There is such strength and warrantise of skill
That in my mind thy worst all best exceeds?   8
Who taught thee how to make me love thee more,
The more I hear and see just cause of hate?
O though I love what others do abhor,
With others thou shouldst not abhor my state.   12
    If thy unworthiness raised love in me,
     More worthy I to be beloved of thee.

b

In loving thee thou know'st I am forsworn.
But thou art twice forsworn to me love swearing,
In act thy bed-vow broke and new faith torn
In vowing new hate after new love bearing.   4
But why of two oaths' breach do I accuse thee,
When I break twenty? I am perjured most;
For all my vows are oaths but to misuse thee
And all my honest faith in thee is lost.   8
For I have sworn deep oaths of thy deep kindness,
Oaths of thy love, thy truth, thy constancy,
And to enlighten thee gave eyes to blindness,
Or made them swear against the thing they see.   12
    For I have sworn thee fair – more perjured eye,
     To swear against the truth so foul a lie.

c

Canst thou, O cruel, say I love thee not,
When I against myself with thee partake?
Do I not think on thee when I forgot
Am of myself, all-tyrant, for thy sake?   4
Who hateth thee that I do call my friend?
On whom frown'st thou that I do fawn upon?
Nay, if thou lour'st on me, do I not spend
Revenge upon myself with present moan?   8
What merit do I in myself respect
That is so proud thy service to despise,
When all my best doth worship thy defect,
Commanded by the motion of thine eyes?   12
    But (love) hate on, for now I know thy mind –
    Those that can see thou lov'st, and I am blind.

Triad 4 – notes (Q 150, 152, 149)

tr 4 *a* 1 *power* (one syllable) *powerful* (two syllables) (cf. **te** 12 *d* 2)
2 *insufficiency* (w-p) too little worth possessed, too little bestowed *sway* control
3 *give the lie to* deny, contradict 5 *becoming* embellishment
6 *refuse of thy deeds* (w-p) the most foul of your acts, your acts of refusing
7 *warrantize* proof, certainty
13 *raised love* (w-p) stirred love, caused an erection

tr 4 *b* 1 *am forsworn* have broken my vows (of marriage)
2 *love swearing* swearing love
3 *torn* (i.e. as if the pledge were a written bond)
7 *but to misuse* (w-p) simply to use you sexually, to slander (misrepresent) you
11 *enlighten thee* (w-p) illuminate your image, make you out fairer than you
are *gave eyes to blindness* (w-p) purported to tell the truth to those who could
not see it, made my own eyes blind not to see the facts
13 *eye* (w-p) I

tr 4 *c* 2 *partake* take sides
4 *all-tyrant* (w-p) wholly tyrannical (like you), O you utter tyrant (vocative)
7 *thou lour'st* you frown
7–8 *spend Revenge* indulge in revenge, take it out on myself
8 *present moan* immediate lamentation
10 *is so proud* makes me so proud as to
11 *defect* (w-p) lack of goodness (cf. 'insufficiency' of *a* 2), lack of physical beauty,
of fairness
14 *can see* i.e. recognize your foulness (This line winds up the first Ennead by
referring back to the opening line of **tr** 2 *a*.)

Triads 2–4 (Ennead 1): Each triad begins with a vocative, the second and third with an 'o',
the first addressing not the woman but Love himself (called blind at the opening, the poet
calling himself blind at the end). The first line of **tr** 2 recalls the first line of **tr** 1.

Autumn 1597: Two Enneads

Second Ennead: winding up another charm: a spell to loose

Triad 5: truths about blackness
Triad 6: states of unfreedom
Triad 7: insatiability and corruption

Triad 5

a

In the old age black was not counted fair,
Or if it were it bore not beauty's name,
But now is black beauty's successive heir
And beauty slandered with a bastard shame;   4
For since each hand hath put on nature's power,
Fairing the foul with art's false borrowed face,
Sweet beauty hath no name, no holy bower,
But is profaned, if not lives in disgrace.   8
Therefore my mistress' hairs are raven black,
Her eyes so suited and they mourners seem
At such who not born fair no beauty lack,
Slandering creation with a false esteem,   12
   Yet so they mourn becoming of their woe
   That every tongue says beauty should look so.

b

Thine eyes I love, and they as pitying me,
Knowing thy heart torments me with disdain,
Have put on black and loving mourners be,
Looking with pretty ruth upon my pain;   4
And truly not the morning sun of heaven
Better becomes the grey cheeks of the east,
Nor that full star that ushers in the even
Doth half that glory to the sober west   8
As those two mourning eyes become thy face.
O let it then as well beseem thy heart
To mourn for me, since mourning doth thee grace,
And suit thy pity like in every part.   12
   Then will I swear beauty herself is black
   And all they foul that thy complexion lack.

c

Thou art as tyrannous, so as thou art,
As those whose beauties proudly make them cruel,
For well thou know'st to my dear doting heart
Thou art the fairest and most precious jewel.   4
Yet in good faith some say that thee behold,
Thy face hath not the power to make love groan;
To say they err, I dare not be so bold,
Although I swear it to my self alone.   8
And to be sure that is not false I swear,
A thousand groans but thinking on thy face
One on another's neck do witness bear
Thy black is fairest in my judgment's place.   12
  In nothing art thou black save in thy deeds,
  And thence this – slander (as I think) – proceeds.

Triad 5 – notes (Q 127, 132, 131)

tr 5 *a* 1 *old age* olden times *black* (w-p) dark (in hair-colour), ill-favoured *fair* (w-p) lovely, blonde (In the w-p on bastardy and legitimacy that follows 'Fair' is almost treated as if it were a family-name.)
 3 *successive* by right of succession
 4 *slandered* ill-reputed *bastard shame* the slur of spuriousness
 5 *each hand* (w-p) everybody, right and left hand *put on* (w-p) assumed, applied (cosmetically)
 6 *Fairing* (w-p) making lovely, making blonde *foul* (w-p) dark, unlovely
 8 *profaned* abused, vulgarized 9 *hairs* (Q's text has 'eyes')
 10 *suited* (w-p) dressed, coloured to match
 11 *At such* over those who *not born fair* although they were not born fair
 12 *Sland'ring* mis-representing, abusing *esteem* repute, opinion, valuation
 13 *becoming of* making attractive

tr 5 *b* 2 *torments* (Q has 'torment') 4 *ruth* pity
 5, 9 *morning . . . mourning* (w-p) 6 *becomes* makes attractive, suits
 7 *full star* (The planet Venus, called Hesperus, arising in the West)
 10 *beseem* befit
 12 *suit . . . like* (w-p) dress . . . alike, make . . . the same
 14 *complexion* (of hair, eyes – and temperament)

tr 5 *c* 1 *so as* just as (*i.e.* with your natural colouring)
 9 *dear* loving *doting* (w-p) foolish, fond 5 *that* who
 9 *that . . . I swear* that that which I swear is not false
 10 *but thinking on* when I merely think of
 11 *on . . . neck* pell mell, one after another
 13 *black* (w-p) dark, evil *save in thy deeds* (a deadly slash)
 14 *slander* (w-p) false repute, ill repute *as I think* (qualifies 'slander') (Line 14 is spoken quietly with bitter irony.)

183

Triad 6

a

Beshrew that heart that makes my heart to groan
For that deep wound it gives my friend and me;
Is't not enough to torture me alone,
But slave to slavery my sweet'st friend must be?   4
Me from myself thy cruel eye hath taken
And my next self thou harder hast engrossed;
Of him, myself, and thee I am forsaken,
A torment thrice three-fold thus to be crossed.   8
Prison my heart in thy steel bosom's ward
But then my friend's heart let my poor heart bail;
Whoe'er keeps me, let my heart be his guard;
Thou canst not then use rigour in my gaol.   12
    And yet thou wilt, for I being pent in thee
    Perforce am thine and all that is in me.

b

So now I have confessed that he is thine
And I myself am mortgaged to thy will,
Myself I'll forfeit, so that other mine
Thou wilt restore to be my comfort still.   4
But thou wilt not, nor he will not be free,
For thou art covetous and he is kind –
He learned but surety-like to write for me
Under that bond that him as fast doth bind.   8
The statute of thy beauty thou wilt take,
Thou usurer that put'st forth all to use,
And sue a friend came debtor for my sake;
So him I lose through my unkind abuse.   12
    Him have I lost, thou hast both him and me,
    He pays the whole, and yet am I not free.

c

Lo as a careful huswife runs to catch
One of her feathered creatures broke away,
Sets down her babe and makes all swift dispatch
In pursuit of the thing she would have stay,   4
Whilst her neglected child holds her in chase,
Cries to catch her whose busy care is bent
To follow that which flies before her face,
Not prizing her poor infant's discontent;   8
So run'st thou after that which flies from thee,
Whilst I thy babe chase thee afar behind;
But if thou catch thy hope, turn back to me
And play the mother's part, kiss me, be kind.   12
   So will I pray that thou mayst have thy Will,
   If thou turn back and my loud crying still.

Triad 6 – notes (Q 133, 134, 143)

tr 6 *a* 1 *Beshrew . . .'* Curse on . . .'
6 *my next self* my alter ego *engrossed* taken over as yours
8 *thus to be crossed* to be thwarted like that (perhaps also w-p: 'which needs requital in this verse – of thrice three sonnets')
9 *ward* lock-up
10 *bail* stand surety for (and so 'release')
11 *keeps me* has custody of me, is my jailer
12 *rigour* physical torment *my jail* my heart, myself
13 *pent* enclosed   14 *perforce* necessarily

tr 6 *b* 1 *now* now that
2 *will* (w-p) power, pleasure, genital organ (the first use of the rhyme in *-ill*, which recurs in the next four sonnets)
3 *so* on condition that *other mine* alter ego (friend)
7–8 (cf. the *M. of V.* situation between Antonio, Bassanio, and Shylock)
9 *Statute* value defined in the bond
10 *Use* (w-p) lending at interest, sexual use
11 *came* who became
12 *my . . . abuse* the cheating, the deceiving, of me

tr 6 *c* 2 *broke away* that has escaped
3 *dispatch* haste
4 *she would have stay* she wants not to escape
5 *holds her in chase* runs after her
5, 6 *her . . . her* (emphatic)
8 *prizing* heeding
13 *thy Will* (w-p) The Will you count yours (Herbert), your aim, your desire, the genital organ you're after (Here and in **tr 7 *a*** 1 Q has Will in italics with initial capital to signify the extra meaning of 'William'.)

a

Whoever hath her wish, thou hast thy will,
And 'Will' to boot, and 'Will' in over-plus;
More than enough am I that vex thee still,
To thy sweet will making addition thus.   4
Wilt thou, whose will is large and spacious,
Not once vouchsafe to hide my will in thine?
Shall will in others seem right gracious
And in my will no fair acceptance shine?   8
The sea all water yet receives rain still
And in abundance addeth to his store;
So thou being rich in will add to thy will
One will of mine to make thy large will more.   12
    Let 'No' (unkind) no fair beseechers kill;
    Think all but one and me in that one 'Will.'

b

If thy soul check thee that I come so near,
Swear to thy blind soul that I was thy 'Will',
And will thy soul knows is admitted there;
Thus far for love my love-suit sweet fulfil.   4
'Will' will fulfil the treasure of thy love,
Ay, fill it full with wills and my will one;
In things of great receipt with ease we prove,
Among a number one is reckoned none.   8
Then in the number let me pass untold,
Though in thy store's account I one must be,
For nothing hold me, so it please thee hold
That nothing me a something sweet to thee.   12
    Make but my name thy love and love that still
    And then thou lov'st me for my name is Will.

c

Two loves I have of comfort and despair,
Which like two spirits do suggest me still;
The better angel is a man right fair,
The worser spirit a woman coloured ill.   4
To win me soon to hell my female evil
Tempteth my better angel from my side,
And would corrupt my saint to be a devil,
Wooing his purity with her foul pride.   8
And whether that my angel be turned fiend,
Suspect I may yet not directly tell,
But, being both from me both to each friend,
I guess one angel in another's hell.   12
    Yet this shall I ne'er know but live in doubt,
    Till my bad angel fire my good one out.

Triad 7 – notes (Q 135, 136, 144)

In 7 *a* and *b* there is dazzlingly ingenious w-p on the name and word, WILL – the first name of Herbert and of Shakespeare and a noun meaning 'intent', 'desire', and 'sexual organ'.

tr 7 *a*   3 *still* continually
          5, 7 *spacious . . . gracious* (each of three syllables)
          6 *vouchsafe* agree   9 *still* ever   10 *his* its
          13 *Let 'No' (unkind)* (Q has 'Let no unkind,') i.e. Let your refusal (unkind word!) *beseechers* those asking your favours (i.e. Grant your favours – don't be unkind! – to all who ask them nicely.)
          (Tucker's brilliant suggestion that the first 'no' should be in inverted commas was improved by Ingram and Redpath's extra comma before 'unkind'; brackets are an alternative.)

tr 7 *b*   1 *check* reproach *come so near* (w-p) am so direct, enter your body
          5 *fulfill* (w-p) satisfy, fill full *treasure* (w-p) richness, treasury (vagina)
          7 *of great receipt* where large numbers are at stake
          9 *untold* uncounted
          10 i.e. I must actually figure among your entries
          13 *my name thy love* (here the w-p on 'Will' 'will' reaches its climax) *still* ever
          14 *for* (w-p) 'since', 'for the reason that'

tr 7 *c*   1 *of comfort* *and despair* i.e. one bringing comfort, the other despair
          2 *suggest me* prompt me, urge me *still* continually
          4 *ill* dark
          8 *pride* (w-p) proud flesh, excitement
          10 *directly* for sure
          11 *from* absent from *both to each* to each other
          12 *hell* (w-p) evil world, vagina
          14 *fire . . . out* (w-p) dismiss, infect with syphilis

1598 April–September: Drama in six episodes
(THREE TETRADS FOR EACH MONTH, ONE EARLY, ONE MIDDLING, ONE LATE)

Episode I (April): new-found security

Tetrad 6: present for a birthday (8 April)
remembrance and the grave
Tetrad 7: at an Easter Service (16 April)
Tetrad 8: refusal of an offer; allegiance and leave-taking

Tetrad 6

a

Thy glass will show thee how thy beauties wear,
Thy dial how thy precious minutes waste,
The vacant leaves thy mind's imprint will bear,
And of this book this learning mayst thou taste: 4
The wrinkles which thy glass will truly show
Of mouthèd graves will give thee memory;
Thou by thy dial's shady stealth mayst know
Time's thievish progress to eternity; 8
Look-what thy memory cannot contain,
Commit to these waste blanks, and thou shalt find
Those children nursed, delivered from thy brain
To take a new acquaintance of thy mind. 12
   These offices, so oft as thou wilt look,
   Shall profit thee and much enrich thy book.

b

Thy gift, thy tables, are within my brain
Full charactered with lasting memory,
Which shall above that idle rank remain
Beyond all date, even to eternity; 4
Or at the least, so long as brain and heart
Have faculty by nature to subsist;
Till each to razed oblivion yield his part
Of thee, thy record never can be missed. 8
That poor retention could not so much hold
Nor need I tallies thy dear love to score,
Therefore to give them from me was I bold,
To trust those tables that receive thee more; 12
   To keep an adjunct to remember thee
   Were to import forgetfulness in me.

c

When to the sessions of sweet silent thought
I summon up remembrance of things past,
I sigh the lack of many a thing I sought
And with old woes new wail my dear time's waste;   4
Then can I drown an eye (unused to flow)
For precious friends hid in death's dateless night,
And weep afresh love's long since cancelled woe,
And moan th' expense of many a vanished sight.   8
Then can I grieve at grievances foregone
And heavily from woe to woe tell o'er
The sad account of fore-bemoanèd moan,
Which I new pay as if not paid before.   12
    But if the while I think on thee (dear friend),
    All losses are restored and sorrows end.

d

Thy bosom is endearèd with all hearts
Which I by lacking have supposèd dead,
And there reigns love and all love's loving parts
And all those friends which I thought burièd.   4
How many a holy and obsequious tear
Hath dear religious love stol'n from mine eye,
As interest of the dead, which now appear
But things removed that hidden in thee lie.   8
Thou art the grave where buried love doth live,
Hung with the trophies of my lovers gone,
Who all their parts of me to thee did give –
That due of many now is thine alone.   12
    Their images I loved, I view in thee,
    And thou (all they) hast all the all of me.

Tetrad 6

te 6 *a*   The birthday-present which this sonnet accompanied seems to have been a novelty-notebook with a mirror for front cover and on its back cover a sun-dial with its gnomon presumably hinged (to serve as a bracket when the mirror was used and to fold away for the use of the book).

3   *The*   (the *non*-vacant leaves may have contained **te** 5 and **tr** 1 as well as, perhaps, **te** 6)
4   *This learning*   i.e. that following in lines 5–12
6   *mouthèd*   yawning
9   *Look-what*   whatever
11   *children*   brain-children, ideas
13   *offices*   regular practices

The first line of this sonnet deliberately recalls the first line of **te** 5 *d*, a link between consecutive sonnets to bridge the gap of more than eight months.

te 6 *b*   1   *tables*   a note-book carried on the person
2   *Full charactered*   plainly written
3   *that idle rank*   i.e. of ordinary, written pages
7   *razed*   wiping out
9   *That poor retention*   i.e. of the pages
10   *tallies*   counters (or any physical things to help counting)   *score*   record
11   *them*   *sc.* the tables (the notebook given by Herbert to Shakespeare in the July before and containing **te** 5 amd **tr** 1)
12   *those tables*   i.e. my brain
13   *adjunct*   physical aid
14   *Were to import*   would indeed mean

te 6 *c*   The extended image of this whole sonnet is accountancy ('sessions' 'waste' 'cancelled' 'expense' 'tell o'er' 'account' 'pay . . . paid' 'losses . . . restored').
4   *dear time's waste*   (w-p)   the value lost through time, the loss of precious time
6   *dateless*   unending
7   *cancelled*   i.e. by previous grieving
8   *expense*   expenditure, utterance   *sight*   sigh (with w-p on 'sight')
9–12   in each line a key syllable is repeated as if a bell were tolling
9   *foregone*   past
10   *tell o'er*   count up

te 6 *d*   1   *endearèd*   enriched
2   *by lacking*   by being separated from them
3   *parts* (w-p)   roles, qualities
5   *obsequious tear*   tear of due mourning
7   *interest*   the due
10   *trophies*   relics, symbols   *Lovers*   dear ones
11   *parts of*   shares in
12   *due of*   owed by, owned by
13   *Their images I loved*   the images of those whom I loved

Tetrad 7 – notes (Q 75, 52, 29, 25)

te 7 *a* 2   *sweet-seasoned showers* April showers

        3   *peace of you* the serenity you bring (also w-p?)

        5   *anon* by and by

        6   *Doubting . . . age* afraid that the dishonest times

        8   *bettered that . . .* my condition made still better if . . .

     10 *clean* quite

     12 *from you* (applies to 'had' as well as to 'be took')

     13 *pine* go hungry

     14 *Or . . . or . . .* either . . . or . . . *all away* having nothing at all

te 7 *b* 4   *For blunting* so as not to blunt *seldom* not often had

        5   *solemn* (w-p) ritual, annual

        8   *captain* principal *carcanet* collar or tiara

        9   *So is . . . as* is just like *chest* strong-box (also w-p?)

   10–12 *the robe* i.e. the pontifical golden robe, for which the dark purple robe was exchanged at a special moment in the Easter service to symbolise the Resurrection

     12 *his* its

te 7 *c* 1   *in disgrace* out of favour

        2   *all alone* isolated (perhaps even in a crowd and not necessarily when alone)

        3   *heaven* (one syllable)

     5–7 (five different men are here glanced at)

        7   *art* experience and skill *scope* opportunity

     10 *state* i.e. mental state

te 7 *d* 4   *unlooked for joy in* unexpectedly rejoice in having

        6   *But* merely

        8   (the marigold closes when the sun's light is withdrawn)

        9   *painful* (w-p) making great efforts, valiant, suffering

     11 *forth* (an almost certain emendation to rhyme with 'worth'; Q has 'quite', which argues an earlier version, rhyming 'might' or 'fight', at the end of line 9) *razèd forth* obliterated

     14 (the line acknowledges the bond of fealty)

This tetrad is at once illuminated when assigned to Shakespeare's experience in St Paul's Cathedral on Easter Day 1598: *a* the waiting in a fasting state in a position from which the Sidneys could be seen *b* the mass *c* the anthem (a special rhyme-scheme) *d* the royal procession out and the family's visit to Sir Philip Sidney's tomb.

a

So are you to my thoughts as food to life
Or as sweet-seasoned showers are to the ground,
And for the peace of you I hold such strife
As 'twixt a miser and his wealth is found: 4
Now proud as an enjoyer, and anon
Doubting the filching age will steal his treasure,
Now counting best to be with you alone,
Then bettered that the world may see my pleasure,   8
Sometimes all full with feasting on your sight,
And by and by clean starvèd for a look,
Possessing or pursuing no delight
Save what is had, or must from you be took.   12
    Thus do I pine and surfeit day by day,
     Or gluttoning on all or all away.

b

So am I as the rich whose blessèd key
Can bring him to his sweet up-lockèd treasure,
The which he will not every hour survey
For blunting the fine point of seldom pleasure.   4
Therefore are feasts so solemn and so rare
Since seldom coming in the long year set
Like stones of worth they thinly placèd are,
Or captain jewels in the carcanet.   8
So is the time that keeps you as my chest,
Or as the wardrobe which the robe doth hide
To make some special instant special-blest
By new unfolding his imprisoned pride.   12
    Blessèd are you, whose worthiness gives scope
     Being had to triumph, being lacked to hope.

c

When in disgrace with Fortune and men's eyes
I all alone beweep my outcast state
And trouble deaf heaven with my bootless cries
And look upon myself and curse my fate,   4
Wishing me like to one more rich in hope,
Featured like him, like him with friends possessed,
Desiring this man's art, and that man's scope,
With what I most enjoy contented least,   8
Yet in these thoughts myself almost despising
Haply I think on thee, and then my state
(Like to the lark at break of day arising
From sullen earth) sings hymns at heaven's gate;   12
    For thy sweet love rememb'red such wealth brings
    That then I scorn to change my state with kings.

d

Let those who are in favour with their stars
Of public honour and proud titles boast,
Whilst I whom fortune of such triumph bars
Unlooked for joy in that I honour most;   4
Great princes' favourites their fair leaves spread
But as the marigold at the sun's eye,
And in themselves their pride lies burièd,
For at a frown they in their glory die.   8
The painful warrior famousèd for worth,
After a thousand victories once foiled,
Is from the book of honour razèd forth
And all the rest forgot for which he toiled.   12
    Then happy I that love and am beloved
    Where I may not remove nor be removed.

a

O how thy worth with manners may I sing,
When thou art all the better part of me?
What can mine own praise to mine own self bring,
And what is't but mine own when I praise thee? 4
Even for this let us divided live
And our dear love lose name of single 'one' –
That by this separation I may give
That due to thee which thou deserv'st alone. 8
O absence, what a torment wouldst thou prove,
Were it not thy sour leisure gave sweet leave
To entertain the time with thoughts of love,
Which time and thoughts so sweetly doth deceive, 12
   And that thou teachest how to make one twain
   By praising him here who doth hence remain.

b

Let me confess that we two must be twain,
Although our undivided loves are one;
So shall those blots that do with me remain
Without thy help by me be borne alone. 4
In our two loves there is but one respect,
Though in our lives a separable spite,
Which, though it alter not love's sole effect,
Yet doth it steal sweet hours from love's delight. 8
I may not evermore acknowledge thee,
Lest my bewailèd guilt should do thee shame,
Nor thou with public kindness honour me,
Unless thou take that honour from thy name; 12
   But do not so, I love thee in such sort
   As thou being mine mine is thy good report.

c

As a decrepit father takes delight
To see his active child do deeds of youth,
So I, made lame by Fortune's dearest spite,
Take all my comfort of thy worth and truth.   4
For whether beauty, birth, or wealth, or wit,
Or any of these all, or all, or more
Entitled in thy parts do crownèd sit,
I make my love engrafted to this store.   8
So then I am not lame, poor, nor despised,
Whilst that this shadow doth such substance give
That I in thy abundance am sufficed
And by a part of all thy glory live.   12
    Look-what is best, that best I wish in thee;
    This wish I have, then ten times happy me.

d

Lord of my love, to whom in vassalage
Thy merit hath my duty strongly knit,
To thee I send this written ambassage
To witness duty, not to show my wit.   4
Duty so great which wit so poor as mine
May make seem bare, in wanting words to show it,
But that I hope some good conceit of thine
In thy soul's thought (all naked) will bestow it,   8
Till whatsoever star that guides my moving
Points on me graciously with fair aspect
And puts apparel on my tattered loving
To show me worthy of thy sweet respect.   12
    Then may I dare to boast how I do love thee –
    Till then not show my head where thou mayst
      prove me.

Tetrad 8

Tetrad 8 – notes (Q 39, 36, 37, 26)

te 8 *a* 1   *worth* (this word will have suggested the idea of changing the fifth rhyme of **te** 7 *d* – from 'fight'/'quite' – to make a link)   *with manners*   with proper humility

      5   *Even* (two syllables here)   *for this*   for this very reason   *divided*   apart

      9–14   (an address to 'Absence' which tells truths now re-emphasized by modern psychology: absence stimulates the use of symbols and the valuing of language ('praise' implies speech and writing) and facilitates the earliest acquisition of separate identity)

      11   *entertain*   beguile

te 8 *b* 3   *blots*   stains (i.e. of being an actor and inferior)

      5   *one respect*   a mutual esteeming, love

      6   *a separable spite*   a malice of fate enforcing a gulf between us

      7   *sole*   without parallel

      9–12   (This had certainly been true immediately upon The Order in Council of 28 July and now, nine months later, the blots that remained offered Shakespeare a powerful excuse for not accepting any invitation to reside in Baynard's Castle, the Pembrokes' vast London residence on the Thames by Blackfriars.)

      13–14   (The couplet will be used again – cf. **te** 26 *b* – to remind the young Pembroke of the circumstances of its earlier use.)   *sort*   fashion

te 8 *c* 1   *decrepit father*   (may be thought to glance at John Shakespeare, William's father, now *c.* 70)

      2   (Hamnet Shakespeare, William's only son, had been 21 months dead by April 1598 but old John Shakespeare would still have talked of him and his deeds.)

      5   *wit*   (i.e. both intellectual ability and its expression in speech)

      7   *Entitled in thy parts*   given nobility (or royalty) in your qualities

      8   *engrafted to this store*   (for giving and receiving) joined to your plenty   *shadow* (w-p)   proximity, image

      12   *part*   share

      13   *Look-what*   whatever

te 8 *d* 3   *this written ambassage*   my approach by letter (the tetrad) (By this line Shakespeare emphasizes the spatial separation.)

      4–5   *wit*   ability (by nature and by education)

      8   *all naked*   unembellished (metaphor of a foundling babe)

      9   *moving* (w-p)   journey to come, life ahead

      10   *aspect*   phase, influence

      11   *tattered*   ragged

      14   *prove*   make trial of

1598 Drama

Episode II (May): Journey to Stratford

Tetrad 9:   setting out
Tetrad 10: upon receiving a portrait
         (TETRAD 10 CONVEYED TRIAD 2)
Tetrad 11: the night before arrival
         (TETRAD 11 CONVEYED TRIAD 3)

Tetrad 9

a

How heavy do I journey on the way,
When what I seek (my weary travel's end)
Doth teach that ease and that repose to say
'Thus far the miles are measured from thy friend.'   4
The beast that bears me, tirèd with my woe,
Plods dully on, to bear that weight in me,
As if by some instinct the wretch did know
His rider loved not speed being made from thee.   8
The bloody spur cannot provoke him on,
That sometimes anger thrusts into his hide,
Which heavily he answers with a groan,
More sharp to me than spurring to his side;   12
    For that same groan doth put this in my mind –
    My grief lies onward and my joy behind.

b

Thus can my love excuse the slow offence
Of my dull bearer, when from thee I speed –
'From where thou art why should I haste me thence?
Till I return of posting is no need.'   4
O what excuse will my poor beast then find
When swift extremity can seem but slow?
Then should I spur though mounted on the wind,
In wingèd speed no motion shall I know –   8
Then can no horse with my desire keep pace,
Therefore desire (of perfect'st love being made)
Shall neigh (no dull flesh in his fiery race),
But love, for love, thus shall excuse my jade –   12
    'Since from thee going he went wilful-slow,
    Towards thee I'll run and give him leave to go'.

c

If the dull substance of my flesh were thought,
Injurious distance should not stop my way,
For then despite of space I would be brought
(From limits far remote) where thou dost stay;   4
No matter then although my foot did stand
Upon the farthest earth removed from thee,
For nimble thought can jump both sea and land
As soon as think the place where he would be.   8
But ah, thought kills me that I am not thought
(To leap large lengths of miles when thou art gone)
But that, so much of earth and water wrought,
I must attend time's leisure with my moan,   12
    Receiving nought by elements so slow
    But heavy tears, badges of either's woe.

d

The other two, slight air and purging fire,
Are both with thee wherever I abide,
The first my thought, the other my desire –
These present-absent with swift motion slide.   4
For when these quicker elements are gone
In tender embassy of love to thee,
My life, being made of four, with two alone
Sinks down to death, oppressed with melancholy –   8
Until life's composition be recured
By those swift messengers returned from thee,
Who even but now come back again assured
Of thy fair health, recounting it to me.   12
    This told, I joy, but then no longer glad
    I send them back again and straight grow sad.

Tetrad 9

te 9 *a*   1   *heavy*   sad-heartedly   (the words for heaviness – slowness, sadness, and (especially) dulness – provide one of the chief unifying ideas in this tetrad)

      2   *travel's*   (w-p)   journey's, labour's, hardship's

      5   *tirèd*   (two syllables)

     14   *grief*   (the chief clue that Shakespeare's 'travel's end' was Stratford, where his wife and daughters together with his parents, sister, and brothers at Henley Street would still be grieving for Hamnet and for John Shakespeare's brother and sister-in-law)

te 9 *b*   1   *the slow offense*   the offense of plodding slowly

      4   *posting*   fast riding

      6   *swift extremity*   the extreme of swiftness

     11   *neigh*   (because galloping home)   *– no dull . . . race*   (the dash added to Q's text)   *dull flesh* (cf. *c* 1)   *fiery race*   spirited breed (for 'fiery' cf. *d* 1, 5)

     12   *jade*   hack-horse

     14   *go*   walk

te 9 *c*   The special idea underlying *c* and *d* is the composition of all matter (including flesh) from four elements – earth, air, fire, water – in varying proportions.

      4   *limits*   regions

      6   *the farthest earth*   the earth farthest

      8   *he*   it (i.e. nimble thought)

     11   *wrought*   composed

     12   *attend*   (w-p)   wait for, serve

     14   *badges . . . woe*   marks of the sadness (of earth and water – salt and wet)

te 9 *d*   1   *slight*   the most refined and light   *purging*   cleansing

      7   *two alone*   i.e. the earth and water mentioned in *c*

      8   *melancholy*   (pronounce here 'mel'ncholy' to scan the line aright)

      9   *recured*   made whole again

     10   *swift messengers*   i.e. air and fire

Robert Sidney, now resident with William Herbert at Baynard's Castle, had as his London agent, when he himself was serving abroad in Flushing, Rowland Whyte, Postmaster General in charge of the courier-service in England. So the sending of messages and packets between Herbert and Shakespeare was very easy.

Tetrad 10 – notes (Q 46, 47, 54, 53)

te 10 *a* 2 *the conquest of thy sight* the possession of your image and of the right to view it
9 *side* allot, share out
10 *quest* panel (jury, as if for treasure trove)
12 *moiety* share

te 10 *b* 1 *a league is took* a treaty has been made
4 *with sighs* (take these words after 'doth smother')
8 *his* its (the heart's)

The unifying idea behind *a* and *b* is that of Herbert's *picture*, the 'painted banquet', which was now clearly with Shakespeare. The simplest way to explain this is to suppose that the Hilliard miniature, painted in July–August for giving to the bride-that-was-to-be, had now been sent to Shakespeare as a birthday-present.

te 10 *c* 2 *truth* reality (i.e. the evidence of more senses than sight alone)
5 *canker-blooms* dog-roses
6 *tincture* colour
8 *maskèd* enfolded, unopened
9 *for* since *their virtue only* their one good quality
10 *unrespected* (w-p) unlooked upon, uncared-for
12 *odours* perfumes
14 *vade* go, disappear *distils your truth* your reality, your substance, is distilled

te 10 *d* 1 *is* (emphatic)
2 *strange shadows* appearances of other beings than your own *tend* are projected
3 *shade* shadow, appearance
4 *but one* though single *can every shadow lend* can accept and offer the appearance of any other
5 *counterfeit* picture, image
8 *tires* clothes
9 *foison* teeming harvest
10–11 *the one . . . the other* i.e. Spring . . . Autumn
14 *constant heart* (there is dramatic irony in this line, since Shakespeare was sending with this tetrad the first of the triads which would tempt Herbert to inconstancy)

Tetrad 10

a

Mine eye and heart are at a mortal war,
How to divide the conquest of thy sight;
Mine eye my heart thy picture's sight would bar,
My heart mine eye the freedom of that right.   4
My heart doth plead that thou in him dost lie
(A closet never pierced with crystal eyes)
But the defendant doth that plea deny
And says in him thy fair appearance lies.   8
To side this title is impanellèd
A quest of thoughts, all tenants to the heart,
And by their verdict is determinèd
The clear eye's moiety and the dear heart's part.   12
    As thus – mine eye's due is thy outward part
    And my heart's right thy inward love of heart.

b

Betwixt mine eye and heart a league is took
And each doth good turns now unto the other;
When that mine eye is famished for a look
Or heart (in love) with sighs himself doth smother,   4
With my love's picture then my eye doth feast
And to the painted banquet bids my heart;
Another time mine eye is my heart's guest
And in his thoughts of love doth share a part.   8
So either by thy picture or my love
Thyself away art present still with me,
For thou not farther than my thoughts canst move
And I am still with them and they with thee;   12
    Or if they sleep, thy picture in my sight
    Awakes my heart to heart's and eye's delight.

c

O how much more doth beauty beauteous seem
By that sweet ornament which truth doth give!
The rose looks fair but fairer we it deem
For that sweet odour which doth in it live.   4
The canker-blooms have full as deep a dye
As the perfumèd tincture of the roses,
Hang on such thorns and play as wantonly,
When summer's breath their maskèd buds discloses;   8
But, for their virtue only is their show,
They live unwooed and unrespected fade –
Die to themselves. Sweet roses do not so;
Of their sweet deaths are sweetest odours made.   12
   And so of you, beauteous and lovely youth –
   When that shall vade, by verse distills your truth.

d

What is your substance, whereof are you made,
That millions of strange shadows on you tend?
Since everyone hath (every one) one shade,
And you, but one, can every shadow lend.   4
Describe Adonis and the counterfeit
Is poorly imitated after you;
On Helen's cheek all art of beauty set
And you in Grecian tires are painted new.   8
Speak of the spring and foison of the year,
The one doth shadow of your beauty show,
The other as your bounty doth appear,
And you in every blessèd shape we know.   12
   In all external grace you have some part
   But you like none, none you for constant heart.

a

Weary with toil I haste me to my bed,
The dear repose for limbs with travel tired,
But then begins a journey in my head
To work my mind, when body's work's expired.   4
For then my thoughts (from far where I abide)
Intend a zealous pilgrimage to thee
And keep my drooping eyelids open wide,
Looking on darkness which the blind do see –   8
Save that my soul's imaginary sight
Presents thy shadow to my sightless view,
Which like a jewel (hung in ghastly night)
Makes black night beauteous and her old face new.   12
  Lo thus by day my limbs, by night my mind
  For thee and for myself no quiet find.

b

How can I then return in happy plight,
That am debarred the benefit of rest?
When day's oppression is not eased by night,
But day by night and night by day oppressed.   4
And each (though enemies to either's reign)
Do in consent shake hands to torture me,
The one by toil, the other to complain
How far I toil, still farther off from thee.   8
I tell the day to please him thou art bright
And dost him grace when clouds do blot the heaven;
So flatter I the swart-complexioned night –
When sparkling stars twire not thou gild'st the even. 12
  But day doth daily draw my sorrows longer
  And night doth nightly make grief's length seem
    stronger.

c

When most I wink then do mine eyes best see,
For all the day they view things unrespected,
But when I sleep, in dreams they look on thee
And darkly bright are bright in dark directed. 4
Then thou whose shadow shadows doth make bright,
How would thy shadow's form form happy show
To the clear day with thy much clearer light,
When to unseeing eyes thy shade shines so! 8
How would (I say) mine eyes be blessèd made
By looking on thee in the living day,
When in dead night thy fair imperfect shade
Through heavy sleep on sightless eyes doth stay! 12
    All days are nights to see till I see thee
    And nights bright days when dreams do show thee me.

d

Shall I compare thee to a summer's day?
Thou art more lively and more temperate;
Rough winds do shake the darling buds of May
And summer's lease hath all too short a date; 4
Sometime too hot the eye of heaven shines
And often is his gold complexion dimmed
And every fair from fair sometime declines,
By chance or nature's changing course untrimmed; 8
But thy eternal summer shall not fade
Nor lose possession of that fair thou ow'st,
Nor shall death brag thou wand'rest in his shade,
When in eternal lines to time thou grow'st. 12
    So long as men can breathe or eyes can see,
    So long lives this and this gives life to thee.

Tetrad 11 – notes (Q 27, 28, 43, 18)

te 11 *a*   2   *travel*   (w-p)   journeying, labour, hardship
     4   *work*   set going   *expired*   finished
     6   *Intend*   (w-p)   set off upon, undertake, propose
     9   *imaginary*   based on memory and imagination
    10   *shadow*   image
    11   *jewel*   (This word was applied to a miniature; so the portrait of Herbert, hanging perhaps at the poet's bed's head, provides the image for his imagined form.)
         ghastly   (w-p)   pallid, ghostly

te 11 *b*   1   *How can I then return*   ('then' is argumentative; the opening suggests an answer to a letter of Herbert's accompanying the gift of the miniature and saying 'You'll be happy to return to your family.')
     6   *in consent shake hands*   combine in alliance
     8   (This line shows that Shakespeare is still on his outward journey.)
    11   *swart-*   black-,   dark-
    12   *twire*   peep   *the even*   the onset of night

te 11 *c*   1   *wink*   keep shut my eyes, sleep
     2   *unrespected*   (w-p)   uncared-for, unlooked-on
     5   *shadow*   (w-p)   ghost, image (cf. *a* 10)   *shadows*   (i.e. of 'ghastly night')
     6   *shadow's form*   body that casts the shadow   *form . . . show*   The reader may choose which word he prefers for the verb and which for the noun; 'make a happy sight' and 'show a happy shape'.)
    13   *are nights to see*   resemble nights

te 11 *d*   2   *lively*   enduring (Q has 'lovely')   *temperate*   restrained (Line 3 negates 'temperate' and line 4 negates 'lively '– but not 'lovely'.)
     3   *lease*   season   *date*   span
     7   *every fair from fair . . . declines*   every loveliness falls away . . . from loveliness
     8   *untrimmed*   losing adornment
    10   *ow'st*   ownest (the same word etymologically)
    12   *eternal lines*   (w-p)   the lines of my poetry, the lines of life   *to time*   (w-p)   with the passage of time, to the world's view   ('grow to time' suggests 'become more and more famous')

The last six lines suggest that Shakespeare is much influenced by memories of his dead son at Stratford.

1598 Drama

Episode III (June): Melancholy at Stratford

Tetrad 12 : 'most rich in youth'
  (TETRAD 12 CONVEYED TRIAD 4)

Tetrad 13 : the ogre, Time

Tetrad 14 : falsities and deceits of the world
  (TETRAD 14 ACCOMPANIED TRIAD 5)

a

Like as the waves make towards the pebbled shore,
So do our minutes hasten to their end,
Each changing place with that which goes before
In sequent toil all forwards do contend.   4
Nativity, once in the main of light,
Crawls to maturity, wherewith being crowned,
Crookèd eclipses 'gainst his glory fight
And Time that gave doth now his gift confound.   8
Time doth transfix the flourish set on youth
And delves the parallels in beauty's brow,
Feeds on the rarities of nature's truth
And nothing stands but for his scythe to mow.   12
    And yet to times in hope my verse shall stand
    Praising thy worth, despite his cruel hand.

b

If there be nothing new, but that which is
Hath been before, how are our brains beguiled,
Which labouring for invention bear amiss
The second burthen of a former child!   4
O that record could with a backward look
(Even of five hundred courses of the sun)
Show me your image in some antique book,
Since mind at first in character was done!   8
That I might see what the old world could say
To this composèd wonder of your frame –
Whether we are mended or where better they,
Or whether revolution be the same.   12
    O sure I am the wits of former days
    To subjects worse have given admiring praise.

c

Sin of self-love possesseth all mine eye
And all my soul and all my every part,
And for this sin there is no remedy –
It is so grounded inward – in my heart.   4
Methinks no face so gracious is as mine,
No shape so true, no truth of such account,
And for myself mine own worth do define,
As I all other in all worths surmount.   8
But when my glass shows me myself indeed
Bated and chopt with tanned antiquity,
Mine own self-love quite contrary I read –
Self so self-loving were iniquity.   12
    'Tis thee (my self) that for myself I praise,
    Painting my age with beauty of thy days.

d

Not marble nor the gilded monuments
Of princes shall outlive this powerful rhyme,
But you shall shine more bright in these contents
Than unswept stone besmeared with sluttish time.   4
When wasteful war shall statues overturn
And broils root out the work of masonry,
Nor Mars his sword nor war's quick fire shall burn
The living record of your memory.   8
'Gainst death and all-oblivious enmity
Shall you pace forth, your praise shall still find room
Even in the eyes of all posterity
That wear this world out to the ending doom.   12
    So till the judgment that yourself arise,
    You live in this and dwell in lovers' eyes.

Tetrad 12

te 12 a
4 *sequent* following (one another) *contend* (w-p) compete, hasten
5 *Nativity, once in the main of light, crawls* a baby, once it is in the light of day, grows slowly *main* (w-p) the sea, the flood-light
6 *being crowned* ('being' one syllable) no sooner is he crowned (with maturity)
7 *Crooked* spiteful, destructive
8 *confound* destroy (as it had taken off Hamnet at puberty)
9 *transfix* (w-p) wreck, score out *flourish* (w-p) bloom, ornamental scroll
10 *delves the parallels* gouges the wrinkles
11 *rarities* outstanding examples *truth* skill, perfection
13 *in hope* to come

te 12 b
2 *beguiled* deceived
3 *labouring* (w-p) striving, being in labour *invention* new creation (thing or process)
3–4 *bear amiss The second burden* (w-p) uselessly produce a mere replica, miscarry with a subsequent pregnancy (there is a hint that a younger child cannot make up for the loss of an older one. Shakespeare himself had been such a younger child; his two elder sisters had not survived.)
5 *record* remembrance (my own and others' records)
6 *courses of the sun* years (But 'days' would here lead back to the first birthday of Hamnet and Judith that followed Hamnet's death and that could have been the unconscious reason for expressing this unfulfillable wish.)
8 *Since . . . done* Since it was in writing that human natures were first portrayed (this line explains 'book'.)
10 *composèd wonder* well-structured marvel *frame* body, person (Also, in this line there may be allusions to the miniatures and to this tetrad, producing a confusion between 'you in your picture' and 'me in my writing' which it will be the job of *c* to undo.)
11 *Whether* (so Q; better 'Where') *where* in what respects *mended* (w-p, as in the first scene of *Julius Caesar*), repaired, improved (modern, 'have progressed')
12 *revolution* be the same: there is no difference in the cycle (as it comes round again)
13 *wits* wise writers

te 12 c
5–8 (these lines describe the self-love)
5 *gracious* handsome
6 *true . . . truth* (w-p) perfect . . . perfection, fidelity
7 *I* (understood) *do define* i.e. I create the very standard of (my own worth)
8 *all other* every other person *all worths* all good qualities
10 *Bated* diminished, shrunk (Q has 'Beated') *chopped* chapped, lined with wrinkles *tanned antiquity'* the leathering of age (old John Shakespeare dealt in gloves)
12 *so* in such an image as that I see *iniquity* (w-p) sin, lack of correspondence
13 *thee (my self)* i.e. my true self (alter ego) *for myself* in my own stead, instead of myself
14 *painting* (w-p) imagining, embellishing (with allusions to limning and to poetry)

te 12 d
2 *powerful* (two syllables)
3 *in these contents* in the substance of my poem
4 *Than* i.e. than if represented in *stone* engraved tablet, monument, statue
6 *broils* quarrels, fights
7 *Nor . . . nor* neither . . . nor *Mars his sword* the sword of war *burn* destroy
9 *all-oblivious enmity* antagonism that effaces all record

12   *That . . . doom*   that live through to the end of the world
13   *the judgment that* (w-p) the Day of Judgment when, your doom comes to pass that
14   *lovers'* (w-p) of those who love you, of those who love each other

The word 'praise', occurring near the end of each sonnet, is one bond of this tetrad. Another is the developing theme of personal destiny – birth, death, youth, mortality, immortality, and resurrection. Memories of Hamnet are never far away. This is the first of the three tetrads which have the couplets of *b* and *c* so closely linked by words and ideas that their tetradic structure may be considered *a bc d* as well as *ab cd*.

Tetrad 13 – notes (Q 64, 65, 63, 19)

te 13 *a*   1 *fell* cruel, ruinous
    2 *cost* wealth, magificence *age* past civilizations
    3 *sometime* formerly
    4 *brass eternal* brass supposed to be indestructible *slave to* at the mercy of *mortal rage* deadly violence
    5–6 *gain Advantage* encroach
    7 *win of* gain from, gain over
    8 *store . . . store* quantity possessed (by one or other)
    9 *state* (w-p) condition, elements
   10 *state* magnificence, power *confounded* brought low, destroyed
   14 *weep to have* weep over the possession of

te 13 *b*   1 *Since* since there is no
    2 *rage* (w-p) violence, fury
   3–4 *plea . . . action* (w-p) (legal metaphor included)
    6 *wrackful* destructive
    8 *decays* makes them decay
   10 *time's best jewel* i.e. William Herbert, the youth in his prime
        time's chest (w-p) the coffin, oblivion
   12 *spoil* (w-p) robbery, damaging

te 13 *c*   1 *Against* to provide for the time when
    5 *age's* old age's *steepy night* abyss of death
    9 *fortify* ensure provision
   12 *my lover's* (w-p on 'his' and 'mine')

te 13 *d*   2 (The Titans and the Giants were the mythical brood of the Earth but the natural fauna is more appropriate here.)
    4 (The phoenix was a mythical bird that consumed and renewed itself in fire; so fire could be thought of as its blood.)
    5 *thou fleet'st* you hasten
   10 *antique* (w-p) agèd, old-world, clumsy
   11 *untainted* unspoilt, undinted

a

When I have seen by Time's fell hand defaced
The rich-proud cost of outworn buried age,
When sometime lofty towers I see down-razed,
And brass eternal slave to mortal rage, 4
When I have seen the hungry ocean gain
Advantage on the kingdom of the shore
And the firm soil win of the watery main,
Increasing store with loss and loss with store; 8
When I have seen such interchange of state
Or state itself confounded to decay,
Ruin hath taught me thus to ruminate
That Time will come and take my love away. 12
    This thought is as a death which cannot choose
    But weep to have that which it fears to lose.

b

Since brass, nor stone, nor earth, nor boundless sea,
But sad mortality o'ersways their power,
How with this rage shall beauty hold a plea,
Whose action is no stronger than a flower? 4
O how shall summer's honey breath hold out
Against the wrackful siege of batt'ring days,
When rocks inpregnable are not so stout
Nor gates of steel so strong but time decays? 8
O fearful meditation, where (alack)
Shall Time's best jewel from Time's chest lie hid?
Or what strong hand can hold his swift foot back?
Or who his spoil of beauty can forbid? 12
    O none, unless this miracle have might –
    That in black ink my love may still shine bright.

c

Against my love shall be as I am now
With Time's injurious hand crushed and o'erworn,
When hours have drained his blood and filled his brow
With lines and wrinkles, when his youthful morn   4
Hath travelled on to age's steepy night
And all those beauties whereof now he's king
Are vanishing or vanished out of sight,
Stealing away the treasure of his spring –   8
For such a time do I now fortify
Against confounding age's cruel knife,
That he shall never cut from memory
My sweet love's beauty, though my lover's life.   12
   His beauty shall in these black lines be seen
   And they shall live and he in them still green.

d

Devouring Time blunt thou the lion's paws
And make the earth devour her own sweet brood,
Pluck the keen teeth from the fierce tiger's jaws
And burn the long-lived phoenix in her blood,   4
Make glad and sorry seasons as thou fleet'st
And do whate'er thou wilt, swift-footed Time,
To the wide world and all her fading sweets,
But I forbid thee one most heinous crime: 8
O carve not with thy hours my love's fair brow
Nor draw no lines there with thine antique pen,
Him in thy course untainted do allow
For beauty's pattern to succeeding men.   12
   Yet do thy worst old Time; despite thy wrong
   My love shall in my verse ever live young.

a

Tired with all these for restful death I cry –
As to behold desert a beggar born,
And needy nothing trimmed in jollity,
And purest faith unhappily forsworn,   4
And gilded honour shamefully misplaced,
And maiden virtue rudely strumpeted,
And right perfection wrongfully disgraced,
And strength by limping sway disablèd,   8
And art made tongue-tied by authority,
And folly (doctor-like) controlling skill,
And simple truth miscalled simplicity,
And captive good attending captain ill.   12
    Tired with all these, from these would I be gone,
    Save that to die I leave my love alone.

b

Ah wherefore with infection should he live
And with his presence grace impiety?
That sin by him advantage should achieve
And lace itself with his society?   4
Why should false painting imitate his cheek
And steal dead seeing of his living hue?
Why should poor beauty indirectly seek
Roses of shadow, since his rose is true?   8
Why should he live, now nature bankrupt is,
Beggared of blood to blush through lively veins?
For she hath no exchequer now but his,
And proved of many lives upon his gains.   12
    O him she stores to show what wealth she had
    In days long since before these last so bad.

c

Thus is his cheek the map of days outworn,
When beauty lived and died as flowers do now,
Before these bastard signs of fair were borne
Or durst inhabit on a living brow;   4
Before the golden tresses of the dead
(The right of sepulchres) were shorn away
To live a second life on second head –
Ere beauty's dead fleece made another gay.   8
In him those holy antique hours are seen
Without all ornament, itself and true,
Making no summer of another's green,
Robbing no old to dress his beauty new;   12
    And him as for a map doth Nature store,
    To show false Art what beauty was of yore.

d

Or I shall live your epitaph to make
Or you survive when I in earth am rotten;
From hence your memory death cannot take,
Although in me each part will be forgotten.   4
Your name from hence immortal life shall have,
Though I (once gone) to all the world must die;
The earth can yield me but a common grave,
When you entombèd in men's eye shall lie.   8
Your monument shall be my gentle verse,
Which eyes not yet created shall o'er-read,
And tongues to be your being shall rehearse,
When all the breathers of this world are dead.   12
    You still shall live (such virtue hath my pen)
    Where breath most breathes, even in the mouths of men.

Tetrad 14

te 14 a 1–2 *all these . . . As* all these things – such as
2 *desert* one who deserves well (Throughout this sonnet abstract nouns are repeatedly used for classes of persons.)
3 *needy nothing* i.e. persons of no account (whether for wit, character, or influence) *trimmed in jollity* 'dressed up to the nines'
4 *forsworn* (w-p) disappointed of promises, forced to break promises
5 *honour* (here not the persons but the positions or the rewards of service)
8 *limping sway* (w-p) the power of limited persons, ministers with a limp (e.g. Lord Burghley) *disablèd* (four syllables)
9 (e.g. by the Order in Council closing the theatres eleven months before)
10 *doctor-like* as if with learning
11 *simplicity* ignorance, stupidity
12 *attending* (w-p) in the service of, at the heels of

te 14 b 1–2 *infection . . . impiety* i.e. corrupt . . . godless persons
4 *lace* make fine
5 *painting* use of cosmetics
6 *dead seeing* lifeless seeming ('seeming' has been thought the correct reading) *hue* (here) complexion
7 *poor* lack-lustre (The word initiates the money-metaphor of 9–14.)
8 *of shadow* of imitation *since* because (or) just because
9–14 (A sustained metaphor from industry, commerce, or finance.)
9 *bankrout* bankrupt
10 *beggared* empty, bereft *lively* living, showing life, long-lasting
11 *exchequer* resources *his* i.e. what he is or what he has
12 *prov'd* (Q has 'proud') i.e. though tested and used by many, herself lives upon his earnings

te 14 c 1 *map* indication, picture *days outworn* olden days
3 *bastard* spurious *borne* (w-p) invented, worn
4 *durst inhabit* dare dwell
9 *antique* (w-p) ancient, simple
13 *store* keep

te 14 d 1–2 *Or . . . or* Either . . . or
3 *from hence* (w-p) from the world, from now on
4 *in me each part* (w-p) each bit of me, each quality of mine
5 *from hence* (w-p) from now on, from these poems
11 *rehearse* tell over
13 *virtue* potency
12–14 *breathers . . . breath . . . breathes* the living . . . life . . . lives

1598 Drama

Episode IV (July): Infidelities

Tetrad 15: discovering the double loss
        (TETRAD 15 ACCOMPANIED TRIAD 6)
Tetrad 16: forgiveness
        (TETRAD 16 ACCOMPANIED TRIAD 7)
Tetrad 17: testament

a

How careful was I, when I took my way,
Each trifle under truest bars to thrust,
That to my use it might unusèd stay
From hands of falsehood in sure wards of trust! 4
But thou, to whom my jewels trifles are,
Most worthy comfort, now my greatest grief,
Thou best of dearest and mine only care,
Art left the prey of every vulgar thief. 8
Thee have I not locked up in any chest,
Save where thou art not, though I feel thou art –
Within the gentle closure of my breast,
From whence at pleasure thou mayst come and part; 12
    And even thence thou wilt be stol'n I fear,
      For truth proves thievish for a prize so dear.

b

Those pretty wrongs that liberty commits,
When I am sometime absent from thy heart,
Thy beauty and thy years full well befits,
For still temptation follows where thou art. 4
Gentle thou art and therefore to be won,
Beauteous thou art, therefóre to be assailed.
And when a woman woos, what woman's son
Will sourly leave her till he have prevailed? 8
Ay me, but yet thou mightst my seat forbear
And chide thy beauty and thy straying youth,
Who lead thee in their riot even there
Where thou art forced to break a twofold truth – 12
    Hers by thy beauty tempting her to thee,
      Thine by thy beauty being false to me.

c

Take all my loves, my love, yea take them all;
What hast thou then more than thou hadst before?
No love, my love, that thou mayst true love call;
All mine was thine before thou hadst this more.   4
Then if for my love thou my love receivest,
I cannot blame thee for my love thou usest;
But yet be blamed, if thou thisself deceivest
By wilful taste of what thyself refusest.   8
I do forgive thy robbery, gentle thief,
Although thou steal thee all my poverty;
And yet love knows it is a greater grief
To bear love's wrong than hate's known injury.   12
    Lascivious grace, in whom all ill well shows,
    Kill me with spites yet we must not be foes.

d

That thou hast her it is not all my grief,
And yet it may be said I loved her dearly;
That she hath thee is of my wailing chief,
A loss in love that touches me more nearly.   4
Loving offenders, thus I will excuse ye –
Thou dost love her, because thou know'st I love her,
And for my sake even so doth she abuse me,
Suff'ring my friend for my sake to approve her.   8
If I lose thee, my loss is my love's gain,
And losing her, my friend hath found that loss;
Both find each other and I lose both twain
And both for my sake lay on me this cross.   12
    But here's the joy, my friend and I are one;
    Sweet flattery, then she loves but me alone.

Tetrad 15

te 15 *a*
1. *my way* i.e. on my journey
2. *truest bars* greatest security
4. *From* away from, (unused) by *wards* strong-rooms
5. *to whom* (w-p) in comparison with whom, (ironical) in whose eyes
12. *part* go
14. *truth* (w-p) honesty, fidelity *thievish* tempting to thieves

te 15 *b*
1. *pretty* (at least implies 'small')
3. *befits* are to be expected from (Thy beauty etc.)
4. *still* ever
6. *therefóre* (a different accent from the line before)
9. *seat* position, place *forbear* avoid, hold off from
11. *riot* disorderly excitement
12. *truth* fidelity

te 15 *c*
The first six lines make much w-p on 'love' as emotion and as person.
6. *for . . . thou usest* for using (knowing carnally)
7. *this self* i.e. me, your alter ego
8. *wilful taste* deliberate (w-p on 'sexual') indulgence *what . . . refusest* i.e. a relationship with a woman (wife)
10. *all my poverty* my poor all
12. *known* i.e. limited
13. *Lascivious grace* charming wanton

te 15 *d*
3. *of my wailing chief* the thing I most lament
4. *nearly* intimately
7. *abuse* cheat, deceive
8. *approve* enjoy
9. *my love's* i.e. the woman's
14. *flattery* self-deception

Tetrad 16 – notes (Q 34, 33, 35, 49)

te 16 *a* 3 *base* black, foul
4 *bravery* splendour *rotten smoke* foul mists
7 *salve* (w-p) ointment, remedy, excuse
9 *shame* sense of shame, admission of wrong done *physic* medicine, cure
12 *cross* (Q has 'loss'; the emendation is usually printed)
13 *sheeds* sheds
14 *ransome* pay for, make up for

te 16 *b* 1 *many a* and *glorious* (two syllables each) *morning* (the actual subject to 'flatter' and 'permit'; 'morning' insensibly becomes 'the sun')
5 *Anon* later
6 *rack* ragged cloud
7 *forlorn* abandoned
9 *sun* (w-p – unconscious?)
11 *out alack!* (exclamation of dismay and grief)
12 *region cloud* (the stratum of cloud in the lower atmosphere)
14 *stain* (intransitive) (w-p) become overcast or obscured, defiled

te 16 *c* 3 *stain* (w-p) obscure, defile
4 *canker* worm in the bud
5 *even I* I myself
6 *Authorizing* (w-p) suggesting (by showing tr 1 *b*), permitting, justifying (and scripting? – dramatic irony) *with compare* by making comparisons (of your fault in this tetrad, of my mistress in tr 1 *b* – and showing them to you)
7 *salving* (w-p) healing, excusing *amiss* misdeed, misbehaviour
8 *more* to a greater extent (than the sins are in degree or in number)
9 *sensual* sexual *bring in sense* (w-p) reason, feeling (w-p incense?)
10 *adverse party* plaintiff
11 *lawful plea* (w-p) legal action, well-grounded argument
13 *áccessary* accomplice
14 *sourly* nastily, to my bitterness

te 16 *d* 1, 5, 9 *against* in anticipation of
2 *defects* (w-p) faults, stains, eclipses, failings
3 *cast . . . sum* reckoned up its final account
4 *advised respects* careful considerations (a formality incompatible with a spontaneous, equal relationship)
5 *strangely* distantly
7 *converted* quite altered
8 *settled gravity* (w-p) definite, unchanging seriousness (a hint at accusations)
9 *ensconce me* establish and secure myself, dig myself in
11 *up-rear* (w-p) raise (to take the oath against myself, to attack myself – by a blow or in writing)
12 *guard* uphold
14 *allege* urge as a plea

a

Why didst thou promise such a beauteous day
And make me travel forth without my cloak
To let base clouds o'ertake me in my way,
Hiding thy brav'ry in their rotten smoke?   4
'Tis not enough that through the cloud thou break
To dry the rain on my storm-beaten face,
For no man well of such a salve can speak
That heals the wound and cures not the disgrace.   8
Nor can thy shame give physic to my grief;
Though thou repent, yet I have still the loss;
Th' offender's sorrow lends but weak relief
To him that bears the strong offence's cross.   12
  Ah, but those tears are pearl which thy love sheeds,
  And they are rich and ransom all ill deeds.

b

Full many a glorious morning have I seen
Flatter the montain tops with sovereign eye,
Kissing with golden face the meadows green,
Gilding pale streams with heavenly alchemy,   4
Anon permit the basest clouds to ride
With ugly rack on his celestial face
And from the forlorn world his visage hide,
Stealing unseen to west with this disgrace.   8
Even so my sun one early morn did shine
With all triumphant splendour on my brow,
But out alack, he was but one hour mine;
The region cloud hath masked him from me now.   12
  Yet him for this my love so whit disdaineth;
  Suns of the world may stain when heaven's
    sun staineth.

c

No more be grieved at that which thou hast done;
Roses have thorns and silver fountains mud;
Clouds and eclipses stain both moon and sun
And loathsome canker lives in sweetest bud.   4
All men make faults and even I in this,
Authórizing thy trespass with compare,
Myself corrupting salving thy amiss,
Excusing thy sins more than thy sins are;   8
For to thy sensual fault I bring in sense
(Thy adverse party is thy advocate)
And 'gainst myself a lawful plea commence.
Such civil war is in my love and hate,   12
    That I an áccessary needs must be
    To that sweet thief which sourly robs from me.

d

Against the time (if ever that time come)
When I shall see thee frown on my defects,
When as thy love hath cast his utmost sum,
Called to that audit by advised respects,   4
Against that time when thou shalt strangely pass
And scarcely greet me with that sun thine eye,
When love converted from the thing it was
Shall reasons find of settled gravity,   8
Against that time do I ensconce me here
Within the knowledge of mine own desert
And this my hand against myself uprear,
To guard the lawful reasons on thy part.   12
    To leave poor me thou hast the strength of laws,
    Since why to love I can allege no cause.

a

O lest the world should task you to recite
What merit lived in me that you should love,
After my death (dear love) forget me quite,
For you in me can nothing worthy prove, 4
Unless you would devise some virtuous lie
To do more for me than mine own desert
And hang more praise upon deceasèd I
Than niggard truth would willingly impart. 8
O lest your true love may seem false in this –
That you for love speak well of me untrue,
My name be buried where my body is
And live no more to shame nor me, nor you. 12
 For I am shamed by that which I bring forth,
 And so should you, to love things nothing worth.

b

No longer mourn for me when I am dead
Than you shall hear the surly sullen bell
Give warning to the world that I am fled
From this vile world with vildest worms to dwell. 4
Nay if you read this line, remember not
The hand that writ it, for I love you so
That I in your sweet thoughts would be forgot,
If thinking on me then should make you woe. 8
O if (I say) you look upon this verse
When I (perhaps) compounded am with clay,
Do not so much as my poor name rehearse
But let your love even with my life decay; 12
 Lest the wise world should look into your moan
 And mock you with me after I am gone.

c

That time of year thou mayst in me behold
When yellow leaves, or none or few, do hang
Upon those boughs which shake against the cold –
Bare ruined choirs, where late the sweet birds sang.   4
In me thou seest the twilight of such day
As after sunset fadeth in the west,
Which by and by black night doth take away,
Death's second self that seals up all in rest.   8
In me thou seest the glowing of such fire
That on the ashes of his youth doth lie,
As the death-bed whereon it must expire,
Consumed with that which it was nourished by.   12
   This thou perceiv'st, which makes thy love more
      strong
   To love that well which thou must leave ere long.

d

But be contented when that fell arrest
Without all bail shall carry me away;
My life hath in this line some interest,
Which for memorial still with thee shall stay.   4
When thou reviewest this, thou dost review
The very part was consecrate to thee;
The earth can have but earth, which is his due,
My spirit is thine, the better part of me.   8
So then thou hast but lost the dregs of life,
The prey of worms my body being dead,
The coward conquest of a wretch's knife,
Too base of thee to be rememberèd.   12
   The worth of that is that which it contains,
   And that is this and this with thee remains.

Tetrad 17 – notes (Q 72, 71, 73, 74)

te 17 *a*
1 *task* (w-p) command, challenge *recite* describe
2 *lived* there really was *that* such that *should love* (refers to te 16 *d* 14)
7 *deceasèd I* me when I am dead
8 *niggard* stingy *impart* allow, tell of
10 *untrue* untruthfully
11 *My name be* let my name be
12 *nor . . . nor* either . . . or (after 'no more')
13 *that which* i.e. triad 7
14 *should you* sc. 'be ashamed' *things nothing worth* (w-p) i.e. the sonnets of triad 7, the worthless woman

te 17 *b*
4 *vildest* vilest
11 *rehearse* mention
12 *even* along
14 *with* (w-p) together with, because of

te 17 *c*
2 *yellow leaves, or none or few* either no more or just a few dead leaves
4 *choirs* (w-p) singing-places (trees or chancels; this was almost 50 years after Henry VIII's destruction of the monasteries)
8 i.e. sleep
10 *that* as *his* its
12 *that which* i.e. the fuel now become ash
13, 14 *thou* (Herbert? Shakespeare himself?)
14 *that which* (Shakespeare? The world?) *leave* (w-p) take leave of, go from

te 17 *d*
1 *fell* evil, ruthless, cruel
2 *all bail* any remittance
3 *line* sc. of verse (w-p on family-line) *interest* (three syllables) (w-p) share, concern
4 *still* ever
7 *his* its
8 *spirit* (monosyllable, as mostly in the sonnets)
11 *coward* made in a cowardly way *conquest* victim *wretch's* i.e. Death's or Time's
13 *the worth of that* i.e. the value of my person *that which* i. e. my spirit
14 *this* this poem

1598 Drama

Episode V (August): poetic contest before a patron

Tetrad 18: plain loving praise as poetry
Tetrad 19: polished fluency or dumb eloquence?
Tetrad 20: the lesser and the greater craft

a

So oft I *have* invoked thee for my muse
And found such fair assistance in my verse,
As every alien pen hath got my use
And under thee their poesy disperse.   4
Thine eyes, that taught the dumb on high to sing
And heavy ignorance aloft to fly,
Have added feathers to the learnèd's wing
And given grace a double majesty.   8
Yet be most proud of that which I compile,
Whose influence is thine and born of thee;
In others' works thou dost but mend the style
And arts with thy sweet graces gracèd be.   12
　　But thou art all my art and dost advance
　　As high as learning my rude ignorance.

b

Why is my verse so barren of new pride?
So far from variation or quick change?
Why with the time do I not glance aside
To new-found methods and to compounds strange?   4
Why write I still all one, ever the same,
And keep invention in a noted weed,
That every word doth almost tell my name,
Showing their birth and where they did proceed?   8
O know, sweet love, I always write of you,
And you and love are still my argument;
So all my best is dressing old words new,
Spending again what is already spent;   12
　　For as the sun is daily new and old,
　　So is my love still telling what is told.

c

How can my muse want subject to invent
While thou dost breathe, that pour'st into my verse
Thine own sweet argument, too excellent
For every vulgar paper to rehearse?   4
O give thyself the thanks if aught in me
Worthy perusal stand against thy sight,
For who's so dumb that cannot write to thee,
When thou thyself dost give invention light?   8
Be thou the tenth Muse, ten times more in worth
Than those old nine which rhymers invocate,
And he that calls on thee let him bring forth
Eternal numbers to outlive long date.   12
    If my slight muse do please these curious days,
    The pain be mine but thine shall be the praise.

d

If thou survive my well-contented day
When that churl death my bones with dust shall cover
And shalt by fortune once more re-survey
These poor rude lines of thy deceasèd lover,   4
Compare them with the bett'ring of the time
And though they be outstripped by every pen,
Reserve them for my love, not for their rhyme
Exceeded by the height of happier men.   8
O then vouchsafe me but this loving thought:
'Had my friend's Muse grown with this growing age,
A dearer birth than this his love had brought
To march in ranks of better equipage;   12
    But since he died and poets better prove,
    Theirs for their style I'll read, his for his love.'

Tetrad 18

Tetrad 18 – notes (Q 78, 76, 38, 32)

te 18 *a* 3 *As* that *alien* i.e. of other poets *got my use* copied me
4 *under thee* dedicating to you *disperse* publish, spread abroad
5 *the dumb* i.e. such as I was *on high* (w-p) clearly, sublimely
6 *ignorance* myself unlettered (metaphor perhaps of the great bustard, a bird not then extinct on Salisbury Plain, on the edge of which Wilton was)
8 *grace* (w-p) high position, accomplishments, learning
9 *compile* compose
10 *influence* inspiration
14 *rude* uneducated

te 18 *b* 1 *pride* finery, merit
3 *with the time* (w-p) as time passes, modishly *glance aside* (w-p) alter my course, swerve, look around
4 *compounds* (w-p) mixtures (verse-forms), compound words
5 *still all one* always in one vein and one form
6 *noted weed* well-known garb
9 *where* the source from which *proceed* comes forth
10 *argument* theme

te 18 *c* 1 *want subject* lack matter *to invent* for composition
2 *that* who
3 *argument* theme
4 *vulgar* common *rehearse* recount
5 *worthy perusal* worth reading *stand against* should meet
8 *invention* composition, literary creation
10 *invocate* call upon
12 *numbers* verses *long date* ages ahead
13 *curious* (w-p) seeking novelty, sophisticated

te 18 *d* 1 *my . . . day* that day which I am well content to face
2 *churl* boor, miser
5 *bett'ring* progress (in poetique technique)
7 *Reserve* keep (with w-p on 'resurvey' of line 3)
8 *happier* better endowed, luckier
12 *equipage* furnishing (of poetic technique)

To read **te** 18 – **te** 20 as one whole, triple poem brings out their remarkable unity – a unity not only formal (e.g. in the similar rhymes opening the two halves of **te** 18 and in the matching couplets that close **te** 18 and **te** 20) but organic. They display an increasing personal vulnerability but form an increasingly powerful answer to – a challenge to comparison. With **te** 19 begins the theme of Shakespeare's silence, his tongue-tied state, his remissness in not praising, and his self-defence. The explanation for this would be that, having received the slight of a comparison of his verse with Chapman's grandiloquent poetry, he held back, did not deliver the usual tetrad in early August, and received a teasing reproof for his silence in mid August, when again he came without a tetrad, but that at the end of the month he produced all these three tetrads together – one poem forming a bigger composition than any since the 17 marriage-sonnets, but still a saucy bark to take on a mighty galleon.

This would explain the change of tense to the past historic in **te** 19 *d* 2, 3, and 9, in which Shakespeare acknowledges the facts of his recent silence and of the reproof it had earned him and also his reason for it. Then in **te** 20 *c* he explores the possible psychological reasons for his silence, rejecting all but the loss to his rival of Herbert's interest and attention. (The present tense of **te** 20 *c* 9 proves the rival to be alive and currently producing, if not in proud full sail!)

Tetrad 19 – notes (Q 85, 84, 82, 83)

te 19 *a*   1   *in manners* with proper humility   *her* herself   *still* i.e. neither singing nor writing
3   *Reserve* (w-p)   keep, stake claims for, draw scrolls around (cf. 'resurvey' and 'reserve' of **te** 18 *d*)   *character* (w-p) lettering, style   *quill* pen
4   *filed* (w-p)   polished, drawn up
5   *other* others
6   *still* continually
7   *able spirit* anybody's talent   *affords* produces, utters
10   *the most of* the extremest
12   *hindmost* unreadily   *rank* position, value
14   *breath of words* (w-p)   utterance, empty speech of writing

te 19 *b*   1   i.e. Who, of all who utter the extremest praise, can say more . . .?
3   *confine* treasury   *the store* the whole stock
4   *should example* might be able to show
5   *penury* poverty
6   *his* its
10   *clear* bright, splendid
11   *counterpart* portray d   *fame his wit* make his ability celebrated
13   *beauteous blessings* blessings of beauty
14   *Being fond on* (w-p)   having a weakness for, being easily pleased by, liking because of

te 19 *c*   1   *married to* (and therefore sworn to hear and read no other)
2   *attaint* dishonour   *o'erlook* read through
3   *dedicated* (w-p)   worshipful, dedicatory
4   *hue* (w-p)   colouring, form
5   *limit* extent, degree
8   *time-bett'ring* progressed beyond further times
11   *sympathized* portrayed

te 19 *d*   2   *fair* loveliness
4   *barren tender* fruitless offering   *debt* obligation, payment
5   *slept . . . report* been silent about your qualities
5–6   *therefore . . . that* for the very reason that, simply because
6   *being extant* ('being' one syllable)   being alive and visible
7   *doth come too short* is too limited
8   *what* to tell what
11   *being* if I remain
14   *both your poets* i.e. I and my chiefest rival (probably George Chapman, who had published his greatest poetry earlier that year).

a

My tongue-tied Muse in manners holds her still,
While comments of your praise richly compiled
Reserve their character with golden quill
And precious phrase by all the Muses filed.   4
I think good thoughts, whilst other write good words,
And like unlettered clerk still cry 'Amen'
To every hymn that able spirit affords
In polished form of well refinèd pen.   8
Hearing you praised, I say, 'Tis so, 'tis true',
And to the most of praise add something more;
But that is in my thought, whose love to you
(Though words come hindmost) holds his rank before.   12
   Then others for the breath of words respect,
   Me for my dumb thoughts, speaking in effect.

b

Who is it that says most, which can say more
Than this rich praise – that you alone are you?
In whose confine immurèd is the store
Which should example where your equal grew.   4
Lean penury within that pen doth dwell
That to his subject lends not some small glory,
But he that writes of you, if he can tell
That you are you, so dignifies his story.   8
Let him but copy what in you is writ,
Not making worse what nature made so clear,
And such a counterpart shall fame his wit,
Making his style admirèd every where.   12
   You to your beauteous blessings add a curse,
   Being fond on praise, which makes your praises worse.

c

I grant thou wert not married to my muse
And therefore mayst without attaint o'erlook
The dedicated words which writers use
Of their fair subject, blessing every book. 4
Thou art as fair in knowledge as in hue,
Finding thy worth a limit past my praise,
And therefore art enforced to seek anew
Some fresher stamp of the time-bettering days. 8
And do so, love; yet when they have devised
What strainèd touches rhetoric can lend,
Thou, truly fair, wert truly sympathized
In true plain words by thy true-telling friend; 12
   And their gross painting might be better used
   Where cheeks need blood; in thee it is abused.

d

I never saw that you did painting need
And therefore to your fair no painting set;
I found (or thought I found) you did exceed
The barren tender of a poet's debt. 4
And therefore have I slept in your report
That you yourself being extant well might show
How far a modern quill doth come too short,
Speaking of worth, what worth in you doth grow. 8
This silence for my sin you did impute,
Which shall be most my glory being dumb;
For I impair not beauty being mute,
When others would give life and bring a tomb. 12
   There lives more life in one of your fair eyes
   Than both your poets can in praise devise.

a

As an unperfect actor on the stage
Who with his fear is put beside his part,
Or some fierce thing replete with too much rage
Whose strength's abundance weakens his own heart,   4
So I for fear of trust forget to say
The perfect ceremony of love's rite
And in mine own love's strength seem to decay,
O'ercharged with burthen of mine own love's might.   8
O let my looks be then the eloquence
And dumb presagers of my speaking breast,
Who plead for love and look for recompense
More than that tongue that more hath more expressed.   12
   O learn to read what silent love hath writ;
   To hear with eyes belongs to love's fine wit.

b

Whilst I alone did call upon thy aid,
My verse alone had all thy gentle grace,
But now my gracious numbers are decayed
And my sick muse doth give an other place.   4
I grant (sweet love) thy lovely argument
Deserves the travail of a worthier pen,
Yet what of thee thy poet doth invent
He robs thee of and pays it thee again.   8
He lends thee virtue and he stole that word
From thy behaviour; beauty doth he give
And found it in thy cheek; he can afford
No praise to thee but what in thee doth live.   12
   Then thank him not for that which he doth say,
   Since what he owes thee thou thyself dost pay.

c

Was it the proud full sail of his great verse,
Bound for the prize of (all too precious) you,
That did my ripe thoughts in my brain inhearse,
Making their tomb the womb wherein they grew? 4
Was it his spirit, by spirits taught to write
Above a mortal pitch, that struck me dead?
No, neither he nor his compeers by night
Giving him aid my verse astonishèd. 8
He nor that affable familiar ghost
Which nightly gulls him with intelligence
As victors of my silence cannot boast;
I was not sick of any fear from thence; 12
    But when your countenance filled up his line,
    Then lacked I matter – that enfeebled mine.

d

O how I faint when I of you do write,
Knowing a better spirit doth use your name
And in the praise thereof spends all his might,
To make me tongue-tied speaking of your fame. 4
But since your worth (wide as the ocean is)
The humble as the proudest sail doth bear,
My saucy bark (inferior far to his)
On your broad main doth wilfully appear. 8
Your shallowest help will hold me up afloat,
Whilst he upon your soundless deep doth ride,
Or (being wrecked) I am a worthless boat,
He of tall building and of goodly pride. 12
    Then if he thrive and I be cast away,
    The worst was this, my love was my decay.

Tetrad 20

Tetrad 20 – notes (Q 23, 79, 86, 80)

te 20 a
1   *As*   like
2   *with his fear*   from stage-fright   *put besides his part*   made lost for his words
5   *for fear of trust* (w-p)   from lack of confidence, from fear to trust
6   *rite* (w-p on 'right') the due procedure of the poetic contest in homage
9   *looks*   (a very early emendation of Q's 'books', which both is incompatible with te 19 and gives a jolt anyway)
10 *presagers*   forth-tellers (cf. **te** 19 *a* 14)
12 *that tongue* (i.e. my rival's)   *more hath more expressed*   more readily has said more
14 *wit*   mental ability, perceptiveness

te 20 b
3   *gracious numbers*   verses that had grace
4   *give another place*   give way to somebody else
5   *thy lovely argument*   the subject of your beauty
6   *travail*   efforts
7   *thy poet*   the poet you now favour
11 *afford*   offer, utter
14 *what he owes thee*   i.e. the 'tender of a poet's debt', his obligation

te 20 c
3   *inhearse*   enclose (for burial)
5   *spirit* (one syllable)   *spirits* (two syllables)
6   *dead* (w-p)   silent, abortive
7   *compeers*   companions, cronies
8   *astonishèd*   amazed to dumbness
9   *affable* (w-p)   friendly, speaking with him
10 *gulls*   deludes   *intelligence*   information, ideas
11 *of my silence* (w-p)   'victors of . . .'   (i.e. when I did not compete), 'boast of . . .' (i.e. that they had reduced me to silence)
12 *of*   owing to
13 *your countenance* (w-p)   your features, your approval   *filled up*   (Q has 'fild up' which gives w-p on 'filed up', i.e. 'polished')

te 20 d
1   *faint*   grow weak
2   *spirit*   (one syllable)
3   *all his might* (w-p)   his best efforts, the utmost he can do
4   *to make* (w-p)   so that he makes, in order to make (ironical)
6   *humble*   humblest   *as*   no less than
8   *wilfully*   deliberately
10 *soundless* (w-p)   bottomless, unechoing
11 *wracked*   wrecked
12 *tall building*   stately rig, high hull
14 *decay*   ruin

1598 Drama

Episode VI (September): accepting the end

Tetrad 21: living in uncertainty
Tetrad 22: the pains of waiting
Tetrad 23: last promises: farewell

a

Some glory in their birth, some in their skill,
Some in their wealth, some in their body's force,
Some in their garments though new-fangled ill,
Some in their hawks and hounds, some in their horse;   4
And every humour hath his adjunct pleasure,
Wherein it finds a joy above the rest,
But these particulars are not my pleasure –
All these I better in one general best.   8
Thy love is better than high birth to me,
Richer than wealth, prouder than garments' cost,
Of more delight than hawks and horses be,
And having thee of all men's pride I boast.   12
    Wretched in this alone, that thou mayst take
    All this away and me most wretched make.

b

But do thy worst to steal thyself away.
For term of life thou art assurèd mine,
And life no longer than thy love will stay,
For it depends upon that love of thine.   4
Then need I not to fear the worst of wrongs,
When in the least of them my life hath end;
I see, a better state to me belongs
Than that which on thy humour doth depend.   8
Thou canst not vex me with inconstant mind,
Since that my life on thy revolt doth lie;
O what a happy title do I find –
Happy to have thy love, happy to die!   12
    But what's so blessèd-fair that fears no blot?
    Thou mayst be false and yet I know it not.

c

So shall I live, supposing thou art true,
Like a deceivèd husband; so·love's face
May still seem love to me, though altered new –
Thy looks with me, thy heart in other place.   4
For there can live no hatred in thine eye,
Therefore in that I cannot know thy change;
In many's looks the false heart's history
Is writ in moods and frowns and wrinkles strange;   8
But heaven in thy creation did decree
That in thy face sweet love should ever dwell –
Whate'er thy thoughts or thy heart's workings be,
Thy looks should nothing thence but sweetness tell.   12
    How like Eve's apple doth thy beauty grow,
    If thy sweet virtue answer not thy show!

d

They that have power to hurt and will do none,
That do not do the thing they most do show,
Who (moving others) are themselves as stone,
Unmovèd, cold, and to temptation slow –   4
They rightly do inherit heaven's graces
And husband nature's riches from expense;
They are the lords and owners of their faces,
Others but stewards of their excellence.   8
The summer's flower is to the summer sweet,
Though to itself it only live and die,
But if that flower with base infection meet,
The basest weed outbraves his dignity;   12
    For sweetest things turn sourest by their deeds;
    Lilies that fester smell far worse than weeds.

Tetrad 21

te 21 *a*   3   *new-fangled ill*   unbecomingly fashionable

          5   *humour* nature, temperament *his* its *adjunct* related

          7   *measure*   scale of values

       12   *pride*   delight

te 21 *b*   6   *the least of them*   (i.e. the slightest withdrawal of your favour)

          8   *humour*   mood

          9   *mind*   attitude

       10   *revolt* change *lie* depend

       11   *title*   deed of entitlement

te 21 *c*   7   *the false heart's history*   the real attitude of the false heart

       12   *virtue* (w-p) power, essence, substance, action

te 21 *d*   2   *do not do*   i.e. do not (either) act in accordance with their looks (of sweetness)

          6   *husband* (w-p) conserve (play the husbandman) *expense* wastage

          9   *stewards* managers, guardians *their* (ambiguous – ironically so)

       12   *out-braves* makes a better showing than *his* its

       14   (A line repeated from *The Reign of K. Edward III* (II.i.451), a play of uncertain authorship, dating to 1595–6. We can only suppose that previous talk between Herbert and Shakespeare had referred to the topic and to the quotation.)

Tetrad 22 – notes (Q 58, 57, 61, 56)

te 22 *a* 4 *stay your leisure* wait until you are free
   6 *Th' imprisoned absence* the lack of freedom due to having to wait (for you)
     your liberty (w-p) your freedom not to be there for me, to do as you please
   7 *patience-tame* (w-p) made docile by patience, docile to the point of
     patience (Ingram and Redpath's hyphen is absent in Q, which yet has a comma
     after 'tame', so linking 'tame' with 'patience'.) *to sufferance bide each check*
     (w-p) endure each set-back to my patience, endure each rebuke to my meekness
     (i.e. accept each new blow or insult) (If 'to sufferance' is taken with 'tame', one
     meaning, without the comma, is 'accustomed to suffering'; another, with a
     second comma or with brackets round 'to sufferance', is 'submissive – to the
     extent of acceptance'. 'Sufferance' could scarcely mean 'my privilege of
     exercising my rights' (Booth) – and be taken with 'check' – without any 'my'
     attached.)
   8 *injury* doing me wrong
   9 *list* please *charter* special right
   10 *privilege* unrestrictedly allot
   12 *self-doing* (w-p) done to yourself, done by yourself
   13 *I am to* I must

te 22 *b* 1 *tend* attend
   5 *world-without-end* never-ending
   7 *Nor* nor dare I
   9 *question* speculate
   10 *suppose* imagine
   12 *those* (*sc.* who are with you)
   13 *will* (w-p) desire (sexual or not)

te 22 *c* 4 *shadows* images
   8 *scope and tenure* intention and drift (tenor)
   11 *defeat* make impossible
   13 *watch I* I stay sleepless, waiting for you *wake* (w-p) stay awake, revel

te 22 *d* 1 *love* the personified emotion
   4 *in his former might* to its previous strength
   6 *wink with fulness* close as if in sleep after taking their fill
   9 *int'rim* interval, episode
   10 *contracted new* just betrothed
   12 *love* (w-p on emotion and person)
   13 *else* (Q has 'As')

a

That god forbid, that made me first your slave,
I should in thought control your times of pleasure
Or at your hand th' account of hours to crave,
Being your vassal bound to stay your leisure.   4
O let me suffer (being at your beck)
Th' imprisoned absence of your liberty,
And patience-tame to sufferance bide each check
Without accusing you of injury.   8
Be where you list; your charter is so strong
That you yourself may privilege your time
To what you will; to you it doth belong
Yourself to pardon of self-doing crime.   12
    I am to wait, though waiting so be hell,
    Not blame your pleasure, be it ill or well.

b

Being your slave what should I do but tend
Upon the hours and times of your desire?
I have no precious time at all to spend
Nor services to do till you require.   4
Nor dare I chide the world-without-end hour,
Whilst I (my sovereign) watch the clock for you,
Nor think the bitterness of absence sour,
When you have bid your servant once adieu.   8
Nor dare I question with my jealous thought
Where you may be or your affairs suppose,
But like a sad slave stay and think of nought
Save where you are how happy you make those.   12
    So true a fool is love that in your will
    (Though you do any thing) he thinks no ill.

c

Is it thy will thy image should keep open
My heavy eyelids to the weary night?
Dost thou desire my slumbers should be broken,
While shadows like to thee do mock my sight?   4
Is it thy spirit that thou send'st from thee
So far from home into my deeds to pry,
To find out shames and idle hours in me
The scope and tenure of thy jealousy?   8
O no, thy love though much is not so great,
It is my love that keeps mine eye awake,
Mine own true love that doth my rest defeat,
To play the watchman ever for thy sake.   12
   For thee watch I, whilst thou dost wake elsewhere,
   From me far off, with others all too near.

d

Sweet love, renew thy force; be it not said
Thy edge should blunter be than appetite,
Which but to-day by feeding is allayed,
To-morrow sharpened in his former might.   4
So love be thou; although to-day thou fill
Thy hungry eyes, even till they wink with fulness,
To-morrow see again and do not kill
The spirit of love with a perpetual dulness.   8
Let this sad interim like the ocean be
Which parts the shore where two contracted new
Come daily to the banks, that when they see
Return of love, more blest may be the view.   12
   Else call it winter, which being full of care
   Makes summer's welcome thrice more wished,
      more rare.

a

When thou shalt be disposed to set me light
And place my merit in the eye of scorn,
Upon thy side, against myself I'll fight
And prove thee virtuous, though thou art forsworn.   4
With mine own weakness being best acquainted,
Upon thy part I can set down a story
Of faults concealed, wherein I am attainted,
That thou in losing me shalt win much glory.   8
And I by this will be a gainer too,
For, bending all my loving thoughts on thee,
The injuries that to myself I do,
Doing thee vantage, double-vantage me.   12
   Such is my love, to thee I so belong,
   That for thy right myself will bear all wrong.

b

Say that thou didst forsake me for some fault
And I will comment upon that offence;
Speak of my lameness and I straight will halt,
Against thy reasons making no defence.   4
Thou canst not (love) disgrace me half so ill,
To set a form upon desirèd change,
As I'll myself disgrace, knowing thy will;
I will acquaintance strangle and look strange,   8
Be absent from thy walks, and in my tongue
Thy sweet belovèd name no more shall dwell,
Lest I (too much profane) should do it wrong
And haply of our old acquaintance tell.   12
   For thee, against myself I'll vow debate,
   For I must ne'er love him whom thou dost hate.

c

Then hate me when thou wilt; if ever, now –
Now while the world is bent my deeds to cross;
Join with the spite of fortune, make me bow,
And do not drop in for an after-loss.   4
Ah do not, when my heart hath 'scaped this sorrow,
Come in the rearward of a conquered woe;
Give not a windy night a rainy morrow,
To linger out a purposed overthrow.   8
If thou wilt leave me, do not leave me last,
When other petty griefs have done their spite,
But in the onset come; so shall I taste
At first the very worst of fortune's might.   12
    And other strains of woe, which now seem woe,
    Compared with loss of thee will not seem so.

d

Farewell! thou art too dear for my possessing
And like enough thou know'st thy estimate;
The charter of thy worth gives thee releasing –
My bonds in thee are all determinate.   4
For how do I hold thee but by thy granting?
And for that riches where is my deserving?
The cause of this fair gift in me is wanting
And so my patent back again is swerving.   8
Thyself thou gav'st thy own worth then not knowing,
Or me to whom thou gav'st it else mistaking;
So thy great gift, upon misprision growing,
Comes home again on better judgment making.   12
    Thus have I had thee as a dream doth flatter –
    In sleep a king, but waking no such matter.

Tetrad 23

te 23 *a* 1 *set me light* disparage me
2 *place my merit in the eye of* ridicule my claims (*sc.* for my skill and devotion)
4 *virtuous* (two syllables)
7 *wherein I am attainted* (w-p) with which I am infected, with which I am charged
8 *That* so that
12 *Doing thee vantage* being gain for you *double-vantage me* are gain as well for me
14 *right* (w-p) privilege, blamelessness

te 23 *b* 1 *Say that* give out that
3 *halt* assume a limp
4 *reasons* claims
5 *disgrace* disparage
6 i.e. by giving substantial support to the version of the facts you would like to be known
8 *acquaintance* familiarity *strange* distant
11 *profane* common, vulgar
12 *haply* perchance
13 *debate* argument, struggle

te 23 *c* 4 *drop in for an after-loss* (metaphor uncertain – some game, the weather, or sieges – e.g. fall in like a cannon-ball doing damage after the main bombardment is over)
6 *in the rearward of* after *a conquered woe* a grief (loss) I have mastered
8 *linger out* protract *a purposed overthrow* a demolition you all along intended
13 *strains* sorts

te 23 *d* 2 *like enough* very likely *estimate* worth, value
3 *charter* inherent rights
4 *bonds in* holding of *are all determinate* have all run out
7 *cause of* justification for *wanting* lacking
8 *patent* privileged right *back again is swerving* is reverting to you
11 *upon misprision growing* originating from a misunderstanding

Envoi
the inevitable reckoning

O thou my lovely boy who in thy power
Dost hold Time's fickle glass, his sickle hour,
Who hast by waning grown and therein show'st
Thy lovers withering, as thy sweet self grow'st   4
If Nature (sovereign mistress over wrack)
As thou goest onwards still will pluck thee back,
She keeps thee to this purpose – that her skill
May time disgrace and wretched minutes kill.   8
Yet fear her, O thou minion of her pleasure,
She may detain but not still keep her treasure!
   Her audit (though delayed) answered must be
   And her quietus is to render thee.   12

Envoi

Envoi – notes (Q 126)

2   *glass*   mirror   *sickle hour*   (w-p)   razor-sharp time, crescent-shaped time-piece

3   *by waning grown*   improved by moving nearer death   (Brent Cohen pointed out to Booth that 'sickle' and 'waning' both allude to the 'fickle' moon.)

5   *mistress over*   (i.e. to inflict or to check)   *wrack*   ruin, destruction

8   *disgrace*   disconcert, humiliate, inflict loss upon

9   *minion*   darling, plaything, serving-boy

10   *detain*   hold back

11   *answered*   met

12   *quietus*   last payment, full settlement   *render*   (w-p)   surrender, submit (accounts) (In the last three lines Nature herself is spoken of as owing a debt to time.)

Poems for eight birthdays 1

1599

    Tetrad 24 : singing resumed

Tetrad 24

a

Where art thou, Muse, that thou forget'st so long
To speak of that which gives thee all thy might?
Spend'st thou thy fury on some worthless song,
Darkening thy power to lend base subjects light? 4
Return, forgetful Muse, and straight redeem
In gentle numbers time so idly spent,
Sing to the ear that doth thy lays esteem
And gives thy pen both skill and argument. 8
Rise, resty Muse, my love's sweet face survey,
If time have any wrinkle graven there;
If any, be a satire to decay
And make time's spoils despisèd everywhere. 12
  Give my love fame faster than Time wastes life,
  So thou prevent'st his scythe and crookèd knife.

b

O truant Muse, what shall be thy amends
For thy neglect of truth in beauty dyed?
Both truth and beauty on my love depends;
So dost thou too and therein dignified. 4
Make answer, Muse; wilt thou not haply say,
'Truth needs no colour with his colour fixed,
Beauty no pencil beauty's truth to lay,
But best is best if never intermixed'? 8
Because he needs no praise, wilt thou be dumb?
Excuse not silence so, for't lies in thee
To make him much outlive a gilded tomb
And to be praised of ages yet to be. 12
  Then do thy office, Muse; I teach thee how
  To make him seem long hence as he shows now.

c

'My love is strengthened though more weak in seeming;
I love not less, though less the show appear;
That love is merchandized whose rich esteeming
The owner's tongue doth publish every,where.   4
Our love was new and then but in the spring,
When I was wont to greet it with my lays,
As Philomel in summer's front doth sing
And stops her pipe in growth of riper days.   8
Not that the summer is less pleasant now
Than when her mournful hymns did hush the night,
But that wild music burthens every bough
And sweets grown common lose their dear delight.   12
   Therefore like her I sometime hold my tongue,
   Because I would not dull you with my song.'

d

Alack, what poverty my muse brings forth,
That, having such a scope to show her pride,
The argument all bare is of more worth
Than when it hath my added praise beside.   4
O blame me not if I no more can write!
Look in your glass and there appears a face
That over-goes my blunt invention quite,
Dulling my lines and doing me disgrace.   8
Were it not sinful then, striving to mend,
To mar the subject that before was well?
For to no other pass my verses tend
Than of your graces and your gifts to tell;   12
   And more, much more than in my verse can sit
   Your own glass shows you, when you look in it.

Tetrad 24 – notes (Q 100, 101, 102, 103)

te 24 *a* 3   *fury* 'poet's rage', inspiration
       4   *base subjects* (w-p) the population of one of Shakespeare's most recent plays
            (perhaps *Much Ado about Nothing*), his audiences
       6   *numbers* verses *idly* (w-p) lazily, wastefully
       7   *lays* songs
       8   *argument* theme
       9   *resty* sluggish
     10   *If* to see if
     11   *be a satire to* satirize, mock
     12   *spoils* (w-p) ravages, booty

te 24 *b* 3   *my love* (personal)
       4   *dignified* given standing and honour
       6   *colour* (w-p) embellishment, cover
       7   *pencil* fine brush *lay* apply
       8   *intermixed* adulterated (i.e. with art or poetry)
     10   *so* in that way *it lies in thee* it is in your power
     13   *office* duty

te 24 *c*   **The Muse's song**
       2   *the show* my display of love
       3   *merchandized* commercialized *esteeming* valuation
       6   *lays* songs
       7   *Philomel* the nightingale *front* early days
       8   *his* its ('her' would be consistent with line 10) *riper* later
       9   *But that* but my reason is that *wild* unrestrained
     14   *dull* bore

te 24 *d* 1   *poverty* poor stuff
       2   *scope* occasion *pride* splendour
       3   *argument* subject, theme *all bare* unadorned
       7   *overgoes* surpasses *blunt invention* stunted powers of composition
       8   *disgrace* discredit, humiliation
       9   *mend* embellish, improve
     10   *mar* detract from, spoil
     11   *pass* direction, result

Poems for eight birthdays 2

1600

Tetrad 25 : third anniversary

a

From you have I been absent in the spring,
When proud-pied April (dressed in all his trim)
Hath put a spirit of youth in every thing,
That heavy Saturn laughed and leaped with him.   4
Yet nor the lays of birds nor the sweet smell
Of different flowers in odour and in hue
Could make me any summer's story tell
Or·from their proud lap pluck them where they grew.   8
Nor did I wonder at the lily's white
Nor praise the deep vermilion in the rose;
They were but sweet, but figures of delight
Drawn after you, you pattern of all those.   12
    Yet seemed it winter still and, you away,
    As with your shadow I with these did play.

b

The forward violet thus did I chide,
'Sweet thief, whence didst thou steal thy sweet that smells,
If not from my love's breath? The purple pride
Which on thy soft cheek for complexion dwells
In my love's veins thou hast too grossly dyed.'   5
The lily I condemnèd for thy hand
And buds of marjoram had stol'n thy hair,
The roses fearfully on thorns did stand,
One blushing shame, another white despair.   9
A third, nor red nor white, had stol'n of both
And to his robbery had annexed thy breath,
But for his theft in pride of all his growth
A vengeful canker eat him up to death.   13
    More flowers I noted, yet I none could see
    But sweet or colour it had stol'n from thee.

c

How like a winter hath my absence been
From thee, the pleasure of the fleeting year!
What freezings have I felt, what dark days seen!
What old December's bareness everywhere!   4
And yet this time removed was summer's time;
The teeming autumn, big with rich increase,
Bearing the wanton burden of the prime,
Like widowed wombs after their lords' decease.   8
Yet this abundant issue seemed to me
But hope of orphans and unfathered fruit,
For summer and his pleasures wait on thee
And thou away the very birds are mute;   12
    Or if they sing, 'tis with so dull a cheer
    That leaves look pale, dreading the winter's near.

d

To me, fair friend, you never can be old;
For, as you were when first your eye I eyed,
Such seems your beauty still; three winters cold
Have from the forests shook three summers' pride,   4
Three beauteous springs to yellow autumn turned
In process of the seasons have I seen;
Three April perfumes in three hot Junes burned
Since first I saw you fresh which yet are green.   8
Ah, yet doth beauty like a dial hand
Steal from his figure and no pace perceived;
So your sweet hue, which methinks still doth stand,
Hath motion and mine eye may be deceived.   12
    For fear of which, hear this, thou age unbred –
    Ere you were born was beauty's summer dead.

Tetrad 25 – notes (Q 98, 99, 97, 104)

te 25 *a*   2   *proud-pied*   splendidly variegated   *trim*   finery
               3   *spirit*   (one syllable)
               4   *That*   such that   *heavy*   melancholy
               5   *nor . . . nor*   neither . . . nor   *lays*   songs
               6   *different flowers in*   flowers various in
               7   *any summer's story tell*   give any account of Summer, make any poem fit for
                   Summer
               8   *proud*   (w-p)   gorgeous, swelling
             11   *figures of*   symbols for
             14   *shadow*   (w-p)   image (recalled or painted)

te 25 *b*   1   *forward*   (w-p)   early, presumptuous
               2   *sweet*   perfume
               3   *pride*   glory
               6   *condemnèd for*   held guilty of stealing the whiteness of
               7   *stol'n*   stolen their scent from
               8   *fearfully*   dreading punishment
             11   *robbery* (two syllables)   *annexed*   appropriated
             12   *in pride*   in the glory
             13   *canker*   canker-worm

(The sonnet has five lines instead of a first quatrain; this and the suspicious punctuation in Q – a question-mark only at the end of line 4 – suggest that Shakespeare had not finished its revision.)

te 25 *c*   2   *pleasure*   pleasantest season   *fleeting*   swiftly passing
               6   *teeming*   fruitful, pregnant
               7   *the wanton burden of the prime*   the fruit of the Spring's sexuality
             10   *unfathered*   destined to know no father
             11   *his*   its

te 25 *d*   2   *your eye I eyed*   (a phrase often condemned for cacophony but surely deliberately
                   used to recall a moment of the meeting of which this was the third anniversary)
               8   *green*   young
             10   *his figure*   i.e. the number on which it is set   *his*   its
             11   *still*   (w-p)   unchanging, ever
             12   *hath motion*   is changing
             13   *unbred*   unborn
          13–14   *thou . . . you*   ('you' – the plurality of the people in the future age)

Poems for eight birthdays 3

1601

    Tetrad 26 : warnings of the world's verdicts

a

How sweet and lovely dost thou make the shame,
Which like a canker in the fragrant rose
Doth spot the beauty of thy budding name!
O in what sweets dost thou thy sins enclose!   4
That tongue that tells the story of thy days
(Making lascivious comments on thy sport)
Cannot dispraise but in a kind of praise –
Naming thy name blesses an ill report.   8
O what a mansion have those vices got
Which for their habitation chose out thee,
Where beauty's veil doth cover every blot
And all things turns to fair that eyes can see!   12
   Take heed (dear heart) of this large privilege;
   The hardest knife ill-used doth lose his edge.

b

Some say thy fault is youth, some wantonness;
Some say thy grace is youth 'and gentle sport'.
Both grace and faults are loved of more and less;
Thou mak'st faults graces that to thee resort.   4
As on the finger of a thronèd queen
The basest jewel will be well esteemed,
So are those errors that in thee are seen
To truths translated and for true things deemed.   8
How many lambs might the stern wolf betray,
If like a lamb he could his looks translate!
How many gazers mightst thou lead away,
If thou wouldst use the strength of all thy state!   12
   But do not so, I love thee in such sort
   As thou being mine mine is thy good report.

c

Those parts of thee that the world's eye doth view
Want nothing that the thought of hearts can mend;
All tongues (the voice of souls) give thee that due,
Utt'ring bare truth even so as foes commend.   4
Thy outward thus with outward praise is crowned,
But those same tongues that give thee so thine own
In other accents do this praise confound
By seeing farther than the eye hath shown.   8
They look into the beauty of thy mind
And that in guess they measure by thy deeds;
Then churls their thoughts (although their eyes were kind)
To thy fair flower add the rank smell of weeds.   12
   But why thy odour matcheth not thy show —
   The soil is this, that thou dost common grow.

d

That thou art blamed shall not be thy defect,
For slander's mark was ever yet the fair;
The ornament of beauty is suspect,
A crow that flies in heaven's sweetest air.   4
So thou be good, slander doth but approve
Thy worth the greater (being wooed of time),
For canker-vice the sweetest buds doth love
And thou present'st a pure unstainèd prime.   8
Thou hast passed by the ambush of young days
Either not assailed or victor being charged,
Yet this thy praise cannot be so thy praise
To tie up envy, evermore enlarged.   12
   If some suspect of ill masked not thy show,
   Then thou alone kingdoms of hearts shouldst owe.

Tetrad 26

Tetrad 26 – notes (Q 95, 96, 69, 70)

te 26 *a*   2   *canker*   canker-worm
5   *That tongue*   e.g. of the popular ballad-monger
6   *sport*   philandering
13   *large privilege*   wide freedom of indulgence
14   *his*   its

te 26 *b*   2   *grace*   charm   *gentle sport*   love-making
3   *of more and less*   by those of high and low degree
4   *faults . . . that to thee resort*   faults which take refuge with you
8   *translated*   changed
9   *stern*   ruthless
10   *like a lamb . . . his looks translate*   change his appearance to a lamb's
11   *gazers*   admirers   *lead away*   (w-p)   take off, seduce
12   *state*   eminence   (William Herbert had just become the Third Earl on his father's death.)
13–14   (The couplet repeated from **te** 8 *b*, presumably reminding Pembroke of Shakespeare's earlier refusal to be led away.)

te 26 *c*   1   *parts*   features, qualities
2   *Want*   lack   *the thought of hearts*   repentance
4   *so as foes commend*   in the way the enemies praise (i.e. just factually)
5   *Thy outward*   your visible aspect
6   *thine own*   your due
7   *confound*   destroy
10   *in guess*   roughly estimating
11   *churls their thoughts*   their boorish, miserly thoughts
13   *why*   to explain why
14   *soil*   (w-p)   solution, ground, dirtying   *common*   (w-p)   too accessible, ordinary

te 26 *d*   3   *ornament*   apanage, attendant attribute   *suspect*   (substantive) suspicion (i.e. suspicion is the inevitable accompaniment of beauty)
5   *So*   if   *approve*   prove
6   *wooed*   courted and seduced   *of time*   in a lengthy siege
7   *canker vice*   cankerous vice
9   *ambush*   the most treacherous period
10   *Either*   (one syllable)   *assailed . . .*   charged accused
11   *so thy praise*   so powerfully to your credit
12   *To tie up*   as to restrict   *evermore enlarged*   continually spreading
13   *suspect*   suspicion   *masked not thy show*   (metaphor again from buds and blooms)   did not obscure the blooming of your splendour
14   *owe*   own

Poems for eight birthdays 4

1602

      Tetrad 27 : the haven of confinement
               after the stains of motley here and there

a

Alas 'tis true, I have gone here and there
And made myself a motley to the view,
Gored mine own thoughts, sold cheap what is most dear,
Made old offences of affections new. 4
Most true it is that I have looked on truth
Askance and strangely; but, by all above,
These blenches gave my heart another youth
And worse essays proved thee my best of love. 8
Now all is done, have what shall have no end;
Mine appetite I never more will grind
On newer proof to try an older friend,
A god in love to whom I am confined. 12
   Then give me welcome, next my heaven the best,
   Even to thy pure and most most loving breast.

b

O never say that I was false of heart,
Though absence seemed my flame to qualify,
As easy might I from myself depart
As from my soul, which in thy breast doth lie. 4
That is my home of love; if I have ranged,
Like him that travels I return again
Just to the time, not with the time exchanged;
So that myself bring water for my stain. 8
Never believe, though in my nature reigned
All frailties that besiege all kinds of blood,
That it could so preposterously be stained
To leave for nothing all thy sum of good – 12
   For 'nothing' this wide universe I call
   Save thou, my rose; in it thou art my all.

c

O for my sake do you wish Fortune chide,
The guilty goddess of my harmful deeds,
That did not better for my life provide
Than public means which public manners breeds. 4
Thence comes it that my name receives a brand
And almost thence my nature is subdued
To what it works in, like the dyer's hand.
Pity me then and wish I were renewed, 8
Whilst like a willing patient I will drink
Potions of eisel 'gainst my strong infection –
No bitterness that I will bitter think
Nor double penance to correct correction. 12
  Pity me then, dear friend, and I assure ye
  Even that your pity is enough to cure me.

d

Your love and pity doth th' impression fill
Which vulgar scandal stamped upon my brow;
For what care I who calls me well or ill,
So you o'er-grain my bad, my good allow? 4
You are my all-the-world and I must strive
To know my shames and praises from your tongue;
None else to me nor I to none alive
That my steeled sense o'er-changes, right or wrong. 8
In so profound abysm I throw all care
Of others' voices that my adder's sense
To critic and to flatterer stoppèd are –
Mark how with my neglect I do dispense! 12
my ⋏ You are so strongly in⹀purpose bred
  That all the world besides – methinks th' are dead.

265

Tetrad 27

Tetrad 27 – notes (Q 110, 109, 111, 112)

te 27 a
1 *Alas, 'tis true* (acknowledging some reproach, supposedly in a letter)
2 *a motley* a clown, a fool *to the view* on show
3 *Gored* (w-p) torn into (for material), patched
4 *old offences* repetitious hurts *affections* friendships
5 *looked on truth* (w-p) regarded loyalty, regarded fact
6 *Askance and strangely* obliquely and distantly
7 *blenches* side-slippings, swerves
8 *worse essays* overtures to worse people
9 *Now* now that *what shall have no end* i.e. my devotion
10 *grind* (w-p) whet, chew
11 *proof* trial *try* (w-p) test, give pain to
12 *confined* i.e. as you to your estate (by royal command) so am I to you – no hardship but a grace
13–14 (an announcement that Shakespeare is coming to Wilton, which he loves next after his own home; a tactful reply to Herbert's boredom with Wilton)

te 27 b
2 *qualify* lessen
5 *ranged* gone here and there
7 *Just* punctually *to the time* (supposedly Pembroke's birthday) *exchanged* altered
8 *myself* I myself
10 *kinds of blood* different natures, temperaments

te 27 c
1 *do you wish* please wish *Fortune chide* that fortune should frown on me, be harsh to me (the wish and Shakespeare's submission are re-stated in lines 8–12)
2 *guilty goddess of* goddess guilty of
3 *That* who *life* living, survival
4 *public means* i.e. the stage *public manners* (derogatory)
5 *brand* i.e. a mark branded on a wrong-doer
6 *subdued To* (w-p) completely affected by, made like
8 *wish I were renewed* (i.e. by my submission to fortune's chiding)
10 *eisel* vinegar (supposedly useful as a medicine for preventing or for treating plague)
12 *to correct correction* i.e. to intensify my punishment

te 27 d
1 *impression* i.e. the depression in the flesh stamped by the branding-iron
4 *o'er-grain* (Tucker's likely emendation of Q's 'o'er-greene') dye afresh (to cover stains) *allow* acknowledge
6 *shames* faults, bad manners
7 *alive* (w-p) is (in my eyes) living, am attentive (to any other)
8 *steeled* (w-p on 'stelled' – cf. **te** 5 *c* 1) set down, fixed *o'er-changes* (Tucker's emendation of Q's 'or changes') *right or wrong* (i.e. whichever it is)
9 *profound abysm* deep abyss
10 *my adder's sense* my ears (adders were popularly believed deaf.)
12 *with my neglect I do dispense* (w-p) how lavish I am with my unheeding, how far I permit (excuse) my inattention
13 *in my purpose bred* become part of my nature and attitudes
14 *all the world besides* all other people *th'are* they are (a contraction found in early C17 literature; Q has 'y' are', a common compositor's form)

This, one of the loveliest of the tetrads, seems to have been Shakespeare's response to a peevish letter from the young Pembroke, contrasting Shakespeare's lot (freedom to range) with his own (confinement to Wilton). Uncertainty whether the Queen will sign the passport for his travel has exacerbated his chafing.

266

Poems for eight birthdays 5

1603

Tetrad 28: devotions interrupted by joyful news

a

When in the chronicle of wasted time
I see descriptions of the fairest wights,
And beauty making beautiful old rhyme
In praise of ladies dead and lovely knights,   4
Then in the blazon of sweet beauty's best –
Of hand, of foot, of lip, of eye, of brow –
I see their antique pen would have expressed
Even such a beauty as you master now.   8
So all their praises are but prophecies
Of this our time, all you prefiguring,
And, for they looked but with divining eyes,
They had not still enough your worth to sing;   12
    For we which now behold these present days
    Have eyes to wonder but lack tongues to praise.

b

Let not my love be called idolatry
Nor my belovèd as an idol show,
Since all alike my songs and praises be
To one, of one, still such, and ever so.   4
Kind is my love to-day, to-morrow kind,
Still constant in a wondrous excellence;
Therefore my verse to constancy confined,
One thing expressing, leaves out difference.   8
Fair, kind, and true is all my argument,
Fair, kind, and true, varying to other words,
And in this change is my invention spent –
Three themes in one, which wondrous scope affords.   12
    Fair, kind, and true have often lived alone;
    Which three till now never kept seat in one.

c

Not mine own fears nor the prophetic soul
Of the wide world, dreaming on things to come,
Can yet the lease of my true love control,
Supposed as forfeit to a confined doom.   4
The mortal moon hath her eclipse endured
And the sad augurs mock their own presage;
Incertainties now crown themselves assured
And peace proclaims olives of endless age.   8
Now with the drops of this most balmy time
My love looks fresh and death to me subscribes,
Since spite of him I'll live in this poor rhyme,
While he insults o'er dull and speechless tribes;   12
    And thou in this shalt find thy monument,
        When tyrants' crests and tombs of brass are spent.

d

What's in the brain that ink may character,
Which hath not figured to thee my true spirit?
What's new to speak, what now to register,
That may express my love or thy dear merit?   4
Nothing, sweet boy, but yet like prayers divine
I must each day say o'er the very same,
Counting no old thing old, thou mine, I thine,
Even as when first I hallowed thy fair name.   8
So that eternal love in love's fresh case
Weighs not the dust and injury of age,
Nor gives to necessary wrinkles place
But makes antiquity for aye his page,   12
    Finding the first conceit of love there bred
        Where time and outward form would show it dead.

Tetrad 28 – notes (Q 106, 105, 107, 108)

te 28 *a*   1   *wasted*   olden
        2   *wights*   persons
        5   *blazon*   heraldic enumeration set forth (as the next line sets forth)
        8   *master*   own
     11   *for*   because   *divining*   imagining the future (emphatic)
     12   *still*   as yet   *enough*   i.e. eyes enough
     13   *For . . .* (explaining a different limitation which amounts to the same result)

te 28 *b*   3   *since*   just because
        4   *still*   always
        8   *difference*   distinctions, change
        9   *argument*   theme
     11   *change*   i.e. of words   *invention*   poetic creativeness

te 28 *c*   3   *the lease . . . control*   limit the span   *my true love* (w-p on sentiment and person)
        4   *forfeit to* (w-p)   subject to, condemned to   *confinèd doom* (w-p)   early end or fate, punishment of confinement
        5   *the mortal moon*   i.e. Queen Elizabeth I   *her eclipse endured*   suffered her extinction (death)
        6   *sad*   i.e. in their mourning   *mock*   belie   *presage*   prophecy (of the Queen's recovery)
     10   *subscribes*   pays tribute, enrols under
     12   *insults*   lords it
     14   *spent*   worn out

te 28 *d*   1   *character*   write
        2   *figured*   set out
        9   *fresh case* (w-p)   young form, new poem
     10   *Weighs not*   makes light of, does not care about
     12   *antiquity*   old age ('wasted time' – personified)   *for aye*   for ever   *page*   attendant
     13   *conceit*   notion

Poems for eight birthdays 6

1604

    Tetrad 29: amazement; then pledges reaffirmed

a

Since I left you, mine eye is in my mind
And that which governs me to go about
Doth part his function and is partly blind –
Seems seeing but effectually is out;   4
For it no form delivers to the heart
Of bird, of flower, or shape which it doth latch;
Of his quick objects hath the mind no part
Nor his own vision holds what it doth catch;   8
For if it see the rud'st or gentlest sight,
The most sweet-favoured or deformed'st creature,
The mountain, or the sea, the day, or night.
The crow, or dove, it shapes them to your feature.   12
  Incapable of more, replete with you,
  My most true mind thus maketh mine untrue.

b

Or whether doth my mind being crowned with you
Drink up the monarch's plague, this flattery?
Or whether shall I say, mine eye saith true
And that your love taught it this alchemy –   4
To make of monsters and things indigest
Such cherubins as your sweet self resemble,
Creating every bad a perfect best
As fast as objects to his beams assemble?   8
O 'tis the first, 'tis flattery in my seeing,
And my great mind most kingly drinks it up;
Mine eye well knows what with his gust is 'greeing
And to his palate doth prepare the cup.   12
  If it be poisoned, 'tis the lesser sin
  That mine eye loves it and doth first begin.

c

Let me not to the marriage of true minds
Admit impediments; love is not love
Which alters when it alteration finds
Or bends with the remover to remove.   4
O no, it is an ever-fixèd mark
That looks on tempests and is never shaken;
It is the star to every wand'ring bark,
Whose worth's unknown, although his height be taken.   8
Love's not Time's fool, though rosy lips and cheeks
Within his bending sickle's compass come;
Love alters not with his brief hours and weeks
But bears it out even to the edge of doom.   12
    If this be error and upon me proved,
    I never writ noι no man ever loved.

d

Those lines that I before have writ do lie,
Even those that said I could not love you dearer;
Yet then my judgment knew no reason why
My most full flame should afterwards burn clearer;   4
But reckoning time, whose millioned accidents
Creep in 'twixt vows and change decrees of kings,
Tan sacred beauty, blunt the sharp'st intents,
Divert strong minds to the course of alt'ring things –   8
Alas why, fearing of time's tyranny,
Might I not then say 'Now I love you best'
When I was certain o'er incertainty,
Crowning the present, doubting of the rest?   12
    Love is a babe; then might I not say so
    To give full growth to that which still doth grow.

Tetrad 29

Tetrad 29 – notes (Q 113, 114, 116, 115)

te 29 a
2 i.e. my physical vision
3 *part his* divide its
4 *effectually* actually *out* non-functional
6 *it* (i.e. the physical eye) *latch* seize (Q has 'lack')
7 *his* its (the eye's) *quick* (w-p) living, transient
8 *his own* its own (the mind's) *it* (the mind's vision)
10 *sweet-favoured* (Q has 'sweet-favor')
13 *incapable of* unable to hold
14 *true* (w-p) telling true, faithful *mine untrue* (w-p) my falsehood, my falsity

te 29 b
1, 3 *Or whether* . . . i.e. which explanation to choose (of the 'untrue' which my mind experiences)?
1 *crowned* made supremely happy
2 *this flattery* i.e. the eye's
4 *that your love* (w-p) that love of yours, of you *alchemy* power to transmute
5 *indigest* amorphous
7 *Creating* manufacturing out of
8 *to his beams assemble* come together to its (the eye's) rays
9 *flatt'ry in my seeing* (the alternative explanation of the 'untrue' – the eye is a practised courtier)
11 *with his gust* to his taste *is 'greeing* is acceptable
14 *That* in so far as

te 29 c
1–2 (Emphasis on 'me' . . . 'true' . . . 'Admit')
5 *mark* sea-mark
7 *the star* the North Star
8 *worth* (w-p) inherent value, usefulness (to sailors) *taken* observed and calculated
10 *compass* reach (w-p on the instrument)
11 *his* its (time's)
12 *bears it out* stands fast *doom* end of the world
13 *upon me* against me (but with a hint of the poisoned cup of *b*)

te 29 d
5 *millioned accidents* countless chances
7 *Tan* spoil the bloom of *intents* purposes
8 *Divert* change *th' course of altering things* the behaviour of inconstant physical objects
10 *Might I not then say* was it not right for me then to say, should I not then have said
12 *Crowning* making supreme
13 *then might I not say so* it was not right for me to say that then

Poems for eight birthdays 7

1605

Tetrad 30: proofs of fidelity

Tetrad 30

a

What potions have I drunk of Siren tears
Distilled from limbecks foul as hell within,
Applying fears to hopes and hopes to fears,
Still losing when I saw myself to win!   4
What wretched errors hath my heart committed,
Whilst it hath thought itself so blessèd never!
How have mine eyes out of their spheres been fitted
In the distraction of this madding fever!   8
O benefit of ill, now I find true
That better is by evil still made better,
And ruined love when it is built anew
Grows fairer than at first, more strong, far greater.   12
   So I return rebuked to my content
   And gain by ills thrice more than I have spent.

b

Accuse me thus – that I have scanted all
Wherein I should your great deserts repay,
Forgot upon your dearest love to call,
Whereto all bonds do tie me day by day;   4
That I have frequent been with unknown minds
And given to time your own dear-purchased right,
That I have hoisted sail to all the winds
Which should transport me farthest from your sight.   8
Book both my wilfulness and errors down
And on just proof surmise accumulate,
Bring me within the level of your frown
But shoot not at me in your wakened hate –   12
   Since my appeal says, I did strive to prove
   The constancy and virtue of your love.

c

Like as to make our appetite more keen
With eager compounds we our palate urge,
As to prevent our maladies unseen
We sicken to shun sickness when we purge,   4
Even so, being full of your ne'er-cloying sweetness,
To bitter sauces did I frame my feeding
And sick of welfare found a kind of meetness
To be diseased ere that there was true needing.   8
Thus policy, in love t' anticipate
The ills that were not, grew to faults assured,
And brought to medicine a healthful state,
Which rank of goodness would by ill be cured.   12
    But thence I learn (and find the lesson true) –
    Drugs poison him that so fell sick of you.

d

That you were once unkind befriends me now,
And for that sorrow which I then did feel
Needs must I under my transgression bow,
Unless my nerves were brass or hammered steel.   4
For if you were by my unkindness shaken
As I by yours, y'have passed a hell of time,
And I a tyrant have no leisure taken
To weigh how once I suffered in your crime.   8
O that our night of woe might have rememb'red
My deepest sense how hard true sorrow hits
And soon to you as you to me then tend'red
The humble salve which wounded bosoms fits!   12
    But that your trespass now becomes a fee;
    Mine ransoms yours and yours must ransom me.

Tetrad 30

Tetrad 30 – notes (Q 119, 117, 118, 120)

te 30 a   2   *limbecks*   alembics (alchemists' vessels for heating and distilling substances)
3   *Applying*   i.e. as medicinal remedies, e.g. salves
4   *Still*   ever   *saw*   imagined
6   *so blessed never*   never happier, never more fortunate
7   *spheres* (w-p)   sockets, natural courses   *fitted*   wrenched by fits (seizures in which there may be extreme eye-rolling)
8   *distraction* (w-p)   violence, madness
9   *benefit* (w-p on 'been fitted')
14   *my content* (w-p)   what I contain (and possess), what really contents me

te 30 b   1   *scanted all*   given short measure in everything
5   *frequent*   closely associated, mingling
6   *given to time*   wasted
9   *Book . . . down*   record against me
10   *surmise accumulate*   collect all your suspicion
11   *level*   aim
13   *appeal*   legal defense   *prove*   test

te 30 c   2   *eager compounds*   sharp mixtures (appetizers – 'bitter sauces')   *urge*   stimulate
3   *prevent*   act to avoid
6   *frame*   apply
7   *sick of*   having had too much of   *welfare* (w-p)   being well, kind treatment, rich food   *meetness*   appropriateness (w-p – nourishment?)
8   *to be diseased* (opposite to 'welfare')   to count myself ill, to undergo a cure
9   *policy*   wariness   *in love t'anticipate*   ever prone to foresee and forestall
10   *grew to faults assured* (w-p)   developed definite symptoms, became convinced of things really wrong (the dominant sense, though strict syntax favours the other)
11   *medicine* (three syllables)   medical treatment (metaphor for 'drinking siren tears')
12   *rank* (w-p)   stuffed, sick   *would . . . be cured*   wished to be treated
13   *so*   like that (i.e. in the way I did)

te 30 d   1   *befriends me now*   is now to my advantage
2   *for*   because of
4   *nerves*   sinews, muscles, feelings
7   *leisure*   time
8   *weigh*   consider, reflect
9   *our night of woe*   our quarrel   *rememb'red*   reminded
11   *soon*   as soon
12   *The humble salve*   the balm of humility (saying 'sorry')   *fits*   is right for
13   *that your trespass*   that offence of yours (i.e. that wrong you did)
14   *ransoms . . . ransom*   pays for . . . pay for (w-p 'set free'?)

It is worth while to speculate upon the 'trespass' of each – patron and poet. The tendency has been to think of it as a sexual offence. It seems more likely that it was an offence against the poet–patron bond, e.g. simply not to have been available when needed and called upon (cf. **te 22**) – i.e. when the other might have assumed presence; this is the kind of accusation that Shakespeare seems to be rebutting in **te 26** *a* and *b* and in *a* and *b* of this tetrad (not to dwell upon the apology for absence of 24 *a* and *b* and the mention of it in **te 25** *a*). (Another conceivable trespass would be for one to have 'set the other light' (**te 23** *a* 1); patron might have disparaged poet and poet have taken off patron (or relative) in a recent play – say, *Measure for Measure*.)

Poems for eight birthdays 8

1606

Tetrad 31: protestations against slanders
and assurance of constancy

a

'Tis better to be vile than vile esteemed
When not to be receives reproach of being,
And the just pleasure lost, which is so deemed
Not by our feeling but by others' seeing.   4
For why should others' false adulterate eyes
Give salutation to my sportive blood?
Or on my frailties why are frailer spies,
Which in their will count bad what I think good?   8
No, I am that I am, and they that level
At my abuses reckon up their own;
I may be straight though they themselves be bevel;
By their rank thoughts my deeds must not be shown,   12
   Unless this general evil they maintain –
   All men are bad and in their badness reign.   ·

b

Were't aught to me I bore the canopy,
With my extern the outward honouring,
Or laid great bases for eternity,
Which proves more short than waste or ruining?   4
Have I not seen dwellers on form and favour
Lose all (and more) by paying too much rent –
For compound sweet forgoing simple savour,
Pitiful thrivers in their gazing spent?   8
No, let me be obsequious in thy heart,
And take thou my oblation, poor but free,
Which is not mixed with seconds, knows no art –
But mutual render, only me for thee.   12
   Hence, thou suborned informer, a true soul
   When most impeached stands least in thy control.

c

If my dear love were but the child of state,
It might for Fortune's bastard be unfathered,
As subject to time's love or to time's hate,
Weeds among weeds or flowers with flowers gathered.   4
No, it was builded far from accident,
It suffers not in smiling pomp nor falls
Under the blow of thrallèd discontent,
Whereto th' inviting time our fashion calls;   8
It fears not policy, that heretic
Which works on leases of short-numbered hours,
But all alone stands hugely politic,
That it nor grows with heat nor drowns with showers.   12
    To this I witness call the fools of time,
      Which die for goodness who have lived for crime.

d

No! Time, thou shalt not boast that I do change;
Thy pyramids built up with newer might
To me are nothing novel, nothing strange;
They are but dressings of a former sight.   4
Our dates are brief, and therefore we admire
What thou dost foist upon us that is old
And rather make them born to our desire
Than think that we before have heard them told.   8
Thy registers and thee I both defy,
Not wond'ring at the present nor the past,
For thy records and what we see doth lie,
Made more or less by thy continual haste.   12
    This I do vow and this shall ever be —
      I will be true despite thy scythe and thee.

te 31 *a*
1 *than vile esteemed* than to be thought vile
2 *of being* of being such
3 *just* right and proper, reasonable *lost* is lost *so deemed* thought vile
4 *adulterate* corrupted (w-p on 'adulterous')
6 *Give salutation to* claim to recognize and know *my sportive blood* my sexual nature
7 *frailer* frailer men
8 *wills* (w-p) decisions, sexual desires
9 *that I am* simply what I am *level* aim, shoot
10 *abuses* vices, wrongs done
11 *bevel* bent, warped
12 *rank* (w-p) lascivious, foul, sick *shown* represented, interpreted
14 *in their badness reign* are powerful thanks to (in the midst of) their badness

te 31 *b*
1 *Were 't aught* would it mean anything *I bore* if I did bear *canopy* cloth held over a person of rank ceremonially entering, leaving, or processing
2 *extern* outward behaviour *the* (perhaps a misprint for 'thy')
5 *dwellers . . . favour* (w-p) those who overvalue show and grace, those who live in 'grace and favour' cottages
6 *rent* obedience, duty, dues (praise)
7 (Q has a semi-colon after 'sweet')
8 *Pitiful thrivers* (w-p) i.e. to be pitied for their thriving, thriving pitiably *gazing* admiration *spent* exhausted, achieving nothing else
9 *obsequious* obedient, devoted
10 *oblation* offering
11 *seconds* stuff of inferior quality (especially used of flour)
12 *mutual render* exchange
13 *suborned* bribed, procured
14 *impeached* accused

te 31 *c*
1 *dear love* (the sentiment but w-p on person) *but* merely *child of state* (w-p) Ward of Court, illegitimate, contingently created
2 *unfathered be* lose its father (legally or by death)
4 (i.e. cast away or chosen specially)
5 *accident* chance
6 *smiling pomp* overtly joyous ceremony *falls* (i.e. as might oppressor or oppressed)
7 *the blow of thralled discontent* (w-p i.e. struck by, suffered by, the oppressed) *discontent* (w-p) unhappiness, resentment
8 *Whereto* (i.e. to one extreme or the other) *inviting* (implies 'untrustworthy') *our fashion* our present habit, tendency
9 *policy* (w-p) wariness, manipulation, selfish prudence *heretic* unfaithful one
10 *works on leases* serves by limited commitments *short-numbered* (Q without hyphen)
11 *hugely politic* tremendously prudent (ultimately)
12 *That* (w-p) since, and so *nor . . . nor* neither . . . nor
13 *To this* i.e. to the truth that policy is ultimately impolitic *fools of time* (w-p) those who have foolishly followed inconstant fashion, those who are helplessly at the mercy of time
14 *die for goodness* (i.e. as martyrs) *for crime* (e.g. for trying to inflict on those in power a 'blow of thralled discontent') (It is easy to take 'the fools of time' as the Gunpowder Plotters – executed 31 January 1606 – but the phrase of course may include others besides.)

te 31 *d*   2   *pyramids*   tombs and monuments (At about this time Shakespeare would have been reading for   *Antony and Cleopatra*.   Also, knowing that this was to be his last sonnet to Pembroke, he used the language of Horace in the epilogue (*Odes*, III. 30) which he had made for the three books of odes that he had published together and dedicated to *his* Maecenas (the real one). That ode too mentions 'pyramids' – for comparison – in the second line and is a poem defying time. Pembroke could not have failed to understand – 'The End'.)

4   *dressings*   new versions

5   *Our dates*   our lives   *admire*   wonder at (as novel)

6   *foist upon us*   cheatingly display to us

7   *make them born to our desire*   imagine them newly created, as we would wish them to be

8   *told*   described

9   *registers* ⎱
10   *records* ⎰ i.e. written annals or other surviving artefacts

11   *what we see*   i.e. present reality

13   *This* . . . i.e. 'But one thing . . .'   The manner of the publication of Q in 1609 and Shakespeare's own subsequent silence show that he almost certainly kept his pledge, whether or not the Herbert family had kept faith with him. There are three facts which give grounds for thinking that only a few copies of Q were sold (although 13 survive) and therefore that Shakespeare may have protested at the publication done without his knowledge and, if he did, may have persuaded Pembroke to order the withdrawal of the edition from further public sale:

(1)   We have only two likely references to the Sonnets (actually to the *dedication* of the first edition) in other works published during Pembroke's own lifetime. One is from 1613 – a dedication by George Wither of a book of satiric poems: 'G.W. to himself wisheth all happiness' (as if to imply that 'Mr. W.H.' had in effect wished all happiness to himself, although 'T.T.' had signed the dedication of the Sonnets). The other is Ben Jonson's dedication to Pembroke of his book of *Epigrams* in 1616; in this he implies that a previous dedicator had changed Pembroke's title and had taken shelter under his patronage because there had been danger in the contents of his book. So Jonson, by hinting that 'T.T.' *had* been the real dedicator, is absolving 'Mr. W.H.' from the slur of self-dedication – or trying to.

(2)   In 1639–40 John Benson published an edition of all but eight of the sonnets with their order changed and runs of them printed together, as if they were longer poems, with titles. This book, which also contains *A Lover's Complaint*, the poems of *The Passionate Pilgrim*, and some poems by other authors, has an 'Advice to the Reader' which makes no mention of the first edition and is worded as if it were bringing the Sonnets before the public for the first time.

(3)   After the first edition there were no further editions of Q's text for a hundred years and all literary references to the Sonnets are to John Benson's edition, the original text of 1609 not becoming generally available again until 1780.

from the traditional order (Q) to tetrads, triads, and pairs and to pages

Q	tetrad	page	Q	tetrad	page	Q	tetrad	page	Q	tetrad	page
1	1 c	153	32	18 d	231	63	13 c	215	95	26 a	260
2	2 a	156	33	16 b	224	64	13 a	214	96	26 b	260
3	2 b	156	34	16 a	224	65	13 b	214	97	25 c	257
4	1 d	153	35	16 c	225	66	14 a	216	98	25 a	256
5	1 a	152	36	8 b	196	67	14 b	216	99	25 b	256
6	1 b	152	37	8 c	197	68	14 c	217	100	24 a	252
7	3 a	158	38	18 c	231	69	26 c	261	101	24 b	252
8	epilogue	164	39	8 a	196	70	26 d	261	102	24 c	253
9	2 c	157	40	15 c	221	71	17 b	226	103	24 d	253
10	2 d	157	41	15 b	220	72	17 a	226	104	25 d	257
11	3 c	159	42	15 d	221	73	17 c	227	105	28 b	268
12	3 d	159	43	11 c	207	74	17 d	227	106	28 a	268
13	4 c	163	44	9 c	201	75	7 a	194	107	28 c	269
14	3 b	158	45	9 d	201	76	18 b	230	108	28 d	269
15	4 a	162	46	10 a	204	77	6 a	190	109	27 b	264
16	4 b	162	47	10 b	204	78	18 a	230	110	27 a	264
17	4 d	163	48	15 a	220	79	20 b	236	111	27 c	265
18	11 d	207	49	16 d	225	80	20 d	237	112	27 d	265
19	13 d	215	50	9 a	200	81	14 d	217	113	29 a	272
20	5 b	166	51	9 b	200	82	19 c	235	114	29 b	272
21	5 a	166	52	7 b	194	83	19 d	235	115	29 d	273
22	5 d	167	53	10 d	205	84	19 b	234	116	29 c	273
23	20 a	236	54	10 c	205	85	19 a	234	117	30 b	276
24	5 c	167	55	12 d	211	86	20 c	237	118	30 c	277
25	7 d	195	56	22 d	245	87	23 d	247	119	30 a	276
26	8 d	197	57	22 b	244	88	23 a	246	120	30 d	277
27	11 a	206	58	22 a	244	89	23 b	246	121	31 a	280
28	11 b	206	59	12 b	210	90	23 c	247	122	6 b	190
29	7 c	195	60	12 a	210	91	21 a	240	123	31 d	281
30	6 c	191	61	22 c	245	92	21 b	240	124	31 c	281
31	6 d	191	62	12 c	211	93	21 c	241	125	31 b	280
						94	21 d	241	126	envoi	249

Index I

Q	triad/pair	page	Q	triad	page	Q	triad/pair	page
127	tr 5 *a*	182	137	tr 2 *a*	174	146	pr 3 *b*	150
128	pr 2 *a*	147	138	tr 1 *c*	171	147	tr 3 *c*	177
129	pr 3 *a*	150	139	tr 3 *a*	176	148	tr 1 *a*	170
130	tr 1 *b*	170	140	tr 3 *b*	176	149	tr 4 *c*	179
131	tr 5 *c*	183	141	tr 2 *b*	174	150	tr 4 *a*	178
132	tr 5 *b*	182	142	tr 2 *c*	175	151	pr 2 *b*	147
133	tr 6 *a*	184	143	tr 6 *c*	185	152	tr 4 *b*	178
134	tr 6 *b*	184	144	tr 7 *c*	187	153	pr 1 *b*	146
135	tr 7 *a*	186	145	proëm	145	154	pr 1 *a*	146
136	tr 7 *b*	186						

Index II

from the groups to Q's numbers and to pages

			page
Proëm		145	145
Extempore	**pr** 1:	154, 153	146
	pr 2:	128, 151	147
	pr 3:	129, 146	150

Commission (urging marriage)

	te 1:	5, 6, 1, 4	152–3
	te 2:	2, 3, 9, 10	156–7
	te 3:	7, 14, 11, 12	158–9
	te 4:	15, 16, 13, 17	162–3
	epilogue: 8		164

Renewing acquaintance

	te 5:	21, 20, 24, 22	— **tr** 1: 148, 130, 138 ——— 166–7 & 170–1

Drama

	te 6:	77, 122, 30, 31	190–1
	te 7:	75, 52, 29, 25	194–5
	te 8:	39, 36, 37, 26	196–7
	te 9:	50, 51, 44, 45	200–1
	te 10:	46, 47, 54, 53 — **tr** 2: 137, 141, 142 ——— 204–5 & 174–5
	te 11:	27, 28, 43, 18 — **tr** 3: 139, 140, 147 ——— 206–7 & 176–7
		— **tr** 4: 150, 152, 149
	te 12:	60, 59, 62, 55	——— 211–2 & 178–9
	te 13:	64, 65, 63, 19	214–5
	te 14:	66, 67, 68, 81	——— 216–7 & 182–3
		— **tr** 5: 127, 132, 131
	te 15:	48, 41, 40, 42 — **tr** 6: 133, 134, 143 ——— 220–1 & 184–5
	te 16:	34, 33, 35, 49 — **tr** 7: 135, 136, 144 ——— 224–5 & 186–7
	te 17:	72, 71, 73, 74	226–7
	te 18:	78, 76, 38, 32	230–1
	te 19:	85, 84, 82, 83	234–5
	te 20:	23, 79, 86, 80	236–7
	te 21:	91, 92, 93, 94	240–1
	te 22:	58, 57, 61, 56	244–5
	te 23:	88, 89, 90, 87	246–7
	envoi:	126	249

Poems for eight birthdays

	te 24:	100, 101, 102, 103	252–3
	te 25:	98, 99, 97, 104	256–7
	te 26:	95, 96, 69, 70	260–1
	te 27:	110, 109, 111, 112	264–5
	te 28:	106, 105, 107, 108	268–9
	te 29:	113, 114, 116, 115	272–3
	te 30:	119, 117, 118, 120	276–7
	te 31:	121, 125, 124, 123	280–1